I0789327

Published by Ed Walker for RedLines Press
ISBN: 9781799186526
First published by the MOPR Verlag, Berlin, 1929 as
Eros im Zuchthaus.
Republished by the Paul Witte Verlag, Hanover 1931.
Cover picture: Brandenburg (Havel) prison, main entrance.
Source: German Federal Archives Picture (Bundesarchiv) 102-06868
Title Page picture: Police photos of Karl Plättner, 1917.
Source: Bundesarchiv Berlin-Lichterfelde (R 1507/2791)

Karl Plättner

Eros in Prison
Tormented cries of yearning for love

An illumination of the sexual distress of prisoners, written on the basis of personal experiences, observations and reports during eight years of imprisonment.

With a foreword by
Dr. Magnus Hirschfeld / Dr. med. Felix Abraham
Doctors at the Institute for Sexual Science, Berlin

Translated from the German, introduced and annotated by Ed Walker

Contents

Introduction: Who was Karl Plättner?

"This is not the face of a propagandist of the deed, but rather that of a cultivated man with artistic leanings."

There were two driving passions in Karl Plättner's life: belief in the possibility and necessity of communist revolution, and belief in the possibility and necessity of sexual liberation.

After the November revolution of 1918-19, which brought the First World War to an end and saw the overthrow of the monarchy, there followed several years of extraordinary upheaval, which in retrospect have been overshadowed by the events in the following two decades. Hundreds of thousands of German workers not only believed that communist revolution was imminent, but were prepared to fight and, if necessary, die for it. After the horror, the hardships and privations of the war, many felt that they really had nothing to lose but their chains. The revolution was held in check, however, by decades of reformist tradition and trust in the conservative leadership of the main working-class party, the German Social Democratic Party (SPD). This was a source of immense frustration for a passionate revolutionary of Plättner's stamp. In his frustration, he turned to non-Marxist methods as the leader of a group of armed bandits, the "Central German Gang Leader". He was sentenced to ten years in prison, regretted his actions, and turned to writing.

The years during and after the First World War also saw a huge change in sexual morality. In the Weimar Republic, more than anywhere else in the industrialized world, a new openness was born. Magnus Hirschfeld established the Institute of Sexual Research in Berlin in July 1919. In the same year Richard Oswald's *Anders als die Andern* ("Different from the Others"), co-scripted by Hirschfeld, was the world's first film to portray homosexuals sensitively and sympathetically. The

Prussian government subsequently ordered police not to enforce Paragraph 175 of the criminal code, which had criminalized homosexuality since 1871. But the changed attitudes extended far beyond homosexuality. Soldiers returning from the front, where their sexual distress had only been held in check, if at all, in army brothels, in which they paid for services with ration-book coupons, certainly had a changed attitude. Prostitution, which had become rife during the war in Berlin and other cities, had become normalized by a combination of economic need and sexual psychosis.

The Austrian novelist Stefan Zweig was perhaps exaggerating only a little when he reminisced in his 1942 autobiography, *Die Welt von Gestern*:

"What we saw in Austria turned out to be only a mild and shy prelude to this witch's sabbath, as the Germans apply all of their vehemence and systematic thoroughness to perversion. Painted boys with artificial bosoms paraded up and down the Kurfürstendamm, and not just the professionals: every high-school boy wanted to earn a little pocket money, and in shady bars one saw secretaries of state and high finance people without shame tenderly courting drunken sailors. Even the Rome of Suetonius knew no such orgies as the Berlin Transvestite Balls, where hundreds of men in women's clothes and women in men's clothes danced under the benevolent gaze of the police. With the collapse of all values a kind of lunacy seized bourgeois circles, which had hitherto been unshakable in their order. Young girls liked to brag about being perverse: at any school in Berlin, to think that anyone might still be a virgin at the age of sixteen would have been considered ridiculous."

Another sign of changing attitudes to sex, but altogether less decadent than what was going on in the shady bars of Berlin, was the rise of *Nacktkultur* (naturism) in northern Germany. The movement was founded in the late nineteenth century but came to prominence in the 1920s. Naturism was promoted as health-giving, but also became politicised by radical socialists who believed it would lead to a breaking down of society and classlessness. It became associated with pacifism. In 1926, Adolf Koch established a school of nudism encouraging a mixing of the sexes, open air exercises, as part of a programme of "sexual hygiene". In 1929, the Berlin school hosted the first International Congress on Nudity. Whereas before the First World War German social democracy had taken a rather prudish attitude towards sex, encouraging abstinence, it was now becoming increasingly common to regard a healthy and active sex life as a human right.

This is the context in which *Eros im Zuchthaus* was written. The author was a diminutive but powerful man, a bulldog. Karl Plättner was barely 5 feet 4 inches tall in heels. A 1919 police report described him as "stocky, powerful figure, rather bent posture, pale facial colour, no beard".

Karl Robert Plättner was born into poverty in the village of Opperode, near Ballenstedt, on the northern edge of the Harz mountains.[1] He was the first of seven children. In 1903 the family moved to Thale, where there was work in the iron foundry (it was at this foundry that the iconic M1916 steel helmet was later developed and produced). After completing elementary school and an apprenticeship in the foundry Plättner worked as a metal caster among well-educated and highly class-conscious workers, nearly all members of the German metalworkers' union (DMV). He was immediately politically active and at the age of 15 was already in trouble with the authorities, arrested for "offensive behaviour" and sentenced to a fine of 45 marks and 15 days in jail. After a

---

[1] The main source for this summary of Plättner's life is Volker Ullrich, *Der Ruhelose Rebell, Karl Plättner 1893-1945*, C.H. Beck Verlag, Munich 2000. Additional sources can be found in the bibliography.

three-year apprenticeship Plättner, as was usual at the time, went on a journeyman's travels *(Wanderschaft)*, eventually settling in Hamburg towards the end of 1912, where he found work in a small factory serving the shipbuilding industry. He joined the Social Democratic Party, soon becoming a leader of the Hamburg-Altona SPD Youth Federation and a member of the Hamburg party executive. But, following the outbreak of the First World War, he distanced himself from the nationalist politics of the SPD leadership, which had voted unanimously for war credits in the Reichstag on 4 August 1914.

Plättner was conscripted into the 66th Infantry Regiment in Magdeburg and transported to the Western Front in October 1914. In the autumn of the following year he suffered a bullet wound and was discharged as unfit for service at the end of that year. With three injured fingers he also had to give up his career as a metal caster. Until 1917 he worked as a clerk with the *Allgemeine Ortskrankenkasse* (AOK) health insurance company. He continued to agitate against the war and was highly active in the underground proletarian youth movement. In February 1917 he took over as editor of the newspaper *Proletarier Jugend* and, together with other radicals such as Johann Knief of Bremen, organized meetings of socialist youth in northern Germany, engaging energetically to set up the *Linksradikalen* (left radicals) party. In September 1917 Plättner was arrested for treasonable activities and held on remand. After being postponed many times, his trial was set for 20 November 1918 but Plättner was released from jail after the outbreak of the November Revolution.

Immediately upon release, Plättner and his comrades worked closely with Otto Rühle to establish the International Communists of Germany (IKD), which tried but failed to move the Dresden Workers' and Soldiers' Council in a revolutionary direction against the Majority SPD. At the end of December 1918 Plättner took part in the founding conference of the Communist Party of Germany *(KPD Spartakusbund)* as a delegate of the IKD's Dresden branch.

In January 1919 Plättner became Chairman of the KPD's north-western region. He had no position in the leadership of the Bremen Council Republic, which was proclaimed on 10 January 1919, but was a member of the Workers' and Soldiers' Council. He demanded that for each Spartakist killed, a leader of the SPD should be killed in revenge. After the Bremen Council Republic was defeated on 4 February 1919, on the orders of Gustav Noske, Plättner fled to Berlin.

On 3 March 1919 a general meeting of the Greater Berlin Workers' and Soldiers' Councils called a general strike. The Prussian authorities imposed a state of siege and gave Gustav Noske full authority to suppress the strike. The cavalry division that had been responsible for the murder of Rosa Luxemburg and Karl Liebknecht entered Berlin and opened fire on unarmed demonstrators. Street battles escalated over the ensuing days. Then on 9 March the military issued a false report that Spartakists had killed sixty police detectives and other prisoners in cold blood. Noske issued a "licence to kill", resulting in the deaths of at least 1,200 people. Plättner was rumoured to be among them but managed to escape and spent the next few months as a travelling speaker in central Germany. In April he published the pamphlet, *Der Weg zur Rätediktatur* (The Path to the Council Dictatorship) in which he vented his rage against the "Nero-Noske" and the leadership of the Majority SPD, whom he characterized as the "hangman's assistants" to the counter-revolution. The Independent SPD, too, were guilty of social treason, through their participation in government, which had enabled capitalist order to re-establish itself after the uprising of 9 November 1918. To Plättner it was now clear that there could no longer be any question of a "parliamentary road" to socialism. Power must be taken through workers' councils. "Only the pure, unadulterated council system, which tolerates no bourgeois parliament besides itself, can save us," he wrote, and to achieve this council dictatorship, the proletariat must be armed and organized into a Red Guard.

A further pamphlet from the pen of Karl Plättner, *Das Fundament und die Organisierung der sozialen Revolution* (The Foundation and Organization of the Social Revolution) appeared in August, published by the KPD's district office in Saxony-Anhalt.

In his travels through central Germany, Plättner built a large following and was able to evade many attempts by the police to arrest him. His luck ran out on 22 September and he was remanded in custody, though only until December, when he made a daring escape, leaping from a moving train.

After the loss of its leading lights, the KPD's course zigzagged according to Russian needs. At its second (Heidelberg) conference.it made participation in parliamentary elections and the old trade unions mandatory for party members. This effectively meant the expulsion of left-communists, who were unable to stomach such a change of direction. The KPD lost roughly half of its members; entire districts, including greater Berlin, Bremen, Hamburg, Lower Saxony, the Rhineland, Mecklenburg, Saxony-Anhalt and Saxony went over to the emerging left-communist opposition. After his escape, Plättner joined the party in Magdeburg, Saxony-Anhalt. He was specifically blamed in a report at the KPD's third party conference for turning the Magdeburg district against the party leadership under Paul Levi.

The KPD's hesitant response to the Kapp-Lüttwitz putsch of 13 March 1920 prompted many communist left oppositionists to establish the anti-parliamentary Communist Workers' Party of Germany (KAPD) in Heidelberg in April 1920. It immediately attracted 38,000 members and within a few months the figure had risen to 81,000. The new party rejected work in the traditional trade unions, instead forging links with the recently established *Allgemeine Arbeiter-Union Deutschlands* (AAUD), based on workers organized by enterprise *(Betriebsorganisationen)* and district rather than craft and industry. Plättner, along with the majority of communists in Magdeburg, joined the new party.

But it was soon riven with factions. This is not the place to examine these splits in detail, but essentially there were major differences on the role of the party, which brought Plättner into conflict with his former mentor, Otto Rühle. Rühle favoured a greatly diminished role, limited to educational activity, with the AAUD taking the lead in economic struggles; Plättner and the majority of KAPD members adhered to the Bolshevik conception of the party as vanguard of the proletariat. Plättner's contribution to the debate was *Rühle im Dienste der Konterrevolution* (Rühle in the Service of the Counter-Revolution). Rühle was expelled in October 1920.

Plättner was one of the most active members of the party in Saxony-Anhalt under the pseudonym *Schuster* ("Cobbler") but was soon forced to flee to Bremen. A life on the run between various German cities began, as Plättner's activities came under close police scrutiny; party branches were infiltrated with informers. On 28 January 1921 the Leipzig police received an anonymous tip-off: "a communist travelling speaker, who has long since been wanted by the police, is residing unregistered with his lover." The lover in question was one Gertrud Gaiewski, who was a few weeks short of her 22nd birthday, and whom Plättner known since their time in the youth movement during the war. The police could not find any reason to arrest Plättner, who had registered retrospectively in the meantime.

As leader of the United Communist Party (VKPD) Paul Levi called for co-operation with the two social-democratic parties in an "Open Letter" dated 18 January 1921. This was rejected by the SPD and Levi was forced to step down in February. On 16 March 1921 the President of Saxony ordered police and military to move, three days later, into the communist strongholds of Mansfeld, Hettstedt and Halle-Merseberg to disarm the workers, who still held weapons from the Kapp Putsch. After nearly two years of opportunist practice, the VKPD now performed an extraordinary volte face: in its edition of 18

March, before the so-called police action against Central Germany was announced, the main party newspaper, *Rote Fahne*, issued an appeal in which it declared that the Bavarian Minister President, von Kahr, was flouting the Disarmament Act by arming right-wing citizens' militias, and that the working class must respond: every worker must get hold of a weapon, wherever he could find it. Under pressure from the emissaries of the Executive Committee of the Communist International the new leadership was pushed in a more militant direction: the so-called "theory of the offensive". These changes of leadership and policy at the VKPD undoubtedly reflected power struggles in Moscow.

However, for the time being, this new approach opened the possibility of an insurrectionary alliance between the VKPD and KAPD. Precisely the moment Karl Plättner had been waiting for; he hurried from Leipzig to Halle. In fact, the local VKPD was very reluctant to take action; it waited until 24 March before it joined in calls for a general strike. Things only got moving when Max Hoelz arrived on the scene. Hoelz was a former mechanic and soldier who had built a reputation as "the German Robin Hood", robbing from the rich to feed the unemployed of Falkenstein after the war and then leading the Red Army of the Vogtland during the Kapp Putsch.[2]

Hoelz's aura and reputation drew hundreds of workers into the armed struggle.

Plättner by contrast played the minor role, attempting but failing to build a second front south of Halle. Hoelz, after successfully holding off the Reichswehr and police in several skirmishes, went down to defeat at Beesenstedt on 1 April. At the Leuna works, a stronghold for the KAPD, where half of the 20,000 strong workforce belonged to the AAUD, workers

---

[2] Max Hoelz's role in the March Action is documented in his biography, *Vom „Weissen Kreuz" zur Roten Fahne. Jugend-, Kampf- und Zuchthauserlebnisse*, translated as *The German Robin Hood* by Ed Walker.

held off the police with rifles and automatic weapons. They even built their own tank. The military and police only retook the plant with the use of artillery on 29 March, showing no mercy: at least 31 of the workers defending the plant were shot on the spot, many others were held for days on end in a silo and horribly abused before being sentenced to long terms in prison.

Otherwise the March Action received more sympathy than active support in the region; moreover, the authorities managed to isolate it from the rest of Germany. Even Leipzig, a bastion of left communism, remained quiet.

After losing his overcoat, Plättner was identified as a leader of the uprising, though only three weeks later. The police learned that on 28 March, Easter Monday, Plättner and his gang had stolen platinum from the Buckau chemical plant near Ammendorf, which they valued at one million marks (this was much exaggerated, the actual value was around 60,000). It was Plättner's first "expropriation of the expropriators".

The raid was facilitated by a member of the Plättner group, the metalworker Karl Meissner, who, before the March Action, headed the works council at the factory. More significantly, Plättner exploited the reputation of the "German Robin Hood" to persuade the factory director to hand over cash and the platinum. According to the director's testimony, "The leader, a small, slender man with appealingly piercing dark eyes, about 160 cm tall, and a sluggish swaying gait, told me ... I am Hoelz! You will immediately open the cash register." The cashier did as requested, handing over 32,000 marks. The factory director handed over a further 1,000 marks of his own money, for which he received a receipt, signed by "Hoelz".

Max Hoelz was particularly upset about this because he arrived later the same day with the intention of robbing the very same plant, only to discover that it had already been plundered by his *doppelgänger*.

Communists drew diametrically opposite lessons from

the defeat of the March Action. The deposed leader Levi took the opportunity to denounce it as "putschism". The KAPD fired back with a pamphlet entitled *Der Weg des Dr. Levis: Der Weg der VKPD* (The Path of Dr. Levi: The Path of the VKPD), which defended the actions of the revolutionary workers, arguing that they had acted in self-defence, while decrying the passivity and opportunism of the two years under Levi's leadership, which, it argued, had made the party congenitally incapable of leading the working class. Max Hoelz, in his autobiography, also complained that the VKPD leadership in Saxony under Brandler was not only unhelpful but obstructive. Karl Plättner went further. In his speech at his trial in 1923 he rhetorically asked, "What does the March Action teach us?" and answered, "It teaches us that there are revolutionaries, but no revolutionary parties". He was even breaking with the KAPD, indeed, with all "party bureaucracy".

The failure of the March Action has been the subject of heated debate – one might call it "Monday morning quarterbacking" – within left-wing circles ever since.

According to Max Hoelz, Plättner had to be compelled to hand over the proceeds from the Buckau raid to the KAPD treasury. But whatever their differences, the rebels decided that the struggle must continue. The KAPD reformed its military wing under the command of a "Supreme Action Council" (*Oberste Aktionsrat – OAR*) consisting of five members. Plättner was in charge of materials procurement, expropriations and purchasing of weapons. The OAR was formally linked to the KAPD leadership. In reality, however, it acted independently. According to the assessment of the Reich Commissar for Public Order, Plättner was the actual leader and organizer of the "Supreme Action Council of the KAPD" which was "in practice, a criminal gang". Plättner was going his own way, and the KAPD rejected his methods, expelling him from the Leipzig district party.

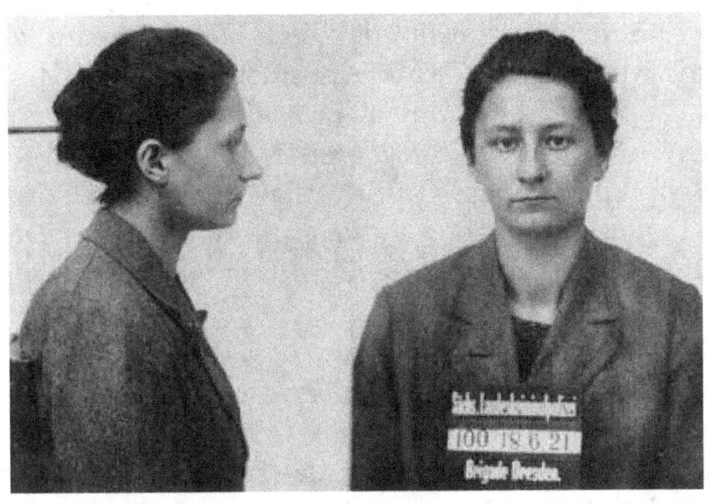

Plättner's first wife, Gertrud Gaiewski, following her arrest in Dresden, 18 July 1921. Source: Bundesarchiv Berlin

After Max Hoelz was arrested on 15 April, Plättner escaped from Hoelz's shadow. He was now Germany's most wanted man. Yet throughout this period of intrigue and dodging the authorities, Plättner managed to stay in touch with his bride-to-be, Gertrud Gaiewski, though they had precious little time together. In mid-May 1921 Gertrud wrote to him: "Maybe it would be nice if we could spend a few more hours together again. But not all day running around Berlin, yes? I would like to seek out a nice little green spot somewhere and be alone with you, so that we both can relax and find, just the two of us ... I gathered in Berlin a bunch of cowslips and forget-me-nots. I have them standing on the table in front of me day after day, and at first, I always imagined that you had presented them to me and made me so happy. And even today the flowers are blooming as fresh as if I had just got them."

This touching letter stands in the sharpest contrast to Plättner's most radical text yet, extolling the anarchistic concept of "Propaganda of the Deed". *Der organisierte rote Schrecken!* (The Organized Red Scare! Communist Parade-ground Armies or Organized Guerrilla Warfare in the Civil War, 1921)

was part political manifesto, part satire (it claimed to be print-ed by the Minister for Public Insecurity, Successor to Gustav Noske, Proprietor Hörsing). It proclaimed terrorist means of struggle: "If you have no weapons, you have matches – blow up the capitalist fortresses, buy matches and set fire to the owners' mansions, also get dynamite and do not leave any stone standing on another, because this world is beyond sav-ing."

There is a millenarian-utopian, religious feel to the lan-guage in *Der organisierte rote Schrecken*: "Thousands climb on the barricades, defying death … to fight for the ancient yearn-ing of mankind, for paradise, for the instinctive memory of the bondless time before the advent of private property." Plättner mocks the VKPD, whose members "strut like Whitsuntide ox-en" with their Soviet medals, and the KAPD for fearing to fol-low up its revolutionary words with revolutionary deeds. The publication of this pamphlet marked Plättner's definitive break with the KAPD and the AAUD but it resonated with many who were equally disillusioned with party politics after the failure of the March Action and were barred from work because of their participation. The "Plättner Gang" grew in number around a core group of roughly 15 members.

From mid-1921 Plättner led and organized a group car-rying out robberies of banks, post offices and collieries follow-ing the slogan of "expropriation of the expropriators". Two of the most daring operations of the Plättner group were their raids on the Deutsche Bank branch in Deuben, near Dresden, on 3 June 1921 and the Grube Alwine mine (near Bruckdorf, not far from Halle) on 13 October 1921, which netted 249,700 marks and 101,530 marks respectively.

Gertrud Gaiewski and another accomplice waited in nearby woods after the Deuben raid, disguised as ramblers, to assist with the escape. She was arrested by Leipzig police on 17 June 1921 and her apartment was watched day and night by policemen, who had been instructed to be on the look-out for a short, stocky man with a "Jewish appearance". On 10 October Gertrud was convicted of receiving stolen goods and sentenced to two years' imprisonment (two other members of the gang were also convicted). Because she was pregnant, Gertrud's sentence was initially suspended.

The Grube Alwine operation was carried out with the utmost audacity, in broad daylight, before dozens of witnesses, and was reported to the revolutionary proletariat in a flyer satirizing the style of a military communiqué. Such was the bravado of the group that a copy of the flyer was deposited in the mailbox of the Grube Alwine plant's chief accountant, who had been forced to hand over the money. Wrapped inside the flyer was the money box containing the trade union's emergency fund, which had been inadvertently taken with the rest of the swag. Plättner wanted to show that he would not take a single penny from the workers, only the unearned profits of the capitalist class.

The last major success was a raid on the Siemens works in Freithal-Döhlen near Dresden, which netted 223,000 marks. Other operations, it must be said, were further and further removed from the already dubious concept of individual "expropriations of the expropriators" and had more to do with common criminality. However, it must be added that (in stark contrast to the violent language of the flyers they distributed after their robberies) the Plättner gang never once used their weapons in anger. Not one person came to any physical harm. Of course, it may be argued that their actions may have caused psychological damage to innocent people, but there seems to have been no maliciousness in these criminal acts. As Karl Meissner stated after his arrest, "We never had any intention of firing on people, on the contrary, we had agreed on the principle that it was better to flee should we meet with energetic resistance." When another prominent gang member, the bricklayer Paul Töpfer, [3] was confronted by police on 10 Janu-

---

[3] Short biographies of Karl Meissner, Paul Töpfer and other members of the Plättner Group can be found in Ullrich p. 109 ff.

ary 1922, he offered no resistance even though he was carrying a loaded pistol.

There was less agreement within the group as to how the stolen money should be used. Given that most were political refugees who were not only unemployed but also stood no chance whatsoever of finding employment, funds were needed to support themselves and their families, in the form of a weekly wage. Plättner kept a meticulous record of all outgoings that would enable him to counter any accusations that he was interested in personal enrichment.

One by one, members of the gang were arrested and interrogated: the noose was tightening. On 2 December 1921 Friedrich Lewandowsky was arrested and subjected to days of psychological torture before he finally broke down, giving names and revealing the Berlin pub where the Plättner group met. By mid-December most of the group's members were under lock and key. Plättner now posted a flyer in the form of a "recruitment ad" for the "Red Scare" calling upon starving workers to join him. Still in a satirical vein, the advertising agency was given as the Hörsing-Noske Chancellery, Hanover. In its purpose, however, it was a failure, which reflected Plättner's complete isolation from even the most radical left-communist elements in the working class.

Plättner was finally arrested on 3 February 1922 along with Karl Meissner at the "Lüdderitzberg" pub in Halle. Both were carrying loaded pistols, but they offered no resistance. The police, by contrast, used maximum force: around 15 detectives entered the pub to effect the arrest, while some 50 paramilitary uniformed police provided cover outside. He was brutally beaten, struck with rifle butts and verbally abused on the way into custody. "On the steps in front of the entrance to the police barracks someone even tripped me up: I stumbled, fell down and half a dozen policemen trampled over me," he later wrote. The torture continued throughout the night.

Plättner was transferred under high security to Halle district court jail, where he was strictly isolated from fellow prisoners. From the very first Plättner argued that his crimes amounted to high treason and demanded that he be tried as a traitor. He chose the lawyer Ernst Hegewisch as his defender. Hegewisch was a member of the KPD, one of a group of mainly Jewish "comrade lawyers" (*Anwaltsgenossen*) and had already spent six months defending proletarians arrested in the aftermath of the March Action.[4] This was in stark contradistinction to the attitude of the KPD party leadership, which distanced itself completely from the Plättner group's methods, condemning them as "adventurism" while simultaneously supporting their wish to be tried as high traitors, i.e. as political rather than common criminals. Between Plättner and Hegewisch there developed a close friendship and mutual respect. The lawyer was impressed by Plättner's readiness to make such great personal sacrifices in the service of his political convictions. "There can hardly be a German revolutionary who has undergone as much persecution as Karl Plättner," he wrote.

The indictment was prepared and brought to Plättner on 22 July. The prosecution case was that the gang were common criminals as most of their takings were put to personal use. Plättner countered: "We are there, the avengers of proletarian suffering, and yet it moves,[5] the proletarian revolution, and still it lives on, the thought of the proletarian revolution! And in the fire of this example we want to keep defiance alive, to arouse enthusiasm – to be those who hail the revolutionary proletariat!" He condemned bourgeois society as organized

---

4 Ernst Hegewisch (1881-1963) later became the lead defence lawyer for participants in the 1923 Hamburg workers' insurrection. From 1924 he worked as a lawyer for Red Aid and the KPD, was barred from professional practice under the Third Reich and interned in Sachsenhausen concentration camp. After the war Hegewisch was Regional Court Director in Sachsen-Anhalt (DDR) before fleeing with his family to the Federal Republic in 1952.

5 This is a reference to the phrase attributed to Galileo, *eppur si muove*.

criminality, claimed the moral high ground for the proletarian revolution and insisted that only people who stood on a yet higher moral plane were fit to judge him and his comrades. In this response he enjoyed the full backing of Hegewisch.

Further delays ensued. First, because state attorneys in Dresden, Neuruppin and Brunswick were conducting their own enquiries and drawing up additional indictments. Then, in Prussia, a law was enacted to amnesty those convicted of crimes during the March Action. Hegewisch grasped at this straw: without the March Action, Plättner and his associates would never have followed the path that they did. It took months for the relevant Prussian committee to consider this appeal before rejecting it.

To break the deadlock, in the spring of 1923 the responsible judicial authorities changed tactics. In July 1922, following the murder of the initiator of the Treaty of Rapallo, German Foreign Minister Walther Rathenau, by right-wing fanatics, the German parliament enacted the Law for the Defence of the Republic, setting up a special court with jurisdiction in such cases. The senior Reich prosecutor argued that it should try Plättner and his associates. But the special court itself rejected this and the legal arguments over jurisdiction carried on.

Meanwhile, behind the scenes, there was a small war going on between the Plättner group and the staff and managers of the jail in Halle where they were being held, who were doing their best to make life as uncomfortable as possible. Apart from a ban on smoking and restrictions on reading material, the authorities strictly controlled Plättner's post, holding back important correspondence and censoring private letters to Gertrud. They also prevented the couple's wedding, which was due to take place on 19 July at the Halle registry office. Gertrud had given birth to their son in March. As a consequence, she was threatened with eviction. The managers of the jail insisted that they would permit a wedding only within the jail's walls, which the registry office, in turn, said was inadmissible. The wedding eventually took place several months later.

The main proceedings finally got underway on 25 June 1923 before the Halle jury court, amid heightened security and intense media interest. Plättner made one of the longest defence speeches in German legal history, eighteen hours over three days, with only short pauses. His biographer Volker Ullrich, an academic not especially sympathetic towards Plättner's acts, was moved to write: "It was a great performance, which wrung respect even out of those who were politically worlds apart." First, Plättner complained about the conditions in the Halle remand jail. Then he gave a long analysis of social conditions under capitalism and the German revolution of 1918, with quotes from Marx. He explained why he regarded the court in Halle as not competent to try him. He described his background and career path and his participation in the various insurrections since the November revolution and the formation of the Plättner group after the March Action. He showed no remorse, only defiance. The other accused showed the same defiance, and none distanced themselves from Plättner.

The KAPD condemned individual acts of terror and robberies as anti-Marxist. Its Berlin newspaper wrote: "In this trial Plättner and comrades have distanced themselves from the KAPD and its tactics [...] Their activity meant that they could have no connection with the mass membership, which is necessary for allowing the party as a whole to decide questions of principle; in this way questions for the party become quite simply questions for military leaders, while the members remain passive. These conclusions attracted Plättner and comrades, who wanted to limit the circle of members to the comrades acting only in their spirit, which amounted to the liquidation of the party in favour of small groups [...] What separates us from Plättner is not the question of principle in itself, but only insofar as we take the view that a revolutionary organization cannot be merely or predominantly a military one

[…] Their opinion is that individual expropriations of the expropriators can also fire up the working class in times of revolutionary stagnation and even in the period of defeat, and thus drive the revolution forwards. The KAPD does not share this position".[6] It continued, "By alarming the bourgeoisie, through the daring deeds of a small vanguard, [Plättner] believes he can arouse the working-class masses out of their lethargy."[7] The KAPD understood that this was the act of the revolutionary who turns to terrorism out of frustration and impatience, but it was clear that this was an error, which had led Plättner away from Marxism.

On the fourth day of the proceedings, the justices began reading the pamphlet, *Der organisierte rote Schrecken*. This led them to the inevitable conclusion on 3 July 1923, after the accused had finished their speeches, that the hearing should be moved to the Constitutional Court in Leipzig. The jury agreed. It had taken 18 months' struggle with the legal authorities for Hegewisch to achieve his objective, that Plättner not be tried as a "common criminal". Nevertheless, it took a further three months of legal wrangling before the Constitutional Court finally declared itself ready to hear the case.

Meanwhile, Hegewisch was feeling the strain. More and more articles were appearing in the KPD's press that were hostile to the Plättner gang. With the great inflation of 1923, his fees from German Red Aid had become worthless and his requests for financial support from KPD headquarters went unheeded. In July he resigned from the party, which he had helped to found in the city of Celle. In his letter of resignation, he wrote, "KPD headquarters systematically hamstrings my activity on behalf of the revolution, which is recognized by proletarians throughout Germany." He appealed for support

---

[6] *Kommunistische Arbeiter-Zeitung*, (KAZ) 1923, Nr. 52.

[7] KAZ 1923, Nr. 54

from Moscow, via Karl Radek, but received none. He suffered a nervous breakdown and had to take a long vacation. By the time he had recovered, and the Plättner trial had begun on 23 November in Leipzig, Germany had undergone further convulsions: the "Red October", a final attempt at communist insurrection in Hamburg, failed. Thereafter the KPD would be firmly under the control of Moscow and would focus on contesting parliamentary elections. Talk of revolution by the party was, more than ever, mere rhetoric, covering opportunistic practice. Hitler's nationalist beer hall putsch had also failed in Munich on 9 November. Currency reform under Hjalmar Schacht would soon restore some stability to the economy.

Plättner was transported from Halle to Leipzig in shackles. The Leipzig senior prosecutor, worried that he might be released under the Amnesty of July 1922, called upon President Ebert to appoint no less a figure than General von Seeckt, the German Chief of Staff, to take Plättner and five associates into protective custody should they be released.

Against this background the trial became a huge media circus, though not all of the coverage was hostile. The court reporter of the *Vossische Zeitung*, the national liberal newspaper of record, was especially impressed by the central German gang leader: "Plättner himself is undoubtedly a person about whom one cannot take anything easily for granted. He comes, as they say, from the simplest of circumstances, has worked his way up from the depths and appropriated an astonishing level of education ... He is of medium size, of squat form. His face is exceedingly striking, pale, and lit up by a pair of clever, fanatical eyes. Above the high forehead stands a neatly brushed parting, which gives his whole face something of the artistic. Actually, this is not the face of a propagandist of the deed, but rather that of a cultivated man with artistic leanings."

The same reporter wrote sympathetically about other members of the gang: "The romanticism of Schiller's *Robbers* wafts from the dock ... There is also a girl of just 19 years of age among the accused. Blond and like a bird of passage, with innocent blue eyes and a cheap gold headband over her childish forehead: the secretary of the organized 'red scare'. All of these people have been sitting in custody awaiting trial for more than two years. Despite everything, the solidarity of the group is unbroken." The group stood the test of the "prisoner's dilemma", as a communist newspaper acknow-ledged: "None incriminated the others, each stood for his own crimes."

As was to be expected, the court showed no such sympathy. As the KAPD's Berlin newspaper, the *Kommunistische Arbeiter-Zeitung* had foreseen when the trial was transferred from Halle, as far as the bourgeoisie was concerned, the defendants were merely "out of the frying pan and into the fire". The President of the Court, Niedner, allowed Plättner no opportunity to make a lengthy speech in his defence, and expelled him from the court's proceedings when he laughed at a witness's testimony. Only when Hegewisch threatened to take no further part did the court relent, stating that there was no intention to exclude Plättner permanently. In his closing speech, the prosecutor demanded 15 years' imprisonment for Plättner, 8 to 10 years for his closest associates, and lengthy custodial sentences for accomplices. In its lengthy 42-page judgment the court discussed the legal issues in depth but found no mitigating circumstances in the political motivation of the group's crimes. "The Plättner people, although they are not to be put on the same level with common street robbers, have moved through the most diverse parts of Germany like robbers with loaded pistols, hand grenades, rubber truncheons, ropes, and in one case also with face masks, and have spread fear and terror. Such a gang is a serious public danger, even if it claims to act for political reasons."

Plättner was sentenced to 10 years' imprisonment; other members of the gang received slightly lower sentences. But these were extremely harsh, especially when compared to another political trial that took place a few months later for an attempt to overthrow the Republic involving multiple fatalities, including four policemen. Adolf Hitler and Rudolf Hess were sentenced to five years' *Festungshaft* for their part in leading the beer hall putsch. This was the mildest of the three types of jail sentence available in German law at the time; it excluded forced labour, provided reasonably comfortable cells, and allowed the prisoner to receive visitors almost daily for many hours. It was the customary sentence for those whom the judge believed to have had honourable but misguided motives, and it did not carry the stigma of a custodial sentence in a *Strafanstalt* (penal institution): either a *Gefängnis* (jail) or *Zuchthaus* (prison). In the end, Hitler served only a little over eight months of this sentence before his early release for good behaviour. Plättner, by contrast, who had not killed or even injured anyone, would serve five and a half years in a *Zuchthaus*, on top of the two and a half years in *Gefängnis*, before being amnestied.

These two judgments made it abundantly clear that the independence of the judiciary in Weimar Germany was an absolute fiction; this was class justice at its most grotesque, pure and simple.

Plättner was transferred to Brandenburg (Havel) jail on 12 December 1923. His group was split up and distributed across three separate penal institutions in an effort to break their solidarity. As was to be expected, Plättner was treated roughly on reception; every attempt was made to humiliate him and break his spirit. And as was equally to be expected, he responded as a rebel. This worked. He managed to secure various privileges: transfer to a less uncomfortable cell, a bookshelf, writing materials, the right to smoke, the right to receive a communist newspaper, and (eventually) a partially unsupervised visit by Gertrud. As soon as one concession was granted, he demanded another, and he got on the Governor's nerves. When Plättner went too far, for example by refusing forced labour, he was placed in an arrest cell. He went on hunger strike, breaking this after the intervention of the Reichstag deputy Wendelin Thomas.[8] Eventually Plättner and the Governor reached a compromise: he would do work in the mornings, after which he was free to read and write.

The authorities were less accommodating when it came to Plättner's request, in February 1924, to visit his mother, who was close to death. The Minister of Justice at the time, Erich Emminger, was a member of the right-wing Bavarian People's Party, the BVP. Gustav Menzel, a KPD deputy in the Prussian parliament, wrote to Plättner that there was little chance of the request being granted: "Yes, if you were Hitler or belonged to that fraternity, the situation would be somewhat different". Plättner's mother died on 16 June 1924.

Plättner was not even allowed to attend her funeral. His hatred of the penal authorities was now boundless, as he later wrote in his prison biography, *Der mitteldeutsche Bandenführer. Mein Leben hinter Kerkermauern*, (The Central German Gang Leader. My Life behind Prison Walls, Berlin 1930). He suspected that the authorities were out to destroy him and his comrades, a suspicion that had increased when Friedrich Lewandowsky died after an operation in the prison hospital early in June 1924. Lewandowsky had complained of intestinal pains but had not been taken seriously until it was too late. Then another member of the group, Friedrich Fischer, was found hanged in his cell in March 1925, after a long period of depression, which the authorities also refused to take seriously. "His suicide was an indictment against a punishment that took no account of mentally ill prisoners," wrote Plättner's biographer.

Plättner himself was at his wits' end. He felt abandoned

---

[8] Wendelin Thomas (1884-1947) was elected to the Reichstag in 1920 as a member of the USPD then joined the (V)KPD following the merger. He worked within the Comintern from 1925 to 1928, then spent two years in jail before the 1930 amnesty. He emigrated to the United States following the Nazi seizure of power and, at the same time, left the KPD. His subsequent existence is disputed.

by Ernst Hegewisch, who was fully occupied defending participants in the Hamburg insurrection of 1923; meanwhile the prison governor was waging a campaign to torment Plättner to the limits of endurance. Plättner suffered frequent crying fits. Hegewisch wrote a 20-page letter to his client, admonishing him for the unfair accusations and pointing out that few other lawyers would have tolerated his behaviour, but also stiffening his spirit of resistance: "He who wrote the pamphlet, 'The Organized Red Scare' cannot allow himself to be broken in prison."

Meanwhile some hope came from an unexpected source. A prominent bourgeois lawyer and criminologist, Moritz Liepmann, penned a sharp criticism of the treatment and sentencing of the Plättner group, arguing that they had been judged not according to their acts but their intentions, and that the sentences were determined by the subjective opinions of the judges. Plättner seized upon this and appointed a new defence lawyer, Felix Halle, to take up the case for an amnesty. He also received support from the German League for Human Rights (DLfM). Plättner had also undergone a change of mind and heart. Towards the end of 1924, according to the DLfM, he declared that he had chosen the wrong path. He based this change of view on a deep study and understanding of the Marxist classics and other theoretical writings. [9]

On 22 January 1925 the KPD fraction in the Reichstag made an intervention on behalf of the Plättner group. The Ministry of Justice rejected their criticism of the verdict and

---

[9] Felix Halle (1884-1937) became Professor of Jurisprudence at Berlin University after the First World War and joined the KPD in 1920. Based on his experiences with Karl Plättner, Max Hoelz and others, in 1929 Halle published a guidebook codifying how proletarian prisoners should defend themselves against the police, prosecutors and courts. It advised against the kind of bravado displayed by Hoelz and Plättner. Following the Nazi seizure of power Halle made his way to the USSR, where he worked in the Moscow Institute for Criminology. He was arrested as a "counter-revolutionary Trotskyist" during the NKVD's German Operation, tortured and put on trial. He was shot on November 5, 1937.

punishment, but at least it had now become a matter for the Reichstag's amnesty committee. Plättner was not invited to appear before it, as he hoped, but he was represented by three lawyers: Felix Halle, Ernst Hegewisch and a member of the Berlin Judicial Council. The committee ducked the question of whether the amnesty law applied but suggested that some members of the group were entitled to clemency. Even this was rejected as "too early" by the judicial authorities and President Paul von Hindenburg.

Plättner's health deteriorated seriously from the autumn of 1924. He suffered lung disorders and panic attacks. The prison doctors, predictably, accused him of malingering. When Plättner then engaged a private physician, Dr. Leo Klaubner, who confirmed that his condition was serious, the prison authorities first tried to undermine Klaubner, because he was sympathetic to the KPD, then diagnosed Plättner with "neurasthenia". This was a very convenient all-purpose term, popular at the time, for a nervous disorder whose causes could not be determined. The prison governor seized on this to reach a subjective and adverse verdict: "Since he considers himself a martyr and is by nature a very restless and arrogant man, he appeared from the outset very presumptuous, and has remained so despite persistent instruction and all attempts to influence him by coercion and benevolence." When Plättner protested against the prison governor's denial of his request to work in the prison garden, in fresh air, the Governor had him transferred to the lunatic asylum at Moabit jail in Berlin. Here, at least, he was treated with respect by the jail's governor, who, Plättner wrote, had a "pleasant appearance – with none of the characteristics of a jailer." This was high praise indeed from Plättner, whose condition started to improve. The governor in question, who had been Rosa Luxemburg's jailer at the Wronke fortress during the First World War, held long conversations with Plättner, and allowed him meetings with Gertrud and representatives of the KPD.

In March 1926 he made a declaration to the KPD, via the

deputy to the Prussian parliament, Gustav Menzel, renouncing his earlier practice of guerrilla warfare and individual expropriations as "criminality disguised as romanticism" and "politically pointless, morally dangerous". Such methods only alienated large sections of the working class, without whose active participation communism was "not viable". And further: "I am repeatedly shocked by what is hidden away under my wing and embellished with my 'programme' … Every miserable person who acts out of despair, every principled hoodlum who is chained to all the vices of the demimonde invokes my 'Organized Red Scare' … My conscience and my sense of responsibility towards the ideological purity of communism command me to put an end to this devilish racket." It is possible to err in politically chaotic times and choose the wrong methods of struggle, but "after such experiments, one must also 'rediscover' the straight line and ways that are driven by the order of a more deeply rooted reason."

The maturity exhibited in this declaration did not help his situation in prison. Against the advice of the medical counsel at Moabit, Dr. Leppmann, Plättner was transferred to the prison of Luckau at the end of July. In Luckau, the prison where Karl Liebknecht had been incarcerated during the First World War, the conditions were similar to Brandenburg. Plättner recommenced his struggle to improve his conditions, but the warders at this institution were determined to make life hell for him.

After petitions by the DLfM and by Plättner's father, who movingly raised the plight of his grandson, had failed, it seemed as though his situation was hopeless. But then, after the elections of 20 May 1928, there was a change of government. The new Minister of Justice, Erich Koch, of the left-liberal German Democratic Party (DDP), was keen to make an impression. Plättner was thus released from prison on 17 July 1928 with the Koch Amnesty, one of a series of amnesties for political prisoners under the Presidency of Paul Hindenburg. On the evening of 18 July Plättner was rapturously greeted, together with his comrade Alfred Menzel, by several thousand workers at Leipzig main railway station, and carried on shoulders to the Rossplatz, where the KPD had organized a major rally. Plättner was so moved that he could barely speak. That same day, Max Hoelz was also released and received a similar welcome in Berlin.

Politically there seemed only one way forward for Plättner after his release: a return to the KPD. The KAPD, long riven by splits, was now in its "groupuscular" phase, with no faction counting more than a few hundred adherents. Not everyone in the KPD welcomed his decision, but the Central Committee could see the propaganda benefits of his return to the "mother party". A further declaration followed, probably in late August, in which Plättner wrote: "I return with joyful agreement to the Communist Party and express the opinion that this move may give impetus to many others who are still reluctant today to decide to join the party, which is determined to overthrow the capitalist economy and to struggle in a disciplined manner under the red Soviet banner."

This blind submission to the party he had once so sharply criticized can perhaps also be explained by the gratitude he must have felt for the support he received from individual party members during his imprisonment. He was not yet in desperate need of financial support, as Gertrud now had a well-paid job as a secretary with a Leipzig publisher, though the party did offer him 200 marks as a bridging loan until he found employment.

At the end of October Red Aid Germany asked Plättner to write a book about the penal system, based on a survey of those released with the Koch Amnesty. He got cracking immediately, with incredible zeal and energy. A 139-page manuscript was ready within a month. The book was published by MOPR, the publishing arm of Red Aid, at the end of 1928, with the title *Gefangen!* (Captive!). Only one of the 30 amnestied prisoners that he interviewed, Paul Töpfer, was a former member of the Plättner group. It seems he had fallen out with some, or perhaps most, of the others, what with the stresses of imprisonment, which had perhaps allowed minor ideological differences and petty personal animosities to get out of proportion. The book took the form of an oral history, with Plättner himself very much in the background, though in the Foreword he stated that one problem faced by prisoners had a particular importance, "the sexual distress of the incarcerated", and he wished to make a special study of this phenomenon.

In his last year in prison, Plättner had begun the preliminary work for such a project. And already in the summer after his release, Plättner helped the director Wilhelm Dieterle on a new film project that had its premiere on 11 October 1928 in the Berlin Tauentzien-Palast, *Geschlecht in Fesseln. Die Sexualnot der Strafgefangenen* (Sex in Chains. The Sexual distress of Convicts). It was an outstanding success, well received in progressive bourgeois circles. Such a film could only have been made in Germany at the time. "German film went to uncanny, erotic and imaginative places where even Hollywood had never been," as James Hawes succinctly put it in "The Shortest History of Germany". The *Vossische Zeitung* now wrote: "The most thrilling, startling trend film ever made. [...] It deals with the sexual distress of the inmates and the equally great misery of their wives. So, an indictment against the modern penal system, which has not yet understood how to solve this certainly difficult problem." The film was restored and rereleased in 1996.

In March 1929 *Weltbühne* (World Stage), a German weekly focused on politics, art and business gave a foretaste of what was come, with an article entitled *Sexualnot der Gefangenen* (Sexual distress of Prisoners). At the time, *Weltbühne* had a relatively small circulation, but considerable reputation and influence, under the editorship of Carl von Ossietzky. [10]

---

[10] Carl von Ossietzky. (1889-1938) was a German pacifist and the recipient of the 1935 Nobel Peace Prize for his work in exposing the clandestine German re-

Eros im Zuchthaus itself was first published by MOPR Verlag in March 1929.[11]

Like the film, this book caused an immediate sensation with its outspoken frankness about topics such as masturbation, homosexuality and the situation of pregnant women in prison. One of the inspirations for this work was *Eros im Stacheldraht* (Eros behind Barbed Wire) by Hans Otto Henel (1926), a collection of stories illustrating the sexual frustrations of front-line soldiers during the First World War. But *Eros im Zuchthaus* goes far deeper, and the speed with which it was published leaves one in no doubt that Plättner had widely read scientific and psychoanalytical literature while in prison, notably the works of Sigmund Freud.[12] On the other hand the book is anything but a dry scientific analysis; it is largely based on Plättner's own sexual distress. As the authors of the Foreword, Magnus Hirschfeld and Felix Abraham state: "Plättner's book provides [...] the first-hand descriptions and reports of a man who lived for years in prison and who went through his own personal suffering and all the agony of sexual abstinence. Here we have a highly trustworthy documentary account of lived experiences."

In reading Plättner's experiences, one should always bear in mind that in the 1920s masturbation was still a highly taboo subject, not just in bourgeois circles but also within the working class, so Plättner must have gone through some considerable self-reflection before writing so openly about the subject. He writes, "My life had developed its form, content and maturity in the Hamburg workers' movement, especially

---

armament. The first such exposé appeared in Weltbühne in 1929.

[11] Carl von Ossietzky. (1889-1938) was a German pacifist and the recipient of the 1935 Nobel Peace Prize for his work in exposing the clandestine German re-armament. The first such exposé appeared in Weltbühne in 1929.

[12] Included in the original German editions is a glossary of scientific and other terms that Plättner thought would be unfamiliar to the ordinary reader.

in the local youth organization, in which sexual abstinence was practised in a more or less strong-willed manner ... The ideas and habits that shaped and ruled my being in this milieu naturally also continued to influence me in this period while I was on remand. I was ruled by the thought that masturbation is a sacrilege against nature, a profanation of sexual life should I resort to forms of relief that would drag down everything that had until now been sacred to me, and for which I worked and lived."

In this respect it is well worth comparing and contrasting what Max Hoelz had to say on the subject in his autobiography. Part 2 of his book deals with Hoelz's prison experience, with considerable focus on the terror of sexual abstinence. Hoelz's solution is the traditional one of physical exercise and cold showers. Certain extracts could even come from Lord Baden-Powell's *Scouting for Boys:*

> "I myself suffered hardly any less than the other prisoners from this forced asceticism. My whole body burned like the fires of hell in my desire for a woman. In order not to be driven crazy by this tormented craving, I often jumped out of bed at one, two, or three o'clock at night and drenched my body with a five-litre jug of icy-cold water. Then I dried myself, wiped the floor and did two to three hours of gymnastic exercises."

Hoelz also believes some of the myths that were still current about the physical effects of masturbation. Perhaps not blindness, but:

> "I had virtually stopped the practice of masturbating and now avoided it for months on end, to ensure that my glands would not wither away, and my sexual organs would not completely lose their functions."

It may be that Hoelz was trying to establish a moral superiority over Plättner in taking this attitude, in which case he failed. Plättner is on the one hand more scientific in his approach to the subject, but on the other, far more authentic in his willingness to admit to his own human weaknesses, succumbing to temptation and the feelings of self-disgust that followed.

The main thrust of Plättner's argument in *Eros im Zuchthaus* is that enforced sexual abstinence in prison inevitably leads to all kinds of psychological and physical problems and repercussions, including moral depravity and, in some cases, sexual crime. Men behave in ways that would be unthinkable while in freedom.

For example, Plättner draws a very clear distinction between those prisoners who are innately homosexual and prisoners who engage in "pseudo-homosexual" activity in the absence of members of the opposite sex, and those who "learn" homosexual practices and prostitute themselves for personal gain. Plättner also asserts that, contrary to received wisdom, it is frequently those who, in freedom, are most sensitive and morally upstanding who fall into the worst excesses of fetishism, bestiality and other forms of sexual corruption when inside. Nor is this limited to men. Plättner provides several personal and first-hand accounts of women behaving as "sexual predators" under the duress of enforced sexual abstinence.

Karl Plättner also offers, at the end of the work, a set of practical proposals for prison reform that would address the issue. Dr. Magnus Hirschfeld of the *Institut für Sexualwissenschaft* (Institute for Sexual Science) in Berlin, considered the greatest sexologist of the twentieth century, joined Plättner in advocating matrimonial visits to lessen sexual tension in prisons. The first edition of *Eros im Zuchthaus* appeared with a jacket design by John Heartfield and a print run of 15,000, sold out in no time at all, and a second edition with a print run of 25,000 appeared early in 1930.[13] The latter was published by

---

[13] Born Helmut Herzfeld, John Heartfield (1891-1968) was a pioneer of art as political propaganda. Some of his most famous photomontages were anti-Nazi and anti-fascist statements. Heartfield created book jackets for book numerous authors, such as Upton Sinclair, as well as stage sets for playwrights, including Bertolt Brecht.

the Paul Witte Verlag in Hanover, as Plättner had apparently parted company with the MOPR publishing house.

Eros im Zuchthaus was also performed on-stage: Friedrich Lichtneker, author and dramatist at the Vienna Volkstheater, wrote a three-act play of the same name, which was first performed at an unknown venue on 23 November 1929, but was later produced at the Lobe and Thaliatheater, Breslau by Max Oppenheimer.

After publication, Plättner went on a lecture tour; the speaking events often took place alongside performances of the film *Geschlecht in Fesseln* (in November 1931 the Hamm magistrates court fined him 30 marks and sentenced him to six days' imprisonment for showing parts of the film that had been censored by the Bavarian government). Karl Plättner rediscovered his revolutionary zeal and rhetoric at these lectures, which landed him in trouble with the authorities once again. Thus, in September 1929 in two Saxon towns he ended his lecture with the call, "Burn down the prisons, open the dungeons, free the prisoners!"

While on the lecture tour Plättner wrote his last book, *Der mitteldeutsche Bandenführer*. Based on the success of *Eros im Zuchthaus*, the publisher promised the public a new sensation. But the book flopped; perhaps this was precisely because the publisher applied too much pressure to capitalize on the recent success. In this respect Plättner fared worse than Max Hoelz. Unlike Hoelz's autobiography, which grips the reader with its picaresque story of personal hardship, the war years, life on the run and guerrilla warfare, before going on to describe Hoelz's dealings with the prison authorities, Plättner's book is for the most part a monotonous account of his petty arguments with prison governors and officials to win special privileges. The hitherto favourable and supportive anarchist poet and author Erich Mühsam wrote a scathing review in his magazine, *Fanal* ("Beacon").

Plättner's political career was also going downhill. The Stalinist KPD headquarters, under the control of Ernst Thälmann, had tightened its grip. Members of the Leipzig district party who supported the opposition were purged. At a conference of Red Aid in the district of West Saxony, Plättner appealed for the former members of the Central Committee to be allowed, at least, to defend themselves. The majority of those present rejected this appeal, even threatening physical violence against opponents. Thereafter, Plättner became less and less involved with Red Aid. The party, in turn, gave him the cold shoulder. "The Moor had done his work, he could go," to paraphrase Schiller. The hopes Plättner had nurtured on returning to the KPD were already in tatters. In any case, despite appearances, the KPD was already facing defeat. As the economic crisis developed, the party, now entirely under the control of Moscow, made electoral gains, but was unable to provide decisive and strategic leadership to the German proletariat, weakened as it was by mass unemployment.

In 1930 Plättner also separated from Gertrud. The love celebrated in the pages of *Eros im Zuchthaus* had evaporated; this is perhaps unsurprising, because Plättner himself provides copious examples of the frequent marital breakdowns that occur between husband and wife after a prisoner's release, as a result of prolonged sexual abstinence, together with unrealistic expectations that harmonious relationships can be re-established. At the end of 1930 Plättner met the woman with whom he would spend the rest of his life in freedom. Hertha Sebastian was 29 years old at the time. She had trained as a day care worker for children; when she met Plättner she was working in Leipzig at Weltfilm GmbH, a company that loaned films to proletarian organizations. She moved in with Plättner in 1931 and their son Rolf was born in June 1934.

Persecution began soon after the Nazi seizure of power. In July 1933 he was interned for five days. He would not compromise his opposition to the new regime, which made it impossible for him to find employment. Attempts to keep the family finances afloat by selling ice cream and eggs failed, before he finally managed to make a go of it selling firewood. It consumed all of his time, the business flourished, and before long he was employing three workers.

In November 1935 Plättner applied for a licence for a delivery vehicle, as it was no longer possible to reach all of his customers using hand-carts. As a consequence, the police looked into his past and concluded that he was "politically unreliable". One report stated, "Before the national uprising [i.e., the Nazi seizure of power] Plättner was the leader of a communist terror-group and an author in the KPD … Until today, he has not changed his opinion and he will not change his opinion." Asked for its advice, the local Nazi party stated tersely that Plättner was a "known communist".

Thus, the application for a licence was refused. To get around this, Plättner persuaded the dealer in Leipzig to sell him the desired three-wheeler but to register it in his own name, in return for a share in his business as a silent partner. This worked for a few months until Plättner was denounced to the police. He was called to the local station on 18 March 1936, where he attempted to persuade the officials that all he wanted was to build a simple existence and a financial basis for an ordered family life. He added that, in the light of developments since 1933, the idea of communism had become a purely passive matter for him, pushed into the background by the pressures of daily work, business concerns and paying his bills. The officials were not convinced, recording that even if he was steering clear of the illegal activities of the KPD, his assurances should be treated with care. Plättner was to be watched from now on. A few days later the Leipzig police headquarters informed him that he was banned from driving his vehicle.

After Plättner wrote a long letter of complaint to the district authorities, stating that without use of the vehicle he would have to close his business and put three men out of work, the police headquarters relented, though only on condition that the vehicle be parked in a shed at night-time. The leader of the local Nazi party, a butcher named Max Fritsch, who lived in the same block as Plättner's business address, was tasked with watching Plättner to ensure that he adhered to this agreement. Fritsch reported back to the police that he had observed Plättner closely from the very first day and could not confirm any suspicions. He said that he considered Plättner too clever to do anything in any way harmful to the state, and that Plättner had told him, in a casual conversation, "It would be mad to undertake anything against the current state, as the state is too firmly anchored."

This was indeed the new reality. The economic upturn and first foreign policy successes had stabilized the regime, while the savage repression of the first two years of dictatorship, mainly directed against communists, meant very few were prepared to risk their necks. In 1934-5 around 1,600 communists were arrested in Leipzig alone. In practice this meant that communists such as Plättner, while adhering to their principles, were not going to raise their heads above the parapet and would do whatever was absolutely essential to avoid arrest. Plättner's successful business venture was a by-product of his hyperactivity in compensating for the end to his political engagement. This was confirmed by Hertha Sebastian, who told the Leipzig District Governor: "He is totally committed to his business nowadays and is focused on raising a family and providing for it as decently as possible."

Nonetheless, the Nazi state kept a close watch on him as a "dangerous communist". For example, when Plättner requested special permission to use his three-wheeler to travel to the Harz mountains to visit suppliers and his family in Thale, he was required to specify in advance the exact route and to register with the police his departure and return. The police in Thale were also informed and asked to keep a watch on him. Such was life under the Nazi dictatorship.

On the morning of 15 April 1937 Plättner was arrested again, this time along with thirteen Leipzig residents suspected of activity for the KPD underground. Plättner and the other prisoners were taken on the same day to the "camp for protective custody" at Sachsenburg near Chemnitz. When this was closed at the end of August, he was transferred to the concentration camp at Buchenwald, on the crest of Ettersberg hill overlooking the city of Weimar. New inmates were greeted with the camp motto *Jedem das Seine*, the literal German translation of the Latin juridical term meaning "to each what he deserves", and then subjected to ritual humiliation and beatings. The SS guards had absolute power of life and death over prisoners, who were subjected to forced hard labour in a nearby quarry. As the communist Gustav Mettin, arrested with Karl Plättner, later testified: "Prisoners were taken to the quarry. There they were burdened with heavy stones until they could no longer bear it and ran through the sentry cordon. Result: shot while trying to escape. Or another method: They gave them a shove so that they fell behind the sentry cordon and then shot them immediately ... People who were lying prone on the muster-ground were kicked with boots and told, 'Die, you dog!' Almost all of the SS people took part in this behaviour."[14]

Plättner was released from Buchenwald on 11 November 1937 and allowed to continue with his business, though he was even more closely watched than ever. He was arrested again on 26 March 1938 but released that evening. Then, owing to a change in the regulations, Plättner had to apply in August 1938 for a driving licence to continue using his three-wheeler delivery vehicle, which he received, again on condition that it was parked overnight at the business address. Despite efforts to trip him up with some minor traffic infringement, a report early in June 1939 confirmed that Plättner had not been involved in or supported any activity against the state and was fully engaged in business activities.

In fact, Karl Plättner had become a model member of the petty bourgeoisie, the class of tradesmen who formed the very

---

14 Gustav Mettin, memoirs, April 1948. Quoted in Ullrich, pp. 203-4

core of the Nazi regime's support: "He always greets his clientele politely and courteously and is generally described as a diligent and correct businessman," says the report. But this was no longer enough to get an ex-communist off the hook. Plättner still opposed the National Socialist movement, though passively, the report added.

Since 1936 the Gestapo had kept lists of potential "enemies of the state" who should be arrested in the event of war, which broke out on 1 September 1939 with the invasion of Poland. That same day Plättner was carted off to the Leipzig police headquarters, along with many other comrades who had suffered alongside him in Sachsenburg and Buchenwald. Seven days later the Leipzig communists and other political prisoners were returned to Buchenwald, where there were already thousands of internees, mostly political, but also the so-called "work-shy", professional criminals and other categories of prisoner. As the war progressed, increasing numbers of prisoners from occupied territories entered the camp, so that by 1944, German inmates were a minority of ten per cent. German communists took on an important role within this minority – despite their ideological differences with the regime – for maintaining order, based on their long experience of camp life. Some even rose to the rank of the so-called "red kapos", in return for which their situation was eased, if only relatively speaking. However, those communists who did not fully fall into line with camp discipline, or who made themselves disagreeable for political reasons, would suffer unpleasant consequences. Both of these applied to Karl Plättner. It seems he commanded high respect among the older KPD inmates who recalled his activity in the years 1917-33, but not among the younger recruits who were keen supporters of Josef Stalin.

As Volker Ullrich put it: "Plättner had never been able to fall into line within power hierarchies, and he had never been an unconditional follower of a ruling party line. Wherever he had appeared, he had acted as a gadfly and played the role of troublemaker and loose cannon. Things were no different in the concentration camp." He made friends with Erich Melcher, a member of the German Socialist Workers' Party (SAPD), formed by ex-social democrats and communist oppositionists in 1931. The two dissidents came into conflict with the KPD camp hierarchy and at the end of January 1944 they were transported to the Lublin-Majdanek concentration camp. As the Dresden communist Walter Reede, who met the pair in Lublin-Majdanek later wrote in memoirs dedicated to his "comrades in suffering", Karl Plättner and Erich Melcher: "It was the same old song: Woe-betide he who opposed the camp aristocracy, he very soon felt the power of these gentlemen. Switch to another labour squad and transport were the most popular means to get rid of the difficult elements."

Unlike Buchenwald, Lublin-Majdanek was not only a concentration camp, but also an extermination camp. Thousands of Jews had already been murdered there. Arrivals from Buchenwald were drafted into forced labour for the Waffen-SS. The work was very demanding, and survival depended on solidarity between the inmates. As the Red Army advanced, the camp was disbanded and Plättner, Melcher and Reede sent on a death-march to Auschwitz-Birkenau, which they barely survived. On arrival at Birkenau, they had to share a single bed for 14 days in the quarantine ward. Thereafter, the work was somewhat easier than at the Lublin-Majdanek camp, but the three soon faced a gruesome choice. As the war entered its final phase, political prisoners were asked to volunteer for the army. Plättner and Reede had no hesitation in refusing. Much to their disappointment Melcher, by contrast, was drafted into the SS Dirlewanger Brigade, a suicide unit composed of criminals and dissidents, and was killed fighting partisans not far from Budapest.

By mid-January 1945 the Red Army was closing in on Cracow. Auschwitz now had to be abandoned. A new death march, this time in the freezing cold. Karl Plättner and Walter Reede survived this too and were among 5,714 arrivals at the concentration camp in Melk, part of the Mauthausen complex, near Linz in Austria. Plättner and Reede were assigned to a force labour unit codenamed "Projekt Quarz", charged with excavating tunnels and galleries in a nearby mountain, where the Steyr-Daimler-Puch company, the largest armaments firm in Austria, could continue production beyond the reach of allied air raids. Work here, hammering out rock and loading wagons and conveyor belts with the debris was especially arduous; hardly a day went by without blows from the guards, and prisoners would be left waiting in snow, wind and rain for transport to and from the camp. Of the 15,000 prisoners at Melk, nearly 5,000 had perished before the end of the war.

On 13 April 1945, the day that Vienna fell to the Red Army, Melk was evacuated. The next destination was the concentration camp of Ebensee. Plättner and Reede were among 2,042 prisoners who were loaded onto freight barges on the Danube and transported to Linz. From there, they were force-marched 70 kilometres to the camp. Once again, many died on the road. Those who could not keep up were simply shot on the spot by the SS; pointlessly, as the end of the war was now a matter of a couple of weeks away. The inmates at Ebensee, located in the Salzkammergut of the Austria Alps, were forced to work on another excavation, in this case to house the German rocket research centre, formerly at Peenemünde in Pomerania. The conditions here were already catastrophic; with the arrival of 18,500 further inmates from Melk, who had to be crammed into a few barracks, they were impossible. Hundreds died of disease and starvation every day. Karl Plättner and Walter Reede now counted among these *Muselmänner*, all skin and bones, dying of hunger fever and incapable of further work. Again, survival depended on solidarity. Reede wrote in his memoirs: "Old comrades from my time in Dachau took us in and hid us in their block. If we were able to experience the hour of liberation, it was thanks to this comradeship."

The SS knew that their days of hegemony were drawing

to a close. The rumours started that they intended to drive the surviving prisoners into the tunnels and slaughter them. On the last morning muster of 5 May, the inmates therefore refused to follow the command to enter the tunnels. The same afternoon the SS guards fled the camp and were replaced by the *Volkssturm* (the German Home Guard). A day later, at two-thirty, the first American armoured cars arrived. Reede: "We fell into their arms [...] Like children, we gave our feelings free rein: we are free, free, free. It was a unique sense of freedom in the middle of the barbed wire perimeter fence."

Driven by a restless impatience, Plättner could not wait to regain his strength before making his way back to Leipzig and his wife and child. On the very day of liberation, 6 May, he and his friend cut through that barbed wire. An army deserter picked them up in Bad Ischl, near Ebensee and drove them to Salzburg. From there they travelled onwards by lorry to Freising in Bavaria, where the military refused to allow them to proceed by motor vehicle. So, they continued on foot. In Thalhausen, near Dachau, they spent the night in a farmer's barn.

The next day, Plättner complained of chest pains. Reede feared that repose would spell death for his comrade; so the pair continued on foot for a few kilometres, then hitched a lift on a cart to Allershausen. Plättner was now completely exhausted. The village doctor prescribed acute bronchitis and sent him in an American jeep to the military hospital in Freising. For the first time in six years the two comrades slept in a proper bed with clean sheets.

But just as Reede had feared, rest could not save his friend. He did not recover. The attempt to organize an ambulance to Leipzig, so that he could say farewell to his wife also failed; on 4 June 1945, shortly before six in the morning, Karl Plättner's life slipped away.

His body was buried in Neustift cemetery in Freising. In 1959 his remains were interred in the Nagelberg War Cemetery in the Franconian town of Treuchtlingen, Bavaria.

This, then, was the tragic but inspiring story of Karl Plättner, a man who matured in his intellectual and emotional intelligence over the years, without ever compromising his fundamental principles. He remains largely unknown outside of German left-communist circles. His masterwork, *Eros im Zuchthaus,* was of course condemned, alongside the work of his mentor, Dr. Magnus Hirschfeld, as "degenerate" by the Nazis, and was never translated into other languages, not even English. In the German Democratic Republic, the name Karl Plättner, like that of other dissident communists, received no mention in official histories of the communist-led upheavals of the early Weimar years.

But *Eros im Zuchthaus* caused a sensation in its time, and its message is still relevant to new audiences today. Reading his words, it is incredible to think that this book was written nearly a century ago. It is a book full of reports of moral depravity, debauchery and perversion, yet at its heart, *Eros im Zuchthaus* is an affirmation of the beauty and dignity of natural, erotic love, as celebrated in the poetry that Plättner dedicates to Gertrud Gaiewski.

As one of Plättner's witnesses said, without erotic love a man is only half alive.

Ed Walker
Mannheim, April 2019

Commentary by Medical Consultants Dr. Magnus Hirschfeld & Dr. med. Felix Abraham

The numerous publications dealing with the sexual distress of our time indicate just how great is the need for reform, in the sense of change and improvement, of people's sex life. It may compromise the illusion of some people that one should approach a human instinct so deeply rooted in psychological experience, and one that has inspired our greatest poets and thinkers to their most sublime works, with the principles of reason and science. But our present epoch, with its social antagonisms and its justifiable desire to reform our way of life, is not inclined to allow sentiment to prevail on its own, and in a more or less vague manner; instead, the mind must intervene to help counterbalance it. The social struggle has also initiated the struggle for birth control, thereby confronting a feeling that has hitherto been one of humanity's most powerful experiences, namely that of motherhood, a development that will also enable us to regulate more strongly than ever our sexual emotional feelings by rational means.

Until now sexual science has accomplished many things in these fields, and it seems as though we have gradually entered an era of sexual fulfilment. But we did not consider a great class of people whose sexual distress is almost immeasurable: those who do not enjoy freedom, those who spend their lives in jails and prisons for years on end and who are excluded from any kind of personal freedom of control over their body and soul. Those of us who have never lived "behind walls" can in no way imagine what kind of torment a sexually mature person must endure when he is damned to spend a period of his life in a closed penal facility. We cannot possibly have our own personal perspective on this, since a short visit to a penal institution will never make us acquainted with this side of prison life. There may well be a few, if not numerous, reports on the sexual life of prisoners; but one cannot view these without a certain amount of scepticism. Most of the work comes from writers who are employed by state institutions in prisons and, so to speak, have dealt with the matter in a purely official capacity. In occasional, perhaps also systematic conversations, prisoners' experiences have been gathered, and conclusions drawn based only on what has been heard. In this respect Plättner's book provides a fundamental remedy; it provides the first-hand descriptions and reports of a man who lived for years in prison and who went through his own personal suffering and all the agony of sexual abstinence. Here we have a highly trustworthy documentary account of lived experiences. However, we are well aware, based on daily consultations in our practice, how things stand regarding people's openness towards the medical professional concerning their sex lives: there is really no other area of the medical profession where greater resistance needs to be overcome. Trust is everything! But if this is already the case for people who are living in freedom, how must it be for those in captivity, where a person does not engage with a doctor of his own choosing, in whom he can put his trust, but, as it were, a superior, whom he distrusts because he does not know whether that person is well-intentioned or not! Only he who has witnessed it, who sees, who can feel, and above all he who knows the soul of the people can count as a true authority. Plättner, in equal measure an unpretentious as well as a keen observer, to a large extent fulfils this requirement, and so his book becomes an indictment, such as would be hard to find presented in a more emotional manner; and, moreover, a book that is not content simply to make the indictment, but also points towards possible remedies!

A person's sex life is the strongest release of his ego. It represents the most primal urge, which connects him most intimately with nature. The analytical researches of the Viennese school, however much exaggerated in terms of their impact and consequences, have demonstrated to us the malign role played by repression of the sexual. By far the most mental disorders, and even a large number of purely organic disorders, can be attributed to an inhibited sex life. This does not only apply to afflictions that are obviously connected with a person's sexuality, such as impotence, but also much more difficult clinical profiles. The sinister influence of earlier childhood experiences, which are pushed into the subconscious and later inhibit the development of sex life, is well known. This has an even more pronounced effect on the adult, who, in purely spiritual terms, has the will and the possibility of subjectively revaluating his subjective feelings, but whose path to fulfilment is blocked. And so it comes to substitute acts, of which there is a myriad, and of whose horror we gain a vivid impression in Plättner's book. Imagine, a man in his prime, married for many years, with children to whom he is devoted, who is suddenly ripped out of all this and moved into an environment that is unloving in every respect! What mental and physical adjustment does this demand of him? And how is it possible to achieve this adjustment? It is often incredibly difficult for the doctor to intervene helpfully, where we confront a phenomenon that is bound up with nature. Why do we need to make people's anguish even greater than it already is in our penal facilities?

The first period of abstinence is usually the most difficult to overcome; we notice that sex drive weakens little by little. But this weakening does not stop at this lower level; rather, if we use a curve for a better understanding, this curve will increase again over time, and longs for a release and relaxation that can only occur through a sexual act. At first, people often fight against self-gratification with superhuman strength, but eventually even the most restrained man succumbs to temptation. Nevertheless, this act soon also becomes insufficient for the senses because, being an act of emergency from the start, the disgust for it grows every time it is undertaken, and other means are resorted to. Only today, as these words are being written, does the news arrive about a young man who has been in prison for some time and who can no longer bear the endless torment of sexual abstinence, who has tried every available means, starting with masturbation, and who now begs to be castrated, because he can no longer see any other way out. As hardly needs mentioning, a sedative is no longer sufficient, only the deed can help in this case!

And what is this deed? The deed consists in allowing prisoners to have regular sex! Among all countries it is above all the new Russia that has done this in an exemplary manner and has largely met the needs of people in this respect by allowing visits and granting holidays. In Germany it came like a thunderbolt when Erich Mühsam first reported, in a lecture at the Institute for Sexual Science in 1926, on the sexual distress in the German jails and prisons, also drawing on his own personal experience.[15] Numerous doctors and lawyers were present to hear the moving indictment and recognized what boundless injustice is going on here. We have been addressing this problem and even if we can still show no tangible results of our activity to this day, we can nevertheless discern some progress in terms of changing attitudes. Even if the Criminologists Day in 1927 dealt with this question, and at that time there were no resolutions that could be formulated in any way, it is to be hoped that the future will bring more tangible outcomes. It is emphasized time and time again that the modern penal system should "educate" rather than "penalize". It is all too obvious that every educational measure is in vain, if the penalty of depriving a man of his liberty is increased many times over by the depriving him of sexual intercourse!

And one other thing should be considered, that is of the utmost importance. The concept of marital fidelity plays an

---

[15] Erich Mühsam (1878-1934), a German-Jewish essayist, poet and playwright, had been sentenced to 15 years for his involvement in the short-lived Bavarian Soviet Republic. He benefited from the amnesty that also freed Hitler and other participants in the beer hall putsch. In 1926 he founded the anarchist magazine, *Fanal* (Beacon). After the Nazi seizure of power Mühsam, along with many other communists and revolutionaries, was interned in the Oranienburg concentration camp, where he was murdered in 1934.

important role in people's consciousness even today, when so much is spoken about individual sexual freedom. It is well known that the imposition of a punishment not only affects the individual person; suffering is also brought upon his family to a very great extent. We are talking in this regard about the sexual distress of the prisoners' wives. If, ultimately, the path is open to extramarital intercourse, no one will be able to recommend it with a clear conscience. We are well aware of the torments and inner struggles that precede the taking of this path, how it reflects on the consciousness of the two spouses, and how it can cast an eternal shadow over their marriage, even if the sentence has long since been served out. In a way more penetrating, perhaps, than such words can describe, the film called "Sex in Chains" brought these issues to our attention.[16] In true-to-life pictures the sexual distress of prisoners and those left at home is depicted in a psychologically flawless way, as the alienation between the spouses takes on more and more importance, so that after the prisoner's release an oft-unbridgeable chasm separates the two. The spectacle of those six women, who once came to us as a deputation, will remain unforgettable. Their request was to initiate a process whereby they should be granted at least a short time alone with their husbands during their visits to the prison, without the constant supervision of a prison warden. Their husbands (these were political prisoners) were on hunger strike since this request had been refused. The torments of jealousy under which these strong men and their equally healthy wives suffered were simply inhumane.

If we do not want unwritten laws to punish people far beyond what is intended by the term of the sentence, if we no longer want sex in chains but want to become truly free people, then a path opens up and an objective becomes clear,

---

[16] Details about "Sex in Chains" (*Geschlecht in Fesseln*) can be found on the IMDB website.

whose attainment makes the effort and travails worthwhile. Plättner's book serves as a landmark and a powerful exhortation along this path. And, for this reason, it is accompanied by our sincere best wishes. May it find open doors wherever there are people who can remedy the situation and comfort those who have already passed through the hell of sexual distress; and may it provide an incentive to all who are minded to alleviate unnecessary human suffering!

Foreword to the Second Edition

The first edition of "Eros in Prison" sold out relatively quickly. There is still a strong demand today. For this reason, the Paul Witte Verlag in Hanover has undertaken a new edition of the work with my permission.

The book has enjoyed a gratifying success. This is confirmed by the numerous and unusually detailed reviews in newspapers and magazines of all genres, apart from publications that represent the interests of the darkest cultural reaction. Moreover, declarations of agreement and sympathy have reached, and continue to reach me in such vast quantities that I could ignore the few calumnies of the most banal and meanest nature that I have received and keep to business as usual.

The form and content of the present edition remains unchanged. I would have been inclined to make changes, if the resonance of the first edition had prompted me to do so. There was just one wish that I could not satisfy: to shorten and cheapen the second edition to publish it as a kind of popular edition. I am sure that this would have achieved mass circulation and that broad sections of the people, who are interested but not solvent, could therefore have come into possession of the book. But all attempts that I made in this direction failed.

Even though the book mainly found its way into the affluent circles of the bourgeoisie, which is interested in cultural politics, proletarian strata have helped themselves through a collectivist process: circles of personal friends, groups with emotional ties or libraries and organizations have bought the book for common use.

The material provided to me on the subject, true cries of pain and equally honest cries of indignation, could not be easily worked into the second edition of the book. I intend to publish this material in a special volume at the appropriate time and thus take a collective position on the topic.

Allow me, if I may, to accompany the second edition of my "Eros in Prison" with a wish that through the study of my book newcomers, like so many readers before them, will be led to an awareness of, and thereby onto the path of tireless struggle against, the sexual barbarism that goes on in penal institutions. This is all the more necessary as still today there are no tangible signs that this barbarism is being curtailed. The bureaucracy of the penal system is content to admit the sexual distress of the imprisoned but does not seek or want a solution to this so important question. Therefore, a solution must be forced by the broad masses. I for my part am fulfilling my duty in this respect in that I have so far commented on this topic in around 250 lectures.

Karl Plättner
Leipzig, October 1930

General introduction

Much has already been spoken, and still more written in public about sexual matters.

Little has been spoken, and still less written about the sexual misery of prisoners. Until now it has been akin to the witness to poverty and misery, whose cheerfulness is disturbed as he passes by.

Erich Mühsam was the first to break through this silence, speaking in 1926 before a more closed circle of participants at the Institute for Sexual Science in Berlin over the abysmal distress of prisoners. The press was present at this first attempt, but then fell silent once again.

In the meantime, the subject of the sexual distress of prisoners was "discussed" behind the closed doors of the Justice Committee of the Prussian Parliament.

One year later, in 1927, the Communist fraction in Saxony brought forward a motion that obliged the Saxon Parliament to accommodate, at the very least, open scrutiny of this subject in parliamentary debate. These discussions did not have a positive outcome, however.

Nearly two further years passed before anything further was undertaken in this area. The result was the film "Sex in Chains" (The sexual distress of lonely people), which was presented to the cinema-going public under the patronage of the German League for Human Rights and is currently on release. The film contains scenes that are astonishingly close to concrete descriptions of situations in my book, though of course this is within natural and in part very narrow limits, which must necessarily be the case since the sexual misery of prisoners cannot be illuminated in film to the full extent of the meaning of the term. The spoken and written word still belong alongside the film, which could be expanded upon and in my opinion, must be expanded upon.

After the film had enthralled, captivated and shocked a limited audience, the Central Office for Prisoners' Welfare in

Berlin was in a position to make a presentation in December 1928 with the support of the Supreme Judicial Counsel Gentz of the Prussian Ministry of Justice on "The Sentence of Sexual Misery".

That is all that has been done so far in this field except for fragments you can find here and there in books. Novorusski suggests sexual distress in his "Memoirs of an Idealist";[17] Bergmann[18] describes it rather more clearly in two chapters of his book, "The Deed"; Wassermann cast the spotlight on the sexual distress of prisoners in his novel "The Maurizius Case";[19] an article on the subject appears here and there, sometimes also a series of articles. But a concrete and systematic treatment of the entire set of issues is entirely absent.

The question arises: why has no-one with a positive view on this subject, the very root of life, yet emerged from the many journalists who themselves languished in prisons and experienced a crippled existence there? Can this fact be interpreted as an expression of disinterest? Is this shortage evidence of the absence of sexual distress in jails?

Since November 1918, more than 20,000 left-wing political prisoners have languished in the dungeons of the German republic, sometimes with extremely long sentences.

Why have they not spoken? Why were they content to treat this subject more or less "discreetly" in "in learning circles" with fragmented, and often also crude phraseology? Why has not one of them exposed this open and bleeding

---

[17] The memoirs of M.V. Novorusski (1861-1925) originally appeared as "Eighteen and a Half Years behind Russian Prison Walls" and was first published in German in 1908

[18] Alexander Bergmann (or Berkman) (1870-1936) was a prominent anarchist, later a critic of the Russian revolution. He served 14 years in prison for the attempted assassination of the businessman Henry Clay Frick.

[19] Jakob Wassermann (1873-1934); German-Jewish novelist. His novel "The Maurizius Case" (1928) deals with a miscarriage of justice.

wound to society?

According to the Reich Statistical Yearbook for 1927, the ruling powers of the German Republic permanently have 450,000 people under lock and key, of whom 65,000 are female prisoners, including pregnant women, and around 22,000 youths aged between 14 and 18, whose sex life is as a rule not yet under control and must necessarily become brutalized in penal institutions.

Are you willing and able to look into these things in the deepest detail? Then behold the convicts who have been isolated from every natural sexual function, from every aspect of life for 5, 10 or 15 years!

Can the human mind, which is capable of grasping things and events and analysing their ramifications, imagine what it is like for physically strong and healthy convicts, endowed by nature with instinctual drives, who must exist for 5, 10 or 15 years without giving any natural satisfaction to their sexual instincts, the very "root of life" as Forel calls it?[20]

And then think of the unluckiest of all the unfortunates: the "lifers" who are isolated from life for a lifetime, who cannot even cling onto the hopeful thought that sooner or later they will be released from the living hell of their daily torment. For the sake of pure common sense, should they not be offered the bare essentials of life so that they can at least have a meagre existence behind prison walls?

Every day new admissions are added to the 500,000 prisoners, and every day people leave prison. That is the "family tree" multiplying the current generation, i.e. begetting children, human life. Under these circumstances human degeneration can, and indeed must take hold in a given organized system, because the question of whether the victims of a

---

[20] Auguste-Henri Forel (1848-1931) was a Swiss myrmecologist, neuroanatomist, psychiatrist and eugenicist, notable for his investigations into the structure of the human brain and that of ants. He was also a pioneer of sexology with his study, "The Sexual Question" (1907).

social system can again separate themselves from what has become a bad habit, and therefore a hardened inner distress, depends entirely on the time-scale of the forced bondage to a destructive perversion of nature. A human being is always a product of his circumstances and that will always remain the case, so long as there are human beings.

Those who leave prison with illnesses are not few. "Sex crimes" increase year on year. In 1925, 5,928 were sentenced for rape and sexual offences, in 1926, however, it was already 6,368. I mention this because we are not mistaken in asserting that among those convicted (those not convicted are not included in the figures) not a few have brought their sexual pathology with them out of prison.

And again, we must ask: why is everyone silent?

Every day loud, shrieking cries of despair from the torture chambers reach the ears of those of us who live in freedom; 500,000 tormented people hurl their screams of agony from the very depths of their soul; 500,000 constantly groan under the effects of the brutal rape of their sensual desires. Why has nobody yet described and illuminated this sexual distress in all its details? It is not so easy. Anyone who feels like dealing with this topic knows that there is little or no use in treating it carefully, tentatively, and only theoretically. Series of articles in the press discussing the topic only show me how it should *not* be done. In one of them I find a solitary concrete description of the condition. Evidence that the author had no other cases and therefore filled 15 columns with commonplace statements and impassioned verbiage. If we want to treat the subject the way it should now be treated, then certain conditions must be met. I will name them: Either the presenter of the material must have lived among prisoners, made purposeful observations and thus had every opportunity to collect material, or he must stand (or must have stood) in the midst of this sexual distress himself; he must extrapolate the feelings of others from what he himself feels within. The first condition is not easy to fulfil, for it is extremely difficult to prompt, move, or consistently induce the tortured individual to make open confessions about their sexual distress while in detention. I have experienced this for myself. For this reason, I worked with all the means at my disposal, doing nothing other than convincing prisoners of the need to speak. But I only achieved a partial success. Even fewer of the prerequisites exist for meeting the second condition. For it requires an unconditional freeing of all inhibitions to write about the subject in a way that is exhaustive and above all convincing.

I will not simply report in the form of statements about the sexual distress of prisoners, but also about my own; not only will I show the products and effects of other people's sexual distress, as far as I am able to gather material, but also shed light on the products and effects of my own sexual distress. And I will do so not in a vacuum, but in the way that sexual phenomena demand: in an inseparable linkage with the correspondent who is drawn, through no fault of his own, into this abysmal distress with all its effects and manifestations. I have to do that, because by the very nature of my presentation, I want to create a sufficiently effective platform from which to illuminate things in their full profundity. If I were to act differently, I would have no absolute guarantee that I would be drawing a true-to-life and authentic portrait. And that is what it is all about. There is no point in looking into the fountain of truth, if you are not prepared to disturb it at its very deepest source. But if you do want to do this, there is no alternative to putting yourself centre-stage, so long as no other more favourable conditions exist. The whole manner, therefore, the whole perspective from which I approach things in my book, is deliberate and well-considered and has nothing to do with making a fuss about the person when what needs to be discussed is the issue and its phenomena.

I felt obliged to do this in the general interest and to help alleviate the immediate distress of many fellow countrymen.

By this I mean those who, as a result of the stubbornly defended traditions and barbarism that are praised as "protecting" society and public order, are outrageously tormented both physically and mentally in prisons.

I submit my text to the public and accompany it with the wish that its content makes an impact. I know that it has shortcomings and do not doubt that in some places it will find no mercy within an entirely outdated professional fraternity, one that has always regarded every breach of its jealously guarded ignorance and false opinions as an unjustified attack on its most sacred assets and fought back. I have laboriously developed my knowledge and formal abilities. There are still large gaps in these. But I have lived through the material that I deal with here, studying it thoroughly and extensively for years. What I state here is based on firm foundations. Much of this is completely unknown to readers; much of it *is* known to them but the majority want to deny any awareness of the sexual pleasures under discussion, which are not entirely natural and to a greater or lesser extent "civilized" – a denial that they make not only before others, but even unto themselves.

I portray things how they are.

While reference is made to sources in scholarly volumes intended for academic students, I cite particularly important passages literally, sometimes even to the fullest extent. I confess that, with this method, I am also pursuing a conscious intention that starts out from the desire to be persuasive and thus to convince without constructing abstractions. I could have interpreted such thoughts in an analogous manner and then limited myself to specifying and, in particular, recommending the source material. This is also the usual practice in publishing. But what use is reference to the source if I have no guarantee that it will be used; often, no use can be made of it whatsoever. I am writing the book not just for academics or other people who are well-read and have broad intellectual horizons, but for the general public. This forces me to make certain concessions. Because one cannot expect of every reader that he should suddenly acquire all the essential literature that I use, and had to use, in my presentation. Having asked here and there if this method is acceptable, I was told: not only acceptable, but even advantageous and convenient. I therefore make this little concession to con-venience, and in the publishing of the thing choose a way that allows anyone who reads this book the opportunity to follow such source material coherently, without relying on interpretations that can often be false.

My text is intended, through its content, to pound at the gates of unreasonableness and wickedness, so that they may spring open, forcing in a fresh, clean draft of air. The lascivious, who seek satisfaction in this book for their own needs, will not get their money's worth. The book is not a novel, but rather reality; it can, will and shall not create the basis for covert fantasies that some perhaps promise themselves based on the title.

I know that my book is not the last word of wisdom; it should simply make a start. It is to be hoped that in the coming weeks and months thousands who until now have held back from doing so will speak out. If they do speak then the public shall hear their voices.

The fact that I have often relied on informants in the presentation of matters leads me to the following statement: I have been tireless in collecting my material and painstaking in its treatment. In no single case have I accepted material from gossips or otherwise unreliable people, but always from prisoners in whom I have been able to verify valuable qualities and who were ruled by their honesty, and who are therefore credible to the highest degree. And despite this, in every single case, I have almost inquisitorially cross-examined all of my informants to ascertain if what they told me about the sexual abnormalities that they observed, or other effects on their violated sensual desire, is genuine; whether I was dealing with true descriptions or if they were presenting me with pictures of themselves as victims in their own sexual fantasy. For me, the deciding factor in making a judgement was always: am I dealing with homosexual predispositions in this case or with pseudo-homosexual activity arising from unavoidable compulsion; am I dealing with acquired perversities, or with fetishists who have brought their pre-existing twisted and stunted sex life with them to the penal institution; or am I dealing with prisoners who have acquired all varieties of sexual deviation only under the pressure of their sexual distress and other circumstances? Over and over again I set the standard for distinguishing between these characteristics, meticulously, sometimes even pedantically. As it did not seem advisable to name the prisons in full in a whole host of cases, I usually refrained from doing so and limited myself to hinting at the names.

Thanks to all who helped me with this and who have already contributed. Most of them are still languishing behind prison walls. Reaching out to you across the barriers is my deepest desire. And in calling upon you, who do not languish behind prison walls, to take up the fight for the sexual freedom of all prisoners in German prisons, I ask that this should not be interpreted as a cheap slogan, but rather as a commitment that should bring amends and hope to those who do languish behind prison walls.

Karl Plättner
Leipzig, January 1929

I. The importance of sexual functions and an introduction to the danger zone of sexual abstinence

1. Facts based on experience versus medical and ministerial assertions

Ranged against a small tier of qualified doctors who know about the sexual hardship of people imprisoned in a single-sex environment, and who recognize the means of self-gratification, there is the mass of prison doctors who deny this kind of sexual distress. At the first Congress of the International Society of Sexual Science in 1926 the Head of Department of the Saxon Ministry of Justice, Dr. Wulffen, dealt with the subject of the sexual distress of convicts and prisoners on remand. According to press coverage he reported on a deliberation of the Saxon prison directors and doctors, the results of which culminated in the collection of relevant material. For his own part, he affirmed sexual distress and believed it possible to reduce this through appropriate measures by the regimes within penal institutions.

A year later, however, the same Wulffen said: There is no sexual distress among prisoners! In the 36th session of the Saxon parliament of 26 June 1927, he justified his point of view thus:

> "The prison doctors and court doctors are of the opinion, and have given us this declaration, that in their opinion there is no genuine sexual distress in prisons, understood in the sense that the only ones who suffer from sexual distress in prison are those who also suffer from it in freedom. I have also listened to our ministerial medical adviser at the Ministry of the Interior regarding this question and he has also told me: significant physical and mental damage cannot be proven, masturbatory excesses develop almost only in psychopathic personalities, not in others."

That is almost the opposite of what the writer Wulffen asserted a few years earlier about the sexual distress of prisoners in his *Criminal Psychology* before he advanced to the position of Under Secretary (cited from the proceedings of the 5th session of the Saxon parliament of 16 December 1926): "One should also consider the sexual distress of the prisoners, which has not been the subject of much discussion. Especially among adolescents and those with highly sexual predispositions, it can increase suffering and lead to injurious extensive onanism."[21]

There is no sexual distress among prisoners, said the medical officer Lumpp in a presentation to the forensic-psychiatric association in Heidelberg in the year 1913. He declared: "According to my experience, only those who have already started onanism on the outside practice it while in solitary confinement." In addition, there are physicians who feel burdened by their conscience, who want to relieve it and therefore stamp the prisoner's self-satisfaction as pathological or attribute it to sexual temperament. Practice, experience and collected facts lead such statements *ad absurdum*. One day, while conversing with friends about prisoners' sexual distress, one of the persons in the circle, whom we knew to be sexually passive in normal life, stated the following:

> "I got over these conditions more easily: I masturbated. I would not know how otherwise I should have relieved the sexual burdens and overcome the urges. By my third month in detention I already realized that it was advisable to bring about the necessary discharges in good time, one way or another. Otherwise I would certainly have been unable to work. I also found that prolonged neglect of sexual functions made my kidney condition worse."

---

[21] Wolf Hasso Erich Wulffen (1862-1936) was a prominent German criminologist and a prolific author on the subject of criminal psychology. A conservative humanist and member of the Saxon parliament, from 1923 he was in charge of the penal system in Saxony.

In Brandenburg prison a mentally very alert prisoner told me:[22]

> "God knows what it is with me, my sexual urges become stronger from day to day and already plague me so much that I am almost incapable of any intellectual pursuits; my thinking almost expires. God knows this power never had me under its control in my normal life, whereas it has now almost defeated me: I was almost impotent out there, it was enough for me to have sexual intercourse every 5 to 6 weeks. But now I am sexually almost hypertrophic; I have to masturbate twice a day or more if I want to avoid worse conditions."

These two examples, which could be multiplied a thousand-fold, already show that it is not just those who already practiced onanism in normal life who do so in solitary confinement. However, these findings are not quite enough in themselves, they must be expanded upon and followed through. I will use my own experiences for this purpose.

During the war I languished, accused of high treason, for 15 months on remand – without resorting to onanism. "There you go" the Under Secretaries and Medical Officers will say, "So it is correct to assert that the only people who practice onanism in solitary confinement are those who already started outside!" No, this assertion is not correct in its general direction.

I want to, or have to, cite some facts to illuminate and explain why I did not resort to masturbation in the 15 months of my wartime custody, even though the sexual urges, which occasionally reached the level of sexual torment, drove me often enough to the early stages of experimentation. But I en-

---

22 As he notes in the General Introduction, Plättner refers to the penal institutions where he was held by their initial letter, in this case "Strafanstalt B". Where these can be identified with a reasonable degree of certainty, I have spelt them in full.

countered inhibitions that were too strong, so I did not succeed. I attribute this state of inhibition to the following: during this period, I was still in good condition from a spiritual point of view, mentally strong and healthy; my ideals were the living source of an optimism giving me the will to resist. The mental impulses worked on me with a kind of effect and activity such that every time I attempted to apply myself to self-gratification, I was automatically distracted and led into completely different realms. Thus, in the years 1917-18, the Dresden remand centre became a university where I tirelessly studied socialism and devoted my attention to the problems with which the imperialist world war had confronted us. The milieu from which I came, and in which I found myself on remand, also played a decisive role. My life had developed its form, content and maturity in the Hamburg workers' movement, especially in the local youth organization, in which sexual abstinence was practised in a more or less strong-willed manner.

The ideas and habits that shaped and ruled my being in this milieu naturally also continued to influence me in this period while I was on remand. I was ruled by the thought that masturbation is a sacrilege against nature, a profanation of sexual life should I resort to forms of relief that would drag down everything that had until now been sacred to me, and for which I worked and lived. This echo of the norms of my milieu remained in the foreground as a defence against acts of self-gratification. Moreover, my nerves were still firm and reliable at that time, giving me the ability to repress my sexuality, giving me the strength and self-discipline required for abstinence.

Finally, the nutritional conditions during the war should not be disregarded when evaluating this matter. These were not very favourable to sexual functions. Sexual functions and sexual instinct should not be confused, in other words sexual impulses can be present as an expression of inner secretory processes and may even occur very strongly, without the bodily sexual functions being able to take effect in the sense of secretion. This can be understood when you take into account that the sexual substances are not produced in just one place, but rather in several places in the body. For example, in men the sperm cells are produced in the testes themselves whereas seminal fluid is produced in intermediary glands. And then you have to take into account the path that the sexual substances must take before they reach a combined state, that is to say to attain the right mix, maturity, and function that finally leads to secretion. If the man is physically under-nourished, in which condition, as is well known, the functions of organs suffer, then the secretion of substances is inhibited, quite aside from the fact that hunger also creates depressive states of a physical nature that promote inhibitions. For example, my hunger in pre-trial detention during the war was so bad that tears came to my eyes day and night from hunger pains and I was constantly suffering from back pain. So much so that I once asked for material for gluing bags to get hold of paste, which I assumed would be edible. Once I convinced myself that this was not the case, I returned the material from my cell: the paste had been made unpalatable as a foodstuff through chemical additives.

At any rate we have here a situation that could not well support acts of masturbation. But few people find themselves in such conditions and they are entirely absent for the average human material found behind prison walls. I will prove that in brief, without lingering further on the subject.

I was arrested for the second time in September 1919 and again engaged in no compensatory sexual acts. But if I got through the second period of detention in this way, it was primarily because it was of short duration, in which I was able, with the help of all willpower, to push back lustful sexual impulses. Also, in this case external factors met me half way. Prosecution material had been collected against me, which I barely managed to work my way through; and apart from this, I was interrogated often and for long periods. When

I was not in the interrogation room, I was buried so deep in these criminal proceedings from morning to night that I often did not even have time to take food. Here then the "evidence" was presented to me, that I was supposedly as though created for detention, and I heard the question, if I never drained myself: one could not day in day out and from early in the morning until late at night hold a pen or a book in one's hand. That must have finished sooner or later. I also busied myself extensively with plans of escape; so much so that each time, after fall of darkness in my cell, when it was no longer possible to work, I started to think about what possibilities could be created to break the shackles.

On 2 February 1922, I was arrested once again and remained in detention for 6 ½ years – the first 15 months again without any compensatory sexual activity.

This fact requires further explanation and with it the correct assessment. Namely, what must be taken into account here is that my wife was at the very last stage of her pregnancy when I was arrested and was thus carried by the rhythm of a joyful spell that can only be very personal to a woman and from which no man with inner experience and spiritual convictions remains unaffected. Like it or not, one is spellbound. It was the first time in my life that I was able to observe the happiness of a mother to be the very depth of feeling and sensitivity. Thus, my wife appeared before me as a transformed being, one that carried the most tender of all languages to me on its wings. The environment of an expectant mother may be narrowly restricted to herself alone, creating the prerequisite for concentrating on just this single object with an intensity that is astonishing. The child alone moves the mother, determines her actions. If it could be organically integrated into the framework of the presentation, I would include the testimonies of the singing soul of an expectant mother and publish the letters of my wife from this period. From the well-spring of her contentment, in which I saw her yearning, her unlimited, natural and simple happiness, I could at least intellectually quench my thirst for the erotic and was delighted by the expectation of that imminent moment when I would be able to see our child and cradle his mother's pride and joy in my arms.

Thus, once again I succeeded in suppressing my sexual functions for an unusually long time and building bridges, which, so to speak, led me into an erotic dreamland. The illusion of eroticism entered into my thoughts in complete purity and portrayed all of the perfectly formed lines of magical femininity before my mind's eye. An element of sexual fulfilment in this satisfied me for a while. Yet sexual functions, in the generally understood sense, were not fulfilled. Even if a fanciful imagination, combined with strict self-discipline helps in overcoming unsatisfied sexual impulses, this question acquires a completely different meaning if the non-fulfilment of sexual functions becomes permanent. "It is in the nature of the lover to seek the satisfaction of the beloved object," says Anatole France in the *Revolt of the Angels*. And the non-gratification of the beloved object, he continues, "is an underserved curse and the deepest humiliation for mature and desirable flesh."

When the above-mentioned mental impulses subsided, I worked off my sexual impulses for a long while by poetical means.

In this regard I would like to make a brief diversion and recall an incident whose concluding scene took place in the Leipzig courthouse. It concerned an illustrated work: *Nights of Venus*, an erotic poetry cycle by Reinhold Eichacker, with paintings by Franz von Bayros, which appeared shortly after the war, published by Walther in an edition of 75,000 copies. Eichacker wrote the poems (according to the Leipzig court records Nr. 24/1927) while serving in the field as a captain. In it, the unfulfilled yearning for woman is artistically abreacted. The full-page illustrations in soft hues by the well-known Munich painter Bayros represent men and women in a restrained manner shortly before or after sexual union. The public prosecutor condemned the "immoral" book with the intention of confiscating it. However, the Leipzig court approved the book with a clean bill of health, took this opportunity to define concepts of morality, and tried to make clear to the prosecutor that not all people shared his notions of morality and that, in recent decades, the general public has become morally purer and spiritually more mature. And for this reason, one should help them to understand or state rationally that every person with normal sexual sensitivities yearns for the surging wave of a healthy eroticism.[23]

One thing is very typical in this respect. A judgemental prison warder once declared to me after I had written my first verses: "I do not believe you ever wrote poetry in normal life, and I do not think you will do so in the future if you return to normal life. But in the way you give new meaning to imprisonment with all its privations and renunciations, especially in sexual terms, your verses are typical. It is a piece of good fortune that you can do so, a nameless misfortune that the great majority of detainees are unable to do so."

This judgement is correct. In fact, sexual distress is to some extent "channelled" in this way, as we shall see in greater detail. An element of sexual distress or even a fantastical-erotic blaze of joy wraps every verse that I created while in custody; in every activity of this kind, suppressed sexual desire breaks through symptomatically. I will demon-strate this with a few verses that came into being at this time. But I would like to emphasize that these verses are not intended for the scalpel of the Academy of Poetical Arts; if they must be dissected, this is the task of sexual science, which can do something useful with these "symptomatic verses". I have decided to include these verses for no other reason.

---

[23] Franz von Bayros (1866–1924) was an Austrian commercial artist, illustrator, and painter, belonging to the Decadent art movement, most famous for his erotic and phantasmagorical illustrations. Reinhold Eichacker (1886-1931) was a German lawyer and author.

Yearning Blood!

Just once would I live
in your spiritual fervour.
Just once entirely imbibe
your love in hot-blooded ardour.

My lips, parched from fever
sensually touch your own.
I will kiss them with my fire
Then my heart will be strong.

Just once, I want to see
love in its full domain.
Embraced by love's sweet dream
I can then make my way.

Just once, I want to read
brilliance in your glances.
Your soulful eyes to lead
where my breath dances.

Wife, you force me to take
you from infinity.
Wife, you will always wake
in me smiling gaiety.

Softly I lay my arm
stretched around your womb.
Now I know: I did not dream
when I shared this joy with you.

This hot-blooded interaction
is impulsive, I confess!
Renewal and liberation
I will find in your flesh.

Evening Still at the Edge of the Forest

Evenings, as light starts to fade
far away from urban hubbub,
I dream beside the forest glade
of long-desired carnal love.

O you holy spark divine
how my eyes watch over you.
Peace so still, so deep, benign
draws so close to me anew.

Nestle with me, raptured hour:
I long so much for your kiss!
In the shady forest bower
closer comes the silent bliss.

Suddenly, through the distant still
I hear the bugle's melody
My very soul is singing
to the forest's harmony.

From the forest's symphony
rises the hour of release.
Everything lives in harmony,
everywhere the world's at peace.

Tears of joy are pouring over,
heartfelt joy freely bursts.
Light and air and sunshine, brother
here at last we'll still our thirst.

In the music of these realms,
mingled with the evening dew,
people are not overwhelmed
no, here is health renewed!

My Happiness!

My child drives my boundless quest
to forms of psychic power.
I hear it call, my dearest
child's all-conquering vigour.

My child: pristine, tiny
witness to light's creation;
my child, our progeny,
from hot-blooded union.

My child, you draw your lifeblood
from your mother's heart.
You, child, heal all discomfort,
and inner strength impart.

My child, you drink life's force
from your mother's breasts.
Never, in such fevered thirst
is a loving heart diminished.

Our child – our common rebirth,
keeps us spellbound in its realm.
We seek and find much mirth
in this single cradled dream.

Embedded in their warmth and grace,
entwined together, mother and child.
Unending faith in my embrace
ease my pain, when I feel reviled.

Courtship Dance!

I seek out taciturn paths,
I seek them through endless night,
when your love-spell is cast,
enveloping me on my flight.

Radiant countenance of love:
laugh, laugh, fleeting hour!
My erotic impulse
Kisses your thirsting mouth.

And let it be dark and dour
around me through the night.
In hot courtship the power
of emotion creates the light.

Oh love, benevolent love,
With you I'll scale the heights.
You'll drive me to distant goals,
to storm the starry sky.

Soft images rise above
from the daylight hours.
Like healing balsam, love
lies soft on my wounded soul.

On sacred lovers' paths
I reach my greatest happiness.
Through my feral blood
runs eternal wishfulness.

Heartfelt Joy!

When I saw you one day,
pure as pearl, in youthful frock,
desire ran through my veins:
come, o come, let us both!

Come, let's fly far away
on the wings of our yearning.
Let us vanquish all pain
with the fruit of our union.

Over hills, over mountains
through skies and heavens apart.
Over a thousand earth-coffins
I lift my mind, you your heart.

In gliding flight we go down,
down to the calming grassland.
There Mars sings us his songs
in his fiery-red raiment.

Then looking deep into your eyes:
pure as pearl, dressed to please.
O in this, my sacred shrine
I find the hour of release.

Love-mania

I know not how to allay
my restless element.
Only you matter in me
so I will harden my intent.

My blood burns like a fire,
love is truly in rut.
Nature will be satisfied,
Yet I must do without.

Love, that my heart fulfilled
is my inner yearning.
Love, when will you be stilled
by tears of joy returning.

Everything pure, everything real
flows from life's greatest good.
All else is but a shell,
Love's joy settles the blood.

Love that you feel in your breast
is an inner wooing.
All the world, East to West
sings its lust for living.

On Green Forest Heights!

I wander with the clouds
across the heavenly haze.
Nothing can cause me discord
In this magical space.

I stand on mountain peaks
and behold the deep-cut vale.
Spread out all around me
I see the fairest day.

Enveloped by fragrant flowers
I lie in the high grass.
And dream about the hour
that will bring me my lass.

And thirsting, my mouth draws
its fill from this wellspring.
Nature, how she conquers
me, my heart is overflowing.

With my arms and all my heart
I embrace you, my lass.

When your warmth pours out,
inside me sings cheerfulness.

Spring Mood

My breast needs more air,
my thirsting eyes a pool of light.
Love's breath is beyond compare,
the source of vital energy.

Then my veins fill in bursts
of wild and passionate blood.
From my young spring fibres
the cord of life is wove.

The symbol of this spring bliss
is my stimulus, so pure.
I kiss, with sensual promise
the sunshine vast and sure.

In growth and vitality,
the blossoming of nature,
there is no mortality,
for life is in full flourish.

Every pain and suffering
borne by man is now allayed.
Every joyful heart now sings
of lovelier days ahead.

Forest Devotion

Gently blowing through my soul
rustling swirls of parched leaves:
I will eavesdrop this hour
in divine humility.

Let your noise not disturb
my silent devotion.

Grant me this godly whisper,
the fullness of emotion.

As if entranced I stand
in the melody of dreams.
Pain to which mankind is damned,
I endure in all extremes.

Few of us can while away
these hours of consolation.
And those who enjoy the stay
think solely of their station.

Pain in me and only pain
destroys the ambience.
Mankind, if you're truly kind
fraternity will triumph.

Erotic Dream!

Dream of dreams! O sweet love
lead me into your life-stream.
Silent passion, she bestows,
joy wafts about my being.

My voice rises, exultant
my heart sings with such zest.
Gossamer spirit, dear love
lie softly 'pon my breast.

Blessed am I, contented!
Desire is my strongest drive.
I must love you, believe it,
rhythmically sings my mind:
Darling, love so long you can
and from love, create life.
Eros' dream's a thrilling dance:
I will make you satisfied!

Confession

I gather the day's strength,
you fill the well with ardour.
And I drink eternal bliss
From the lap of your love.

My yearning belongs to you,
my very life force.
I drink the essential juice
from the loving source.

To you, my red flower
to you I turn my eye.
This delicate rose
brings me my sunlight.

Shine brightly, you delight,
remain, full of warmth!
Throughout my deepest hurt
I kiss your sweet flesh.

Cry of Nature

On verdant turf,
by the stream in spate,
heart's melody sings
the song of breaking day.

In mountain ravines
of the beech forest
my ear perceives the whirring brook:
People, forge the spirit's stylus
and hearken to nature's moods!

In the morning dew
of the great rebirth
my fever bathes, I am at ease:
It would be bleak on Earth

without the song of dreams.

Under green firs,
in sheer solitude,
I dream, desirous
of love's beatitude.

Sun Dream

O sunny morning,
you giving day!
The sun-silver filaments.
What heavy on my humours lay
the sun will sweep away.

Sweet-smelling roses
and ornate lilies,
source of abundant joy.
Ease my heaviness of spirit
burst open the cumbrous sheath.

Carefree summer days,
they bring love of life.
Resentment, that sad malaise
is cast so far aside.

Changing, the days pass by
with hours of escape.
Growing joyful on my mind,
the ode to love takes shape.

2. The beginnings of my psycho-sexual distress while on remand and flight into the first stage of self-gratification

I will first go into the deepest mental distress, in order to show how the path to my sexual distress was prepared before I finally took refuge in self-gratification. More or less all prisoners travel this path. And for this reason, the accounts that follow have general import.

As long as my wife was able to respond to my inner need and compelling requirement to exchange my thoughts, she did so. Therefore, I had core issues and profound objectives before me. Life did not seem completely pointless, and from time to time I inhaled a healthy breath of fresh air from the outside world. But under the impact of the conditions of detention my wife arrived at that fateful moment, the one that becomes the root of all evil: the point at which sex drive is absent. A period of inner dissatisfaction, which welled up like a flood powerful enough to burst any bank, entered into her cycle of existence. In her dealings with me my wife was more and more burdened with inhibitions, given the absence of an adequate exchange of ideas and the fact that the interaction between us, even when it concerned our most intimate affairs, was always carried out under the watchful eyes of a warder. The permanent loss of the person she loved, the father of her child; the perpetual suppression of all feelings and needs killed her mental vivacity and intellectual capacity. This state of affairs weighed down on her flights of fancy like lead weights, thereby driving out everything healthy that she wanted to do, and sensibly would have to do, if the relationship between us was to remain harmonious. The bullying manner of letter censorship meant that she did not hear from me for months: my letters with the best and strongest thoughts went into the files. So my wife's original communicativeness turned into a disastrous passivity. The accumulation of all her bitterness over the treatment by the German remand system, and her understanding that she must passively observe the way in which they wanted to bend me (and of course others) to their will destroyed her every joy and every enlightening perspective, leaving her to grope through the world in darkness, animated by the one desire: to destroy herself. She was literally the plaything of her dissatisfaction, and she was all too well aware of this. In this atmosphere, her intense inner inhibition about revealing her distress, her worries and sensations before the eyes and ears of others had to take effect. Our healthy and heartfelt togetherness, in which we are connected by a bond of inner harmony and purposefulness, had been corroded by the poison of the prison system. There were rifts and fissures opening up between us that could not be bridged and threatened to plunge us into despair at any moment. Not only her dealings but also my own became uncertain; we alienated ourselves and got into a chain of wrongdoing. The uncertainty of our dealings was nourished by the highly sophisticated and complicated nature of my wife, who naturally had to develop in a fateful direction in this gulf that stood between us. Thus, my wife lost the last opportunity, on the basis of the life granted to us, to discuss sexual matters with me subjectively in any form, given that others could eavesdrop upon these discussions. The peculiar nature of my demeanour, intensified by the circumstances of my detention, created a mood of irritation that my wife found unendurable. She felt that the discussion of such things as one has to say personally was a profanation of her sex life under such circumstances. And quite rightly. I, on the other hand, saw in the failure to communicate a complete absence of the desire to communicate with me. I also deduced from this a certain lack of depth and extent in the quality of her sex life. Certainly, I did not ask my wife for any reports. Sex life in the subjective relationship between man and woman is, however, not a matter that anyone lives for himself, but rather something that absolutely demands discussion. No one can deny that, no matter how you might regard the sexual; both sides belonging to each other in a relationship want to be elastically emancipated down to the last detail: no-one can avoid a discussion. The need for sexual satisfaction had been troubling my wife for some considerable time, and she kept pushing it back. She wanted to make sure she could count on my approval. Every time our conversations reached the cardinal point during visits and she logically had to come to the crucial question, she would go off on a tangent. But I noticed nothing of it and later I was shocked when the demand was obliquely put to me, I should grant her permission to seek sexual satisfaction. Even before my wife could realize her intention to be sure, her need had been satisfied. Then she discussed with her friend how and in what manner I should be informed of what had happened. Much was decided, but nothing acted upon, which meant I remained ignorant and judged my wife's condition to be a result of sexual abstinence.

But my wife also found no opportunity to discuss other matters that did not need to be directly stressed in a subjective-sexual manner. The heartbeat of the most self-evident communication was muffled out by the iron curtain of surveillance. The slightest caress that we wanted to offer one another, and which we longed for, was prevented by the uniformed audience. So one character trait after another withered from our being. I no longer yearned for visits; I even went through periods in which I feared them.

Under such circumstances I felt nothing for long periods, but also nothing at all about my wife's inner workings. She stayed resolutely silent, even though she knew that I suffered in the situation. This persisted. I knew as little about her life, how it worked out, what happened, what she did, what she experienced, and what did not happen as I did about a complete stranger. We faced each other like two people who no longer care about one another, who have never been anything to each other. And yet, we were inseparable, united in our basic outlook and with two hearts beating as one.

Out of some inadequately informed or misinformed circumstances, hinted at while I was in a depressed mood, I created all sorts of delusions in my narrow cell. How could a person come to clear judgements of events when the eyes replace the tongue and language takes the form of hand and body movements? The doorway to insinuation is very wide indeed – yet there is no substitute for the impact that three small words can have! So I built Potemkin villages everywhere, tore them down again, and rebuilt them with the material that my wife was inevitably adding. The Potemkin villages were left standing, because my wife did not tear them down, and often could not tear them down, because I did not always put them on show.

In this period I was dependent on the insight and goodwill of the District Court Director Bühnemann in Halle. He was a judge with a right-wing political orientation, but despite this I owe him some respect. I did not have a single conflict with him in a period lasting more than a year. In correspondence by letter with my wife, he allowed me extraordinary freedoms, which is crucial in the absence of any other distractions in detention. In consequence of this freedom to write I was thus able to dress my erotic energy in words for a more prolonged period; I could write about the power of my sexual urges. But taking everything into account one cannot forget that I was already demoralized. Which is to say: certainly I was allowed to write, more than was usual and more than my strength allowed. Over a period of several months I produced such a plethora of letters that later, when I saw them again, I was startled by their volume and to some extent also by their content.

One should not assume that I was simply writing "meaningless drivel" to fill up the page in my letters. If this were the case, my wife would not have been able to write to me three years later, when I requested the letters for journalistic purposes: "What precious wealth is contained in the letters – in spite of everything, in spite of the pain that they inflicted on me at the time." If I had embedded "vacuous rubbish" in the texts, then the dry jurist Bühnemann would have been unable to express to my defence attorney what the latter then informed the Governor of Brandenburg jail by letter: "The District Court Director Bühnemann has personally explained to me that the more he reads Plättner's correspondence with his wife, the more he is won over by the peculiar personality of Karl Plättner."

I have only drawn on this characterization for objective reasons. My defence counsel wanted to give the Brandenburg Governor a judgement on my nature in order to obtain a different form of treatment, in view of the fact that as a result of harassment I was once again playing very strongly with the idea of suicide.

Yet with all the undoubtedly correct thoughts that I wrote, I was writing a rather strange scripture, as though I was speaking a foreign language that my wife, who otherwise knows everything about me, no longer understood. In addition to the basic thoughts were nervous outpourings. I intertwined good with bad, right with wrong, understanding with poisonous doggedness, healthy thoughts with sick; I saw much under the distorted light of a lantern; did not see many things as they were, but rather turned upside down. Under these conditions, my tetchiness had to become pathological and drive me more and more into states of inner conflict.

What I wrote to my wife during this time about improprieties, unfairness, harshness, coarseness and ugliness I later had to feel was unjust. I became the worst possible caricature of myself.

The differences between me and my wife could not have deepened to become chasms if halfway regular sexual relations had taken place, at least a surrogate for normal life; a possibility under which it could formally be said to me: not so, that's just how things appear.

In all, the success of being able to communicate adequately with my wife, at least by letter, without being inhibited by technical means, was sexually surprising. I submitted so much effort to the writing down of my better thoughts that I felt a soothing emotional flow and the outburst of feelings overwhelmed me with its sexual impact; indeed, I felt the touch of my body with that of my wife, with whom I held, in these conditions, long conversations out loud, as one can only do when in isolation. In the truest sense of the word, I felt transposed into "natural" active sexual acts, which kept renewing my ability to work. Sexual feeling grew to the maximum potency, to physical exhaustion. But what took place here was not in the nature of self-gratification; rather, what dominated and controlled me functioned automatically. After such occurrences I then felt sobered; my thoughts were attracted to a quieter pole and maintained on a more even keel: I came closer to an inner balance, enjoyed some *joie de vivre* and felt such a powerful inner force in me following the effects of this sensual pleasure that my thoughts were released and brought into the realm of the spiritual.

The sexual satisfaction that I achieved in this situation, however, cannot be compared to what one would consider normal sexual satisfaction, which is only fulfilled when the path has been cleared for regular enjoyment. Those circumscribed phenomena required extraordinary experiences, strong inner pleasure, and much more besides, namely, a high and indeed the highest spiritual sexual excitement; that means, as far as the actual effusion of semen was concerned, they were only exceptional phenomena, which, when they happened, required extraordinary physical and mental powers and turned my inner existence itself into a sexual volcano, so to speak. What that means, I will illuminate with a terrible experience from penal incarceration. My wife could not subsequently write, by hand or by typewriter, the kind of letters that would arouse me to the extent that they could replace the physical and comprehensible form of the object of love, quite apart from the fact that these forms of satisfaction, however elemental and primitive in the way that they occurred, were and remained unnatural forms of satisfaction. So, I drifted into severe sexual distress. And this distress led me to a cliff edge. My mental exhaustion was so complete that I could not begin anything, nothing at all; I even found it impossible to formulate my thoughts in writing. What stood between my wife and myself had to be given free expression.

In the dilemma we were in, I saw no other way out than applying for an unsupervised visit. I explained the application in detail, first in writing. The exceptionally good relationship between me and district court director Bühnemann justified me in making such a start, without me needing to feel that I was prostituting myself. The fact that, in the progress of our complicated relationship, District Court Director Bühnemann stood as an unbiased observer and mediating factor between me and my wife, led me to assume that he would seek to find a possible and necessary solution in this regard.

So the matter led to a personal interview with him. At first, he tried, as I could hardly have expected otherwise, to take the matter down a blind alley. His feelings were rooting for me, his intellect for the regulations; but in the end sensitivities were stronger and won him over. Seldom have I been able to exchange inner values and inner cordiality with an opponent of my world-view to the extent that I could with the District Court Director Bühnemann. The feeling grew ever stronger in me: Here speaks a father with his child, a child he no longer understands; nevertheless, he listens, because he loves his child. He jumped from one suggestion to another. In every instance I told him that the suggestions had no practical merit. Bühnemann shrank from the consequences of any precedent he might create. But he himself conceded that Justice was being unjust in this case – and that alone determined him to allow me an unsupervised visit by my wife.

I wallowed in the deepest anticipation of the coming days and the extraordinary event that they would bring. My wife came – and our tears flowed together in streams. Tears of sorrow and tears of joy that became a deep spiritual experience! It was all too much, and I burst out of my shell.

My wife went away again, as she must, and I was left alone with my feelings. Overflowing with happiness, I felt as though my thirst had been slated by tears of joy. In one or other edition of *Die Schönheit* I read about dance as a liberator, and created a kind of rhythmic intoxication in myself: "All dissolution of solid forms and bonds will undoubtedly lead to chaos, but chaos is not identical to absolute nothingness; far more it can evolve again and again to newly created forms when it is youthfully and powerfully touched by the procreative spirit."[24] I profited from my wife's unsupervised visit for a relatively long time, and felt myself as though inwardly reborn. Suddenly, I was so cleansed of all the garbage and once again so animated that I hardly recognized myself. All of the barriers that stood between me and my wife were torn down. Even the people with whom I had to deal seemed to me as though changed. It was about three months before the effect wore off. Then my first respiratory arrest occurred. That's how I ended up, as do all prisoners, in the labyrinth of masturbation. All prisoners tread this path before they find themselves on the road to acute sexual distress.

---

[24] *Die Schönheit* ("Beauty") was a German monthly magazine published by the poet and journalist Karl Vanselow between 1902 and by Richard A. Giesecke from 1914 to 1932. Elaborately designed in the art nouveau style, it was in the vanguard of the nudist culture in Germany.

3. Self-gratification as an instrument of coercion in solitary confinement and the suppression of sexual functions as the cause of physical illnesses

The conclusion we can draw from the preceding discussion is as follows: every prisoner, if his sexual instinct is normal, will, after prolonged futile attempts to suppress the impulse, to displace it, will resort to some substitute. He will? No, he must! He must do so, because he cannot overcome the impulse, and he must do so, because the impulse torments him and will not leave him in peace. He must do so while in detention, because the object of his love is absent.

The Christian medical professional Paul Maag, who wrote a book arguing against aspects of Freud's teaching (*Geschlechtsleben und seelische Störungen* (Sex Life and Mental Disorders) Albert Zutavern Verlag, Pforzheim 1924), writes:

"An instinctual act in itself means nothing other than a desire for satisfaction, which is put to the conscious ego as a choice. This is now decided one way or the other, through assent or rejection. If the instinctual desire is approved, fulfilment takes place, it becomes an act, it is lived out. If it is rejected, so the desire is lost more or less quickly, only to return after a while. In the field of sexuality, this willingness can very easily turn to self-reliance; the highly strained organic stimulus then forces the psyche to a solution, an affirmation, and places it more and more in the relationship of the dependence on the organ, which persists in a pathological, almost permanent instinctual tension, one that the will can no longer resist. Thus, the oneness and supremacy of the ego has been lost for this part of the psyche. Management of the impulse is not under the control of the organ. That is the essence of all indiscipline. The increasingly powerful impulse proves to be intractable. It has lost all constancy, all calm, prudence and expediency

and is working towards the ruin of the organism."
It therefore makes little sense and, on the contrary, is highly hypocritical to repudiate self-gratification, as it is insincere to deny sexual distress, which breaks forth in one form or another. I once said to a warder that I estimated 95 out of 100 prisoners indulged in self-gratification. He replied that you could comfortably assume it was 100%. The prisoners who did not satisfy themselves, were either acutely ill, impotent, or had other physical ailments that prevented them from masturbating. Hirschfeld says about this in the first volume of his *Geschlechtskunde* (Julius Püttmann Publishers, Stuttgart 1926):

> "That the sexually normal person in a single-sex environment on ships, in the field, in prison camps, in prisons, in short, wherever there is no opportunity for intercourse – frequently resorts, *brevi manu* (= without further ado) to self-gratification, usually by imagining people of the opposite sex, is an old and well-known fact. Some push the pillow into their arms and cover it with caressing words and kisses, while others make a kind of vagina out of the bedsheet. One wrote from the field: 'Before, my wife was my right hand. Now, my right hand has replaced my wife.'"

These observations also seem to be in accordance with a smaller number of official doctors who approve of masturbation as a necessary surrogate, calling it the "lesser evil," even recommending this remedy in many cases, and quite simply express themselves as comfortable with the remedy of masturbation by people in prison. But these are only the more understanding physicians, who, although hesitantly, always try to fight against the Bastille of an ossified and misanthropic bureaucracy. When official doctors express their bitter-sweet approval of the prisoners' self-gratification, and, beyond this, don felt slippers to tiptoe into the Privy Counsellors' salons to tell them something about the prisoners' sexual distress, it is therefore based on more deeply rooted considerations of maintaining the health of the body. They know that the sexual organs, especially the sexual glands, generate the sexual products that enter the circulation of the blood everywhere, including the brain cells. If the products of the sex organs have no somatic outflow, they must, so to speak, lead to over-production. The sexual substances multiply and become over-charged, overstored and agglomerated; they create a chemical crust around the brain, so to speak. In other words, the effect of the sexual substances takes on excessive, unhealthy forms. The vernacular refers to this condition (usually in jest) as *Samenkoller*.[25] Hirschfeld, the undisputed leading sexologist, describes it thus:

> "Any substance in the physical metabolism unrelated to its purposes has a toxic (poisonous) impact in the blood; why should it behave any differently in the sexual metabolism?"

The Berlin sexologist Max Marcuse says:

> "According to the present state of science and practice, sexual abstinence is a major cause of mental and physical illness."

In order to mitigate the conditions that must necessarily have a toxic impact when semen production is excessive, prison doctors recommend masturbation or at least approve of it.

Let us begin with a somewhat more detailed consideration of sexual abstinence as the "serious cause" of physical complaints, before proceeding to describe concretely complex situations inseparable from the nature of self-gratification, including, for example mental disorders. One day a fellow prisoner told me the following:

> "In the summer of 1923 I came into other communal areas as a result of heavy labour that I was unable to perform. At the time I had stomach troubles. Incidentally, gastric illness is often found among long-term prisoners, but almost never in homosexuals, who also have

---

[25] *Samenkoller* literally translates as "semen-rage".

sexual relations while in detention. There must be a sexual linkage that either provokes, or on the other hand holds in check gastric complaints, though I cannot figure out what that is. At any rate it is strange that in my sharp observations I have almost only encountered onanists with stomach diseases. Homosexuals are virtually never ill while eating the same food; after years, their appetite is still good."

Another inmate in prison W. told me the following:

"I suffered for an entire year from ulcers: furunculosis. A disease with which I have otherwise never been afflicted in my whole life. I went to the doctor, who on this occasion literally advised me to masturbate; but when (a few months later) my weight had fallen to 59 kg (my normal weight is 77 kg) and I asked in vain for dietary supplements, he admonished me not to masturbate so much. When I pointed out this contradiction to him, he left me in a state of outrage and without saying a word."

I considered these formulations to be exaggerated and declared that if I publish such extreme deduction and argumentation in this form, not only will we not seem plausible, but we will have to endure the insults of the medical profession, while the great army of cynics will make us the object of their attacks. And yet there is truth in the synthesis between sexuality and physical illnesses. Nemilow expresses it thus:

"The sex organs, and in particular the sex glands, i.e. the ovary in women and the testicles in men, have a dual function. On the one hand, the sex products are developed, i.e. the ova in the female and the spermatozoa or the seminal filaments in the male; on the other hand, special chemical agents are secreted here, the hormones that are continuously supplied to the blood and reach everywhere with the blood. Distributed over the whole body, they influence all processes taking place in the body in the strongest manner. Now it should be pointed out that the research of the last ten years increasingly confirms the view that the secretion of the sex glands has a tremendous physiological significance. Without normal internal secretion, there is no health. Everything that happens in the body and in the soul of man is related to these sex hormones. They make humans what they are.

"The sex glands are not the only organs in which hormones or incretions are formed. The thyroid gland and the parathyroid gland, the pituitary gland and the adrenal glands among others give the blood very important internal drivers, which ensure the interworking of the bodily organs. But in the array of organs, which together with the nervous system direct all processes of the body, the sex hormones have a very special significance."[26]

So you have to combine the metabolism in the human organism with the sex functions; if prisoners feel physically uncomfortable, ill at ease or simply ill, at the time of diagnosis one must take into account the fact that the sexual functions have been despotically disabled. Which is to say: the metabolism is impaired, when parts of organs that work with it and which drive it, are despotically disabled.

In confirmation of these findings, a statement made to me by the Medical Counsellor Leppmann in his capacity as an official psychiatrist is typical. I was constantly complaining of headaches, heaviness of the limbs, pain in the lungs and the kidneys, severe depression which encouraged my shortness of breath, bronchial catarrh, and other purely physical illnesses. But what did Leppmann say about this? "I have been racking

---

[26] A.W. Nemilow, *Die biologische Tragödie der Frau* Oskar Engel Verlag, Berlin. Nemilow was a Professor at the Leningrad University; his research specialized in the hormonal operation of the sexual organs. The "Biological Tragedy" claimed to offer an ABC of sexual enlightenment and promoted professional management of maternity and infant care.

my brains for days as to how I should explain your overall
condition – especially in physical terms. Tell me: isn't a lot of
this to do with the sexual side of things? Here, the disable-
ment of sex functions must play a major role. Otherwise, with
the best of intentions, I cannot achieve a satisfactory result in
the understanding and judgement of your condition, in the
diagnosis of your bodily condition!"

In a lecture to doctors in Berlin, in the year 1926,
Leppmann spoke exhaustively about the various types of reaction in detention. In this respect he spoke about the physical
reactions; the excessive acid secretion of the stomach, of
"pimples on the face," and the connections between metabolism and sexual functions.

I supplement Leppmann's findings with a quotation
from Hirschfeld's *Geschlechtskunde*:

> "Not only those who adapt man to life, but also those
> who adapt life to man, can help and heal. If not the one,
> often the other leads us to our objective.
>
> "That every struggle by the body against an illness,
> with the many physical and chemical changes that this
> entails, has a strong effect on sexual desire and ability,
> disturbs the fine bodily sexual mechanism, can soon in-
> crease or weaken drive and resistance, should be obvi-
> ous but in fact it rarely is. One would in fact have to go
> through one disease after another to be able to discuss
> the influence that it can have on sex life. It would be a
> good topic for a book in its own right."

In his assessment of sexual neurasthenia, Freud emphasizes
that sexual repression "is often converted into physical symptoms, and translates into breathlessness, tremor, palpitations,
dizziness, diarrhoea, sweating, etc." And Hirschfeld emphasizes "that hysterical ailments of all kinds, states of oppression, especially so-called 'heart cramps' with extreme anxiety,
do not count as rarities after long-term abstinence." From the
Hirschfeld survey material, I use three passages that are
meaningful for assessing the question of the interaction of

sexual functions with the other functions of the human body. Hirschfeld writes in a report:

"Mrs Sch., 40 years, was married from the age of 20 to 25 years. She bore two sons from this marriage. For 15 years she has been abstinent, and for 12 years she has suffered from sleeplessness, lack of appetite, languor, strongly eccentric behaviour, violent fits of crying and sexual obsessions. Her head is as though pressed in. Repeated stays in sanatoriums proved as unsuccessful as medication. Five years ago, she maintained a two month-long sexual relationship with a married author. Even though she had the strongest moral objections, she felt as though liberated during this time. Sleep and appetite returned, her mood became harmonious, she was 'reborn', to use her own expression."

The second report states:

"A second case concerns a man, who, up until his 54th year neither masturbated nor had sexual intercourse. He lived in a small town in conditions that made sexual intercourse very difficult. He was afraid of being in-fected in large cities. His sex drive was relatively mod-erate. Nevertheless, his ability to work was severely impaired, he suffered from 'colossal' inner agitation, travelled all around the world complaining of limb pain, absent-mindedness, aversion to any activity, nightmares, nocturnal crying, and nervous dyspepsia. Medical cures and the natural life (the 'simple life') rec-ommended to him by American doctors for vegetarian, alcohol-free food, fresh air and bathing cures, gymnas-tics, etc. were of no use. Since having sexual intercourse once a week his symptoms disappeared, only the occa-sional nervous dreams still persist. He says it occurred to him that he was previously only half alive."

The third report, which was issued to a seminar teacher, says the following about his wife:

"The married woman named Sch. is a woman of

healthy and natural sexual instincts. She is also in other respects mentally and physically a completely healthy woman. Aside from what has already been stated, she says the following: She suffered all the more from the lack of sexual satisfaction in marital intercourse when she shared her husband's dwelling and bedroom. Previously of a healthy nervous disposition, in the last year she had fallen into a state that had until then been completely alien to her due to unfulfilled arousal and privations. She lost 14 pounds in that one year, sleeps very badly and restlessly, is constantly in an unbalanced and irritable mood, cries very easily and has become very quarrelsome. Palpitations and anxieties are not uncommon."

Maag writes the following about the disturbed interactions between sexuality and physical well-being:

"In other cases, the reflex-wave in the imagination works on the heart, triggering palpitations, cardiac spasms or feelings of tightness. Even more commonly, the stomach is a drainage organ and responds to it by a variety of functional disorders. The gut responds with diarrhoea or obstinate constipation. The skin reacts with outbreaks of sweat and pins and needles of all sorts. The possibilities are specific to the individual and infinite. The greater the impressionability, the easier the transmission. It is quite certain that all sexual abnormalities, more than any other influences, increase the irritability of nervous life and increase sexual to physical conversions and transmissions by at least double. Thus, for example, the sexual aetiology of frequent changes to respiration, which can rise to the most pronounced asthma, is so well known that we only need recall it."

I once went to the doctor in Brandenburg prison in search of suitable therapeutic treatment for my lung and bronchial symptoms. I also drew his attention to my slow metabolism and stressed that improvement might perhaps be achieved through more abundant outdoor exercise and better nutrition. This placed me under "suspicion". Obviously, I just wanted to get better food, wanted "to get over the severity of my punishment"! And so, this official doctor told me: "That is another fanciful idea used to promote a lot of nonsense. You should think less about your illness, then your bodily metabolism will be perfectly adequate." The words of Casanova instinctively occurred to me: "More people die in the care of doctors than are healed by them. In the end, the world would be a lot less unhappy without lawyers and doctors." Quite so. If misanthropic clerics or lawyers with official duties do not recognize in people's sexual functions the natural drive in the blood, then they can simply get back to business as usual. But if a doctor does not recognize the natural facilities in the human organism and ignores their functional significance, that is tragic. Because "the more the organs of the body free themselves from the power of the 'mysterious juices' that pass from the sexual glands into the blood, the more they fall prey to another power, but now a power of destruction, which is called death. We see from this that man is unable to free himself from the power of sex, because outside of sex there is no health, not even a life" (Nemilow). The Christian doctor Maag says, however: "The imagination is constantly accompanied by somatic over-exposures that are unintentional and do not bear the character of conversion." And the eminent doctor Bieg, who has also made a great contribution to the clear definition and crystallization of the importance of internal secretory functions for normal organ flow in the human body, calls the human constitutional formula a glandular formula and speaks in this connection of generational glands. Thus, according to him, "the person shifts his whole being, all the peculiarities of his body and mind, his diet and the activity of nerves under the dependency of sexual functions."

The implied and basic findings may suffice here. For no person who wants to be taken seriously and loves the truth will want to assert that the interaction of glandular functions can be satisfied in the case of prison inmates. One need not even draw the failure of any one of the glandular organs into consideration to realize that the very elimination of the organic glandular functions, or even their reduction, must lead to permanently acute and finally also to chronic organ defects and thus to physical diseases of all kinds. There is no prisoner "in the modern German penal system" who does not suffer from stomach, kidney, heart, chest, nervous or mental illnesses after more than a year's detention. For in this destructive substance no human life can grow, no physical health can flourish. It is enough, even if it has been deter- mined by official medicine with caution and reserve, that the metabolism in the human organism, this basic constitutive factor, is destroyed, or at least disturbed, when the sexual functions are violently and arbitrarily eliminated, while there is a total absence of physiological and psychological precon-ditions for this. That this is the case is proved by the fact that since my release from prison, I have not had any asthmatic seizures, whereas they tortured me to the point of desperation in prison.

4. An illumination of situations of sexual distress in connection with spontaneous ejaculations

No impulse can be transformed into another, the science of sexology teaches us. The Christian doctor Maag nevertheless states in his previously mentioned book: *Geschlechtsleben und seelische Störungen* the opposite assertion which, since it is pursued *ad absurdum*, cannot remain unmentioned. He writes:

> "If reality prevents an individual from satisfying his or her libido normally, this does not cause conflict. It simply leaves the instinctual tension in place and forces it to a spontaneous solution by way of menses or ejaculation. That is the natural way out. The compulsion to choose another, perverse way out, is not based on actual denial. If no normal object is offered consistently for sexual desire then, we would continue, the individual remains dependent on the aforementioned natural safeguards and will not suffer. But Freud seems to consistently support the notion that sexual desire is entitled to more, and that it also enforces its claim and, as it were, chooses a perverse path out of defiance. He personifies the libido."

I already mentioned that after nearly five years' detention I had the first opportunity to discuss sexual distress with the Medical Counsellor Dr. Leppmann. The sensitive, understanding and serious way in which Leppmann treated the battery of questions of a sexual nature, especially in the penal system, naturally brought me into relatively close contact with him in this field. The discussion about the torments and consequences that are rooted in sexual dissatisfaction initially led to an intensification of emotional depressions. I fell into a terrible state of anxiety, whose violence threw me on the bed, I even fell into fits of crying, which were followed by a certain inner relief or at least calm. I struggled hard against the elements of sexual excitement that welled up inside me. My feeling, however, was reluctant to profane the erotic at work within me with a wild, fleeting, superficial sensory intoxication, with grossly sexual activity. I was completely dominated by the desire to feel the body of a woman, to embrace it, to tear off its clothes. My burning eyes sought the beauty of woman in all its forms; the power of my heart demanded affirmation, my ears wanted to hear the soft sound of a female voice. That could not be, because I was locked up in my cell. Nevertheless, over a period of time the stormy waves swept me into a realm of the most beautiful erotic imaginings: I saw myself transposed into an act of procreation. After a while, I longed for an opportunity to communicate with others. Terrible, that you can rarely do this in prison! But for the moment, this would also have been of no help to me, because my desire was for something specific: a woman. It got ever closer to me and around me, however; the demand of my mental yearning became ever more impetuous, the sound in my soul grew louder and louder: break out of the confines of the cell! Get into company and talk openly about what oppresses you! Exchange your thoughts so that you can test who you are, what you are, what you want and can and must be: human! But the iron barrier held me tight, screaming at me: destruction of all the normal and natural laws and functions of life!

Again I threw myself on the bed, again I was overcome by anxiety, and again this was followed by crying fits. Once again, the desire to get hold of a means that could lead me to my death was alive and kicking!

Crying, I would have liked to throw myself on a sweet girl, so that her mouth could drink my streaming tears, and I could bury my pain in her breasts. This was the only atmosphere in which my balance could be established, my torrents of agony brought to calm, level and clean shores. It was a fortunate circumstance that at the time I had fellow inmates, to whom I could at least tell something about what was oppressing me. But, what you can and do say to a woman in such feverish moments you would never tell a man. The relationship that connects a man more inwardly, naturally and deeply to a woman is absent. However, within the ambit of my disposition to think about these things a certain composure and calmness had again become possible. After being locked up in the evening, I felt the emergence of a thought whose outlines I was still trying to refine – when the light was turned off again. It would have been sensible to put my thoughts to paper in the creative state in which I had worked so energetically. Prison regulations prevented me: "The light is to be switched off at 8 p.m." I tried to sleep. My condition made this difficult. Strong sexual arousal was neither satisfied nor overcome. I did not arrive at the only possible and necessary solution: ejaculation. The emotional outpourings flowed to the limit, where they start to be tantalizing. If I had had light, then the necessary release would perhaps have been achieved insofar as the exercise of mental power had "compensated" for the sexual elements. That would have provided satisfaction, even if only of a psychological nature.

Thus the night was sleepless; my head burned like an inferno. On top of the psychological disorders came shortness of breath, which compounded the torment. The following morning I was dull and tired, physically I felt completely whacked out, but at the same time still in a relatively happy mood, because I saw one goal in mind: the study of sexual distress in penal institutions. This ruled my thoughts until the last hour of my detention on 17 July 1928, so a full three years.
Immediately I set to work but was soon exhausted and after a bold hopeful surge I plummeted to the depths once again. Once again, I was in pieces. What would have been child's play the night before, if the technical prerequisites had not been lacking – the light – now presented me with insurmountable difficulty. The source of spiritual creative power had dried up again. A few minutes of sufficient mental vigour was followed by hours of lack of resolve, absolute mental powerlessness. So I idled away most of the day and my thoughts only drove me as though storm-whipped through infinity once again as evening fell.

I know that the reader now wants to know: what development did your sexual urges take? They were pushed back after severe torture, under the will to bring a particular piece of work to conclusion in an uninterrupted progression. This resulted in terrible headaches that plagued me for weeks. It carried on for about five weeks altogether. I worked intensively from seven in the morning until ten in the evening, without any break. I often had little time to eat my meals; I turned down every request from fellow inmates to go with them to a common room for a conversation with them. But the impulses grew stronger and stronger, more and more feisty, impetuous, impulsive, wilder – until they literally drove me into a sexual rage, with perpetual erections; they drove me around the cell like a hunted game. In the nights that followed, I clutched everything that came into the reach of my arms: the whole bed became a substitute for women and remained without satisfaction. A woman's hand in mine, her breath and fragrance, the faintest touch of a woman's body, a kiss would certainly have triggered a release. I was unable to achieve self-gratification through a single ejaculation by means of my hand because in my imagination and yearning I was in the lap of a woman. In my fantasy world, my hands had buried themselves in her full and fleecy hair and my head was embedded in her breasts, my lips imbibed desire; but I was simply not in a position to take my erect member in my hand to achieve, at least, a purely physical release from the tension. Every wilful attempt failed on the very threshold of intent. My hand was repulsed by psychological forces. I was attracted only, and time and time again, by the magnetic pole of woman. I fell into screaming fits and remained for four days and endless nights the victim of these conditions.

Is it really so difficult to grasp such conditions? If so, then allow me a little detour from the current topic. This state of emergency was not unknown to a senior warder, who sought ways out of my situation, but found none and finally he pressed Karl Schleich's *Besonnte Vergangenheit* into my hand, in the belief that the book could help me. That might have done the trick to some extent, because I gained a certain amount of satisfaction reading the book. But that was of lesser importance. With the help of Schleich, the great physician, I want to explain my own conditions and those of prisoners in general.[27]

Karl Ludwig Schleich, who during his lifetime drank from the well-spring of bourgeois ideologies, writes in his memoirs about sexual love: "Now I suddenly stood before my lover in her full bloom, and all the elemental force of an inescapable intimacy took hold of my heart."

As stated, Schleich was a bourgeois ideologue, though as such he was supported by free-thinking ideas and, as a man, determined by strong moral forces that set him beyond the capitalist horizon. As a bourgeois in ordinary garb he had a strong thirst for the "wisdom of pleasure". There was an inspired art of living in the man, on which basis he could also touch his ideological opponents. Stefan Grossmann wrote about him: "At the heart of his nature was faith. He took in the world, people, dreams, the flash of thought, sounds, colours. His bright eye drank in colours, his ear listened to the world's melody, his brain, the mechanism of thought, brought order to impressions. He was not God-fearing in the sense of orthodox pastors, but he never became a believer in force and matter, he never carried the monistic explanation of the world in his back pocket, he always had the humility of the sage, who knows that he knows nothing. And faith of return and resurrection always remained with him, the old childlike faith

---

[27] Carl Ludwig Schleich (1859-1922) was a surgeon and writer born in Stettin, West Pomerania (now Poland). He is best known for his contribution to clinical anaesthesia but was also a philosopher, poet and painter who challenged certain "epistemological monopolies" of current scientific orthodoxies, such as Darwinism, as just as dogmatic as religious orthodoxies. His memoirs *Besonnte Vergangenheit* ("Sunlit Past") was for decades a best-seller and has stamped the image of *fin de siècle* Germany before the First World War.

never died out in his heart."[28]

In sexual matters, too, Schleich loved "spiritual alchemy". This servant of religion, this believer under global horizons, who was carried by the myth of an "immaterial God", had to leave his parents' house prematurely because of his parents' marital quarrels and thereby separate himself from the girl who was the object of his affections. As a result of this separation the young man hurled cries of true pain from his heart: "But then I went through such a love-melancholy, waking up in the nights, crying into my pillows and sad as a sick canary on a small corner window overlooking the market square, that I still believe today real love is a very rare metaphysical entanglement of the soul, an amalgamation of gold of the heart to an invisible lock, which, somewhere in the Holy Land of the beauty of the soul, inextricably enters the chain of our fate and is kept faithful. True love is a supernatural process of attachment, eternally invisible to human eyes in its primary causation, inaccessible to logic, unbreakable by any dexterity."

The following must be said to expand on this cry of pain: Sexual love is more than a metaphysical union of souls; it is more than a supernatural bonding process. If only it were, then the thought of the beloved would fully satisfy; if only it were, then imagination would replace the feminine body, and the sublimated sex drive would enter into the realm of efficacy and would produce heightened spirit rather than impotent cries of sorrow; if it were just that, then you would not have to sit like a sick canary on the corner window of a Pomeranian or East Prussian market square, and weep into your pillows through the nocturnal hours to let the love-melancholy suffocate the breath of life! Nevertheless, in the judgement of

---

[28] Stefan Grossmann (1875-1935) was a left-wing liberal Viennese writer and theatre impressario, founder and first editor of the German political weekly journal *Das Tage-Buch*.

Schleich's cry of pain, it is not the metaphysical secondary effects that matter, but rather the openly professed symptomatic of the natural: "She cast her purifying light into my still darkened soul."

I have turned to this example, because it at least allows us to make striking comparisons and achieve an understanding of situations. Schleich, who lived in freedom, and in whose past, present and future, in whose milieu all the preconditions for the triumph of bodily and mental satisfaction were anchored, gives the best answer to this: "But then I went through such a love-melancholy, waking up in the nights and crying into my pillows." Under the prevailing circumstances of his living environment, which also moulds the inner life, Schleich would have been able to sublimate his sexuality and thereby pay tribute to the alleged "promotion of culture", not working off his sexual energies to transform himself but rather to transform them into "culturally valuable work" as certain apostles call it. Because Schleich held back nothing in his interest in art or science, professional work, sport, travel and enjoyment of nature. Despite all the natural pleasures that Schleich undoubtedly sought, enjoyed, and understood, despite his preoccupation with art, literature, and science, despite his pioneering professional work, he did not think of pushing his awakened sexual instinct into the machinery of sublimation. Sexual impulses cannot be satisfied with religious sentiments, biblical sayings, metaphysical rose water, art, science, literature, professional work, travel, sports, pleasures of nature, etc. These can only be satisfied in the life of the organic functions, once the sexual has been awakened. It has always been like that and it will always stay that way – and humanity will begin to listen, to hear the sound in its own soul and transform it into a conscious harmony.

After my inner urges had taken on ever greater dimensions, I could or rather had to write to my wife in order to avoid destroying myself. Reproducing the letter also cannot be avoided here. I wrote to my wife:

Dear Gertrud! I sat and vegetated for weeks in a chaos of emotions and thoughts, before I put roots into a better soil. My thoughts were so tied up with you that I was unable to sleep at night. What's more, this situation is still not over. And so, I have no choice: I must write to you at least to be able to explain what I am feeling on this path. My fibres are transformed into a melody of intoxicating symphonies. For a few moments, I then drink from this wellspring of procreation, the fluid of life, but it's just moments. Then I immerse myself in Beethoven: *"Freude, schöner Götterfunken!"* Nothing can restrain me in this moment: Joy, joy! Joy to the one who calls himself a soul on the whole planet! Be embraced, millions, this kiss to the entire world! But then the bad nights come in which I need to work – and yet cannot work, because the technical prerequisite, the light, is missing. This condition causes an increase in my sexual longing for satisfaction. It is not random sexual impulses that rule me; no it is a river of sexuality that flows in its single compulsive current into the loving ocean of your body. All of my thoughts are overrun by this. I do not know where to go with the impulses that are so strong, I cannot bring the overflowing current to a standstill. In this situation it is – and this is the cruellest aspect – entirely impossible to bring these impulses to rest somehow through ejaculation. It's just not possible: my soul positively screams for you, yet it gets no answer; my over-tension gets no relaxation, the yearning of my body is not a yearning for satisfaction, not even as a substitute. An entirely cruel game that nature, the fundamental good, is playing here with people, a cruel game because violence closes down, and finally destroys nature.

During the past few nights I had decided and formulated in my mind to write to the Prison Governor, to give me the opportunity to come to inner peace. But as soon as I tried to start writing, my hand lost its resolution. I thought of the words you said to me on my last visit, more reproachful than well-intentioned, thinking of your allegation that, as far as you know, the Prison Governor takes the position not to allow unattended visits in principle, and therefore one should not make requests to such people, because in doing so one would have to reveal inner distress, which is a profanity in this relationship and under these conditions; ultimately I also thought about how and in what way old Hülsberg interpreted the relevant provision of the DVO,[29] according to which he has the right to allow unsupervised visits in special cases, when he thinks that such visits should be allowed only for serious illnesses; namely, when a near death is to be feared. Then in my mental games I came up with the absurd idea of telling Leppmann about the hours of tormented distress in order to ask him if he could help us. My sense of hopelessness, however, meant that I did not act on my intention. But then something is again driving me in two directions. Namely, if I were to act according to Menzel's inspirations then I could confidently turn to the prison governor with a petition, without having to fear receiving a negative decision.[30]

But these ideas are opposed to your feelings. Therefore, I can reach no positive decision on the matter. But that does not get me through the conditions that are

---

[29] *Dienst- und Vollzugsordnung* (DVO): the prison regulations.

[30] Gustav Menzel (1867-1930). From 1921 he was a KPD member of the Prussian Landtag, member of the central committee of the Red Aid and head of the Legal Central Office of the KPD parliamentary group. From 1924 the main field of his activity was the care of political prisoners. Due to his involvement in prisons and prisons, Gustav Menzel was respectfully called the "Prisoners' Uncle". It was precisely to Menzel that Plättner made his March 1926 "declaration" that he renounced guerrilla warfare as a means of waging the class struggle.

playing their cruel game with me. Also, the hint that you made to me in your irritable mood, that it would be enough if we could be together for at least a few hours without supervision, as is currently allowed in the Brandenburg prison, leads to no solution. You don't actually have to know, what I will do with you, if we are alone together. Heavens above, dearest Gertrud, I will hug and embrace and crush you with my powerful loving arms! Just imagine the situation! Do you want to be controlled in a physically naked condition? During the unattended visit in Brandenburg I was more or less able to suppress my need in that direction at the time. I cannot do that now, at least I can make no absolute guarantee. If they now admit you to me without supervision, I will scare you out of your wits. Or not? Or the reverse? During your last visit I was barely able to ward off my inner forces, as I had until then always been able to do. I do not even see it as a solution if they let me see you during the day, as they arranged in pre-trial detention. Even the daylight disturbs me: I must be able to search for you with my hands, not see you, but feel and touch you. My eyes want to drink in the lines of your body in the semi-darkness, so that there is still some scope for fantasy. So that only my mouth will find your body shapes and will kiss you contentedly. I must drink from this heavenly spring; in this magical paradise I will be healed and born anew. Do you understand the fullness of my sexual power, do you feel the ocean waves that wash over me, do you see the wings that take me into the air? If it were up to me, I would rush to you at the speed of a flash of light like the rising sun, undress you and bathe in a flood of kisses. But I must allow myself to be driven by inner hardships in my cell, not obtaining a single satisfying solution that would allow me to drink in a new source of life. Such a hot breath is streaming through my breast, such a hot torrent is flowing through my veins, such a fiery glow is energizing my body as if I were completely connected to your own. It is not just sex drive, but rather sexual desire for you, for your physical love. That it is so, is good, and if it were otherwise, I would have to feel miserable; miserable because then I would no longer know where I should direct my impulses. Thus, my sexual desire can still nest in your soul – which it does. And that gives me a partial power in the midst of the destructive forces, a partial force under which I feel that the one is not without the other; that it is not sex drive that could be fulfilled anywhere, just as sex drive, but that it is the specific that holds me captive, and captivated. This is on the one hand good, but on the other prejudicial, because it inhibits release and destroys attempts at release. I do not know whether one can live under such forces in the long run, for the time being I only know that sometimes it is a wonderful thing to be in this predicament – to live under the strongest forces of desire, to live under the strongest forces of *this* desire so that one has the feeling: this desire will yet be fulfilled, but before fulfilment comes, the desire is always renewed; this desire gets closer and closer, but at the last moment it always retreats half a step; or not even quite half a step, but just enough that you can still feel its closeness, just enough that a glorious imagination keeps release at a distance.

Look, dearest, under such inner forces, I have undressed you and embraced all your tenderness through to reverent breathlessness. May I, dearest of all girls, kiss your voluptuous breasts in thanks? May I, most beautiful of all women, suckle life-force from your breast? Please, please, come: I rest in your soft flesh, enraptured in blissful anticipation, thirsting for your hot spring. Thus, completely surrendered to you in thought, embraced by you with infinite power, caressed by you with all your ardour, you live in me, you live for me – for my sake and for your own. Keep me dear and think of me when you have a happy hour of joy.

I had hardly written ten lines, when the extraordinary happened again, something I had already experienced while on remand: suddenly the inner violence of matter erupted and freed me of all my tribulations. The ejaculations now occurred spontaneously, like Vesuvius, so to speak as both forerunner and trailer to the thoughts I wrote to my wife.

Maag will celebrate and announce that this supports his theory. Maybe he will pick up the blue pencil and highlight a series of passages in his book, among others the following:

"Congestion of the sexual instinct is counterbalanced by many natural outlets. The somatic element (organ-pleasure) through spontaneous ejaculation and menstruation, the psychic element (the need of love and tenderness) through forces that themselves partly reside in the factors of denial, such as mourning for the dead, care for the sick and absent, insults and sorrow about conflicts; and further through a multiplicity of circumstances, such as family relations, kinship, friendship, participating people, new loves. Heightened nervous tension instinctively leads to increased work, it raises the level of professional interest, it awakens new duties, etc. People with an alert conscience and sense of duty always find a way out in such situations. It must also be said that a lot of silly talk goes on about the omnipotence of the sexual instinct. Anyone who has ever learned to control his instinctual life will now find his way without any particular difficulties. Scant food intake, an unappetizing diet, less alcohol, less meat than usual, lots of muscle work and exercise in the open air, cool baths and light clothes support abstinence. It may temporarily influence mood and temperament, but it does not make you sick. We think the danger lies elsewhere – in the temptation to satisfy the accentuated instinct in a forbidden way. Here, the cause may be found when people fall ill under the above-mentioned situations of denial. They have put the demand to keep the sexual instinct under control to one side and have made room for the temptation."

Certainly, in the difficult situation in which I found myself, ejaculation occurred spontaneously. But in the face of these tormenting conditions, does Maag seriously demand that "the individual can remain dependent on the aforementioned natural safeguards and that he will not fare badly"? Purgatory, hellish torments are the initiation for otherwise not even completely spontaneous ejaculations. Spontaneous ejaculations are not natural sexual functions. In the 96 months of detention behind me I had two spontaneous ejaculations, but the conditions described that preceded the ejaculations occurred more than 20 times, without it coming to spontaneous ejaculations. According to my experience and surveys this example can be applied to all prisoners, with few exceptions.

What remains of Maag's "natural outlets"?

Now it is a well-known fact that bromine is consumed on a massive scale in penal institutions. Bromine reduces the sex drive, but at the same time weakens the nerve centre, and thus natural resistance. However, this bromine consumption is not the sole reason for the absence of spontaneous ejaculations; other dangerous remedies must be, and are, given. Incidentally, the physician Maag does not seem to know that spontaneous ejaculations also prefigure a physically dangerous condition. And where all this is not the case, it is simply a mockery of human sex life in all its central importance, if he sees this expression of lust for life fulfilled in ejaculations.

5. Does self-gratification satisfy the laws of normal sexual functions?

It is undoubtedly a good thing that prisoners, under pressure of the general conditions in which they find themselves, use self-gratification as a means of achieving a crude release. But a good thing is not the same as a healthy thing. What self-gratification means can only be measured by recognizing the interaction of these things in all their profundity. If there is no doubt that self-gratification is necessary and certainly the lesser evil where normal functions are forcibly prevented through incarceration, then the question is: can it really satisfy these functions? Can it replace everything that constitutes and crowns a healthy sex life? And can it do so permanently? In people with normal sensitivities, sexual impulses go hand in hand with a spiritual aura; their satisfaction depends strongly on their state of mind. The laws of normal sensual pleasure should then take effect under the conditions of constraint; sex drive should abate, and sensual pleasure will subside. The first complication is anchored in this observation. What self-gratification can achieve from one perspective, it only tears down from another.

Here is what Hirschfeld says about it:

> "There is some evidence that after masturbation, the adverse reaction that occurs, the 'masturbation hangover', as one of my aptly patients called it, also has endogenous causes (due to bodily chemistry), whereby once again sexual loneliness carries considerable, and perhaps decisive weight. In sexual intercourse with a loved partner, of course, in their bodily proximity the arousal dissolves naturally, appears proportionately harmonious, whereas after sexual excitement with an unsuitable, or no object, the fall back to earth is much more abrupt. Just then the factor without which a sex life is not a sex life is absent: the partner."

The affirmation of sex life in humans can – from a moral perspective – only have high meaning where beautiful, up-lifting and edifying ideas are intimately intertwined with it. Respect for the higher self and respect for the delicate impulses of the other being, that is the epitome of an orderly sexual life. The liberating and activating effects, manifestations and consequences of a normal sexual life can in no way be compared with the results of masturbation. This fact has a special meaning where we are dealing with complicated feelings. Here, the demands that mind and soul place on the sexual functions remain unfulfilled. Only where self-gratification is in any way an outgrowth of a person's natural predisposition will sexual misery in the bondage of incar-ceration not take on the same forms that it does where we are dealing with normally predisposed people. Men who have been unable to connect sexually with a woman in normal life can continue to live that life without mental disturbances in detention if they are not prevented from doing so, which of course is the case.

As much Hirschfeld as regards the question of sexual masturbation under the broadest horizon, he sees little "fulfilment" therein, as he emphasizes. I further cite his book, *Geschlechtskunde*.

> "Of course, a completely different question is whether masturbatory sexual activity is a humane and appropriate solution to the individual sexual problem. I would like to reply in the negative. Masturbation is certainly not a sin, a vice or a crime; that was and is a complete misjudgement of its nature, but apart from the developmental years, in which it is the first natural sexual relief for most people, in the rest of one's life it is a pitiful way out, a defective solution, an unsatisfactory surrogate (substitute), a sad remedy for the sexual needs of men and women. Therefore, I cannot agree with Hans Blüher, who notes in his extreme way (which so often overshoots the target): 'There can be no doubt that masturbation is the greatest invention of human beings in the field of sex' (quoted by Prof. Dr.

G. Messer, Giessen, in *Die Freideutsche Jugendbewegung*, 5th edition), Bayer, Langensalza, p. 116). Certainly this sentence does not deserve the name 'disgusting filth', which is why a letter writer who falls into the other extreme in *Der Zwiespruch* (third year, no. 24)[31] turns against the followers of Blüher and Blüher himself, but masturbation is in no way a great invention, for in the first place it is not an invention at all, as little as is eating, drinking, sleeping and intercourse, but a purely instinctual affair, and then it is not a human invention, since it is not peculiar to man and, above all, the adjective 'great' seems inappropriate; on the contrary, it is one of the lowest of all sex acts because it lacks what first gives dignity and consecration to sexuality, the emotional connection and physical union with another person."[32]

The highest purpose of sex life is – medically speaking – only then fulfilled when the secreted sexual substances of the man penetrate the woman, so that blood is reciprocally mixed with the "mysterious juices" as Nemilow expresses it. The intended psychological and physiological purposes of sex life are never fulfilled with masturbation. Both factors – the medical as well as the moral – are therefore disregarded. Between the two is the predicament of the prisoner, who is burdened with a thousand indignities by the prison system.

Usually self-gratification is a perpetually self-increasing tendency. This is the rule, especially among average prisoners, but not to be excluded in the case of other prisoners in higher

---

31 *Der Zwiespruch* ("Dialogue") was a magazine of the *Wandervogel* movement.

32 Hans Blüher (1888-1955) attained prominence as an early member and historian of the *Wandervögel* ramblers' movement and as a taboo-breaking philosopher. He believed that pederasty and male bonding provided a basis for a stronger nation and state. Blüher supported the Nazis but turned against them after the murder of SA leader Ernst Röhm on the Night of the Long Knives.

quality facilities. There are many circumstances involved, and here it is crucial to have certain other remedies at your disposal that can help overcome states of weakness and urgency. But in 99 percent of cases these remedies are entirely absent, in the remainder they are only partially granted. Now, however, one must assume that most prisoners only start to use masturbation when they have been weakened enough and they can no longer rely on their nerves.

In any case, I think the dangers of self-gratification are greater than the benefits one can derive from it, because I believe it prepares the soil that can nourish serious nervous disorders. I assert this to be generally the case and would like to substantiate this claim with some individual experience. For example, I was sexually in a state of high tension for months on end, and then again was sexually in a state of low tension for months on end, until I reached a condition of neither high nor low tension, but suffered the most from sexual distress when sexual functions were performed automatically, mechanically and as a matter of habit. It can be said of this condition: I practiced sexual self-gratification for months at a time when I did not feel any sex drive, and then I did not masturbate for months, and was unsuccessful when I felt strong sexual impulses and was even plagued by strong urges. This may seem contradictory, but it is the truth. It can be seen from this you cannot track such situations in a linear fashion. In particularly bad situations of high sexual tension and tribulations, I went for months when I masturbated every day, often twice a day, without getting any relief. This is not necessarily damaging, because there are many people who regularly engage in sexual intercourse both in the morning and in the evening, even when they have a very weak physical constitution. However, this fact cannot be taken as a yardstick. So, it suffices for me to assert that my constitution was unable to tolerate daily sexual activity that was only half-way satisfying: I have neither the physical strength nor the psychological prerequisites to cope with it. But by the same token it also suffices if I assert that it was just as incompatible with my constitution and with my basic spiritual desires when I experienced a "low sexual tension" for months on end, that is to say, because of my depressive states, I could not gain actual sexual pleasure. Because these depressive states of mind were not the same thing as the absence of sexual impulses. The reciprocal effect of these states is now perfectly rounded out when the physical condition is satisfactory and sufficient sexual urges are produced that can raise, and must raise, sexual lust to the point of intolerability if no discharge takes place, and then no discharge takes place, and no discharge can take place, because mental inhibitions obstruct these discharges. Both states thus embody a certain destructive tendency, for where the physical condition is relatively or entirely healthy, that is to say where bodily forces are not consumed by the insatiable elements of an acute illness, there remains a certain excess of physical forces which, in performing their proper function, produce enough semen. Here stands one indisputable cornerstone upon which sensual pleasure supports itself and upon which its bodily sub-structure rests; but a cornerstone that carries something specific and for which there can be no substitute, in other words under the dictum of a law of nature, semen requires discharge and naturally occurring actions.

If I consider the disadvantages of masturbation to be greater than the benefits, then I am not thinking primarily of the purely physical side of things. But there are other side effects, so to speak necessary accompaniments to masturbation, that Hirschfeld illustrates very aptly and very characteristically:

> "An interruption to the act of masturbation before ejaculation occurs frequently because of mental inhibitions. If the production of the load has already advanced to a certain level, then this restraint, 'at the last moment' is better suited to multiplying rather than diminishing damage to the nerves because of masturbation. These inhibitions then act in a similar way to protracted or

prolonged masturbation, which intentionally post-
pones the climax of pleasure associated with ejaculation for a very long time. As soon as the onanist recognizes that this anticipation of pleasure is reaching its
climax, he stops his movements, to start up again after
a break. There are cases in which the sexual act is
dragged through these interruptions for up to an hour
and beyond. It is obvious that the consumption of
nervous energy is considerably increased by this. Incidentally, the time that elapses from the start of masturbation to discharge is individually just as different as it
is in the case of coitus; it varies from a few seconds,
thus coming close to *ejaculatio praecox* (premature ejaculation) and many minutes, ten, twenty and more."

In fact, the prisoner's whole tragedy in his acts of self-
gratification are crystallized in this conclusion. But with the
difference that in this case the climax aimed at is postponed
not only for hours, but for the whole night, unless two, three
and more acts of self-gratification arise from one. These conditions rob the prisoner of his sleep and must therefore already
have damaging effects. What being could bear to go for
months on end without sleep? A fellow prisoner, sentenced to
15 years, of which he had already served six, wrote me the following on the subject:

"I cannot get women out of my mind; more and more
often my hand reaches for my sexual organ, daily,
hourly and through sleepless nights. Ringing in the
ears, a slight feeling of dizziness that is pleasantly experienced, a hovering in the room with all the pleasant
effects of an opiate, and ejaculation deliberately postponed for hours. One lies there helplessly and vulnera-
ble to self-torture because of one's unsatisfied sex life."

6. External and other influences of a general nature that encourage self-gratification

In addition to local stimuli that trigger masturbation, says Hirschfeld, "there are nervous reasons of a general nature, especially increased unrest, which can also bring about a craving for masturbatory manipulations." Such increased restlessness and inner urges, which at first need not be sexual in nature, permanently exercise control over the prisoner. That would be an expression of nervousness. Hirschfeld writes the following in his *Geschlechtskunde*:

> "The stronger the nervous system is, the stronger the external stimuli it requires, the weaker it is, the weaker the stimuli required to overcome resistance. Based on this experience, the most important means of liberation from masturbation is: strengthening of the nervous system."

By contrast, in Luckau prison the incumbent district doctor declared the following:

> "Masturbation is not only harmful, but it is also only an expression of an incapacity, a weakness of the will, a lack of moral fibre, an expression of a dissolute life. But incarceration is not the cause of this; rather, it is the inferior disposition of those who masturbate. For if it were the case that sexual instinct demands satisfaction as an imperative, then one would also have to allow the prisoner sexual intercourse, and actually grant it. But it is possible to do without sexual pleasure: neither physically nor psychologically does it signify what prisoners falsify to suit their own purposes."

One might refrain from pointing out to people who are being stamped into ground where their willpower must inevitably dry up, that they must control their impulses with self-discipline and volitional tension. I can justifiably believe that in my case, for example, one is dealing with absolute energy of the will. But that is of no use whatsoever in prison. The whole useless existence in the narrow, barren cell simply creates all the conditions for excessive sexual impulses, which brooks no opposition and which, over time, can no longer be diverted into the stream of intellectual creativity. You cannot sit in silence in a confined space for years on end, day in, day out, dreaming in seclusion without knowing what to do with time, how to kill it. Even the healthiest and most spirited, the most enthusiastic of men, the most prudent and most actively intellectual, the most daring artist and idealist, cannot endure such an existence, cannot dismiss inner tribulations; he cannot keep his distance from the destructive. Such people may dream their way into a paradise; they may, with their inner strength and spiritual construction, be able to work their way into another, beautiful world of ideas; they may be able to use the fullness of time and may even, at the start, have an inner desire not to be pulled out of this seclusion too soon; but under the conditions of our incarceration, they will not be able to use the time that is available in a useful and satisfying manner. I am certainly carried aloft by a lively imagination, one that all too often is excessively lively; I certainly know how to use my time and fill it with satisfaction – but that does not alter the fact that the cruel beasts of Reaction manage to creep in, both physically and spiritually-intellectually, imperiously demanding their nourishment. And with the years of incarceration this phenomenon becomes a permanent condition. That is the basis for our severe inner troubles. And these troubles are the connecting paths that lead to unhealthy, unnatural states, including excessive nervous strain, out of which all other actions then evolve, including excessive self-gratification.

A person only sleeps when he is tired; but he only gets tired within the confines of what is healthy if he can fatigue himself by working in a healthy and suitable way. At least 95 percent of prisoners lack all the prerequisites for this. Most prisoners sit in their cells or in prison units and must do the kind of work that does not provide any satisfaction, the kind of work by means of which a person can develop and fatigue himself while in the bloom of life; the prisoner must perform the kind of work – lots of it – that only destroys his nervous energy. On top of this, as a rule, prisoners are forced to go to bed at seven o'clock; first, they must hand over their clothes at this time and then sit naked in the cell, and then the lights are turned off. This is the crucible where excessive masturbation starts and develops through to catastrophe. For, as soon as the average prisoner finishes his mechanical housework, any other employment that could distract and thus lead him into another sphere abruptly ceases. And now all the nonsensical prohibitions first take effect, such as looking out of the window, talking to your neighbour, the ban on independent activity of any kind, the ban on smoking, the withholding of any stimulating reading material that can harness the spiritual powers and interest, the lack of social interaction. And on top of all this there is the confinement of prisoners to their so-called bunks. The exceptions, when prisoners may leave the light on until 8 or 9 in the evening, are of secondary importance. It is obviously impossible for the prisoner, who is not worn out and exhausted and whose nerves are permanently in an inferno, to fall asleep at 7 o'clock. He cannot even do so if he is tired and weary; his churned-up nerves, still in the highest state of unrest, prevent him from dropping off. He lies sleepless on his bunk, in despair, in deep misery for hours, night after night, and satisfies himself until he is physically exhausted enough to be able to find some sleep. The following evening the whole business repeats itself. In his *Geschlechtskunde*, Hirschfeld writes about such situations:

> "Two other causes of onanism have often been mentioned to me in the many thousands of cases that I saw: sleeplessness and abstinence from sexual intercourse. It is not uncommon to hear from older people in particular, but also from younger people, that they treat masturbation as a sleep aid. Only after this relaxation were they able to find the fatigue that is necessary for

rest, and thus for them self-gratification became a nightly habit, just as for others it is necessary to get intoxicated with morphine or alcoholic drinks to achieve the required 'drowsiness'."

If you add to this the fact that the sexual loneliness of people held in custody is "the most important among the manifold reasons for masturbation", then we have the whole complex before our eyes. And indeed, it was sometimes the case that in the evening, when I wanted to sleep, but could not fall asleep, sexual relief brought me the necessary "drowsiness". I also reduced my breathing troubles in this way.

Subsequent to these discussions I will deal with a couple of typical examples. Thus, one fellow prisoner revealed the following to me:

"Two particularly unhappy cases have stuck in my memory, prisoners who recounted every morning how often they had masturbated during the night. They had completely lost the plot and thus started a formal competition between the two of them as to who had done it most often."

In the Brandenburg penitentiary I met several young people who regularly masturbated four, five, six times a day, day in day out. During the day they bragged about it. A sergeant provided the fanfare, i.e. he created the atmosphere of the dirty joke for this tragedy. For him it was also a kind of sport to sneak from cell to cell and to watch the prisoners and see if they were masturbating. This sergeant therefore had a lot of arguments with the prisoners, because he made the pasted-over "spyhole" transparent again. An inmate in Wartenburg prison provided an excellent personal testimony to the degree of cynicism of the average prison warder. He wrote to me: "In cell 23, as I wash my feet after changing my clothes (in my shirt), Sergeant M. quickly closes the door and asks in an echo: 'What are you up to in there? – Ah, I see. I thought you were wanking'."

7. Self-gratification in the isolation cell, intellectual and mental disturbances

If sexual distress causes terrible torments even for those prisoners who are born with nerves of iron, then you cannot possibly imagine the extent to which sexual distress must affect those of a nervous disposition as they languish in detention cells. My heart tenses up, my hands start to shake as I think of those conditions. It is terrifying, the cynicism and frivolity with which people are locked up for nothing, and again for nothing, in the isolation cell for 14 days, three or four weeks at a time! In repeated cases I was told about, or I have overheard in conversations, that prisoners who were in isolation cells for a long time permanently indulged in substitutional sexual activities even when they were completely exhausted. They did it out of sheer desperation, just to kill time, or, as a prisoner told me, just to "work up" some warmth on the hard wooden bunk in the bitter cold of the dungeon. I know from personal experiences that these are not exaggerations or untruths. I sat in the isolation cell at a time when I was still relatively resilient and strong-willed. But already by the third day of the arrest, a state of emergency had set in and would have violated me despite all resistance had I not been released from the dungeon through the mediation of the Reichstag deputy Wendelin Thomas on probation, i.e. "pardoned". Before I went to this torture chamber, I had been deprived of hot food for a period of ten days, so that I was dragged there in an already depressed state. The denial of food was continued in the isolation cell; in addition, I immediately went on hunger strike. None of this prevents prisoners from indulging in sexual activity. Imagine, however, prisoners whose nervous system is severely weakened and who are moved between the prison hospital and the isolation cell. And then imagine: an inmate in Wartenburg, who was taken to the lunatic asylum for the last six months of seven years served in prison and has spent 295 days of the seven years in the detention cellar. He was not a man of coarse and unruly temper. His actions were mostly defensive fights against the Governor of the institution. He was sexually weak, as he told me, by nature. But I also heard from this prisoner that he had suffered cruel sexual torment in solitary confinement.

And then you have to have seen prisoners whose nerves have been worn down so much that they can no longer grasp the reason for their torments. You need to have witnessed such conditions that show us prisoners who were driven out of their human shells during a three, four, or five-year prison term and were then sent to the prisons' so-called psychiatric observation stations as a model for another half year so that they could be examined, observed and assessed there. What is taking place here is no longer a destruction of human beings by the shortest route, no, it is a systematic desecration of human beings, under the cloak of the functioning of retributive justice.

Thus, in the madhouse of Brandenburg prison I saw two totally unnerved prisoners who practiced acts of self-gratification in front of each other in the so-called observation room. If ejaculation occurred the game would pause for a few minutes and then start afresh. One day, one of the unfortunates was taken to the bathroom while I was taking a bath. The *kalfaktor* told me: since seven o'clock this morning he has already masturbated five times and now it was barely eleven o'clock.[33] They threw the man in the tub, and as soon as he was immersed in it and had looked at his new environment he started going through the motions again. After he had been given a cold rub down and brought back into the compound, he continued with these activities. Then a second prisoner joined in, performing the self-gratifying movements

---

[33] The *kalfaktors* were prisoners who had earned special privileges and performed duties that were essential for running the prisons. They were later known as *kapos* in concentration camps during the Nazi era.

as naturally as normal people breathe; yes, there are prisoners who out of sheer desperation often use masturbation with the intention of destroying themselves. The Medical Counsellor Lumpp stated at the Forensic Psychiatric Association in Heidelberg:

> "Such sexual thrills were disgusting to one of our murderers; he thought he could ruin himself through endless masturbation so that he would die of weakness, and when that did not happen, he reached for the knife and wanted to cut off his penis. It came to a colossal loss of blood and the onset of unconsciousness prevented him from further action. Another prisoner, also in such a desperate mood, tried to castrate himself with the bread knife; here too the bleeding put an end to the attempt.

We can overlook the name-calling in the first sentence. Do not imagine that this is an isolated case. If Lumpp wants to make us believe through his statement that this phenomenon can only be confirmed in the case of murderers, then let me remind you of the case that Wilhelm Pinnecke[34] recently published in the Cologne *Sozialistische Republik*. In this case, it concerns a political prisoner. Pinnecke writes:

> "The proletarian political prisoner H., after years of torture endured in prison, asked the prison doctor to effect his sexual sterilization by means of castration. After rejecting this proposal, our unfortunate comrade pierced through both testicles with a needle and darning yarn, allowed the condition brought about in this way to induce pus and forcing his sexual sterilization

---

[34] Wilhelm Pinnecke (1897-1938) was a KPD politician in journalist. In December 1924 he was given a prison sentence for his alleged leadership of a "proletarian hundred" military unit. Shortly after his release he became editor of the *Sozialistische Republik*, KPD organ for the middle Rhine region. He fled over the Dutch border when a second round of arrests occurred in the summer of 1933. Pinnecke was killed in the Spanish Civil War.

after enduring an operation."
So, wherever you look, the terrible evil of prison conditions is everywhere. Every normal person will seek to meet all of the demands that are dictated by good sense in his natural life. And the same applies to your sexual life. Under the effects of the "modern German penal system", however, it is not possible to create healthy conditions. In such an atmosphere, there is no point in giving the advice that, by using all the energy of will power, you must brace yourself against sexual excitation; it is all too easy to conclude that lack of willpower is based on organic weakness of the will. The prisoner already defends himself against all this violence in so far as he can, but he cannot do so by means of his natural powers, given that all of his natural means to spur on or control the will are absent. Where the means that help you to live normally and keep everything on track and in balance are absent, there is just no willpower left; it is broken, smashed, destroyed. Where, ignoring the results of all biological research, individual treatments are applied to situations that fall entirely outside the framework of every norm, where the individual's inner spirit is treated as an anvil, the person must be reduced to a caricature. Here, we are already on the path that leads to the borderlands of an idiocy conditioned from the outside. And once again I see hands fending me off and the cries of: "Exaggerated!" "Subjective!" Therefore, I will let others speak, whom one cannot accuse of exaggerating and being subjective. The Medical Health Officer Dr. Flörsheim in the Berlin-Moabit remand jail often said in conversations with me, when I underlined that I was feeling a certain dwindling of my mental ability: That is all quite explicable. In the bondage of detention and with the elimination of all instinctual joys and necessities of life, a person's mental capacities are broken, and all too often shattered. There are so many negatives piled on top of each other, which have, and must have, a catastrophic impact on intellectual and emotional beings, so that it is completely understandable if people create nothing great and significant while in detention, what-

ever other facilities are available. On top of this there is sexual abstinence, whose evil impact obviously increases the unhealthy situation.

However, before prisoners have developed to an externally observable idiocy, they move through the pre-stages, operating on the fringes of feeble-mindedness. And in prisons the sources of danger lurk in every corner. Literally everything starts here and takes its shape; every development is rooted in the soil of psychological disorders. Psychological disorders, however, signify or condition elimination from intellectual contact, meaning the failure of clear deliberation, the disappearance of the higher consciousness and thus the disappearance of the exercise of free will and volitional resolution. Psychological contact to the intellectual self signifies here the same as what the power generator and the transformer station signify to electricity; it is only in the latter that electricity first becomes usable. In this case what we mean by usable, with regard to psychological contact with the intellect, is purification. If this contact is shut off, only traces of destruction remain.

Hau provides a very good picture of typical feeble-mindedness in his book *Lebenslänglich*.[35] Hau describes the condition of an imprisoned cleric:

> "In one of the neighbouring cells there lay for a long period of time a priest, who was serving a sentence of, I believe, eight years for sex crimes. He went before me in the yard and into the chapel. I never spoke with him. He was still young as he entered the prison, perhaps in his early thirties, but lately he seemed like a tired old

---

[35] Carl Hau (1881-1926) was a German jurist who was sentenced to death following the murder of his mother-in-law. The sentence was commuted to life imprisonment and Hau was released on probation after serving 17 years. His memoirs, *Lebenslänglich (Erlebtes und Erlittenes)*, Verlag Ullstein, Berlin became a bestseller; however, together with a book on the trial it was judged to breach the conditions of his release, provoking much debate about the case and freedom of speech for convicts. Hau fled to Italy, where he committed suicide.

man. He may never have possessed much energy, but in solitary confinement his backbone became mollusc-like. He also tried language studies, but of course he got stuck in the middle. Soon he found only the lightest reading palatable, and he could never get enough of it. 'Do you have a novel for him, your neighbour asks,' was the message the warder brought to me time and again. If I had one from the prison library, I sent it to him; in an incredibly short time he had devoured it and demanded more. But if I sent him a book of my own, such as Shakespeare or Byron, the volume immediately came back with the comment that it was too hard for him. He gradually turned into a troublemaker. He bickered with his confessor, the prison chaplain, over the latter's sermons and accused him of heterodoxy, the two of them sometimes quarrelling so vehemently that I could catch every word. One morning I heard them once again arguing about the personality of the Apostle Paul, of whom my neighbour had a poor opinion, and the row ended up with the prison chaplain slamming the door shut and yelling something from outside that sounded very much like a curse. Upon which he continued his rounds and came to my cell. He stood there for a while, sighed distinctly and then opened up. His face was still flushed, he first wanted to talk about something else, but when one's heart is full, the mouth overflows. He had to take a deep breath. It was no longer possible to get along with the man. He was cracking up. A repulsive person. A disgrace to the clergy. Fortunately, there were only a few of his sort. I replied to him that I could not regard my neighbour as such a *monstrum iniquitatis*; he seemed to be the average sort, more or less, but solitary confinement had worn him down; he was afraid to go out of his cell, and indeed rightly so, as he would have a tough time among the other prisoners. The man was a victim of today's prison system. Which was the case. After his release he had to be sent to an institution, where he vegetated for the rest of his life."

Here we have a typical example of priestly impatience and intolerance; an example of psychological short-sightedness and intolerance regarding pathological conditions. One finds this short-sightedness in virtually all organs of the penal system, not excluding prison doctors. I received the following memo from a fellow prisoner:

"Generally speaking, I am inclined to attribute a purely sexual background to every contravention of the house rules (apparently unmotivated refusal to work, breakout, mutiny etc.) In fact, I was myself present when the very mention of the anticipated pleasures of a sexual nature alone were enough for me to cast aside any lingering doubts at the suggestion of a general breakout."

In the report in *Vorwärts* about the aforementioned lecture by Mühsam at the Institute for Sexual Science about "The Penal System and Sex" it states:

"Erich Mühsam described how the irritability caused by sexual abstinence led to excesses, plans for escape and breakouts, just as the heat of desire can lead to sex crimes after release."[36]

The Medical Health Officer Dr. Lumpp, in his lecture at the Forensic Psychiatry Association in 1913, made the following comments on these phenomena:

"There is no doubt in my mind that some states of agitation among prisoners, in which they are insubordinate and aggressive, can be traced back to sexual origins; they are nervous discharges driven by increased, unfulfilled sex drive. Thus, just as the sex-murderer dismembers his victim, so are prisoners driven to at-

---

[36] *Vorwärts* was the newspaper of the Social Democratic Party of Germany (SPD).

tacking warders or breaking up the furniture in their cells; in the first years of incarceration, this occurs more frequently than later. It is the instinctual men with low self-esteem who lack inhibitions."

The condition that prisoners necessarily get into, when even the emergency means of self-gratification has no effect, was described to me most convincingly and fascinatingly by a fellow prisoner in detention:

"But other phenomena also arise: heavy limbs, aversion to work, being easily irritable, every symptom of neurosis. A moment of self-contemplation makes him aware of these symptoms. Insofar as he fails to identify the true cause, onanism, he becomes a hypochondriac, a repugnant yahoo. The states of agitation increase, and incidents occur, serious clashes with warders, who, because they are unaware of the underlying causes, pay back in the same coin. Reports, disciplinary measures and arrest follow. The prisoner rages and destroys cell inventory, which he must pay for out of his meagre prison wages, and beyond this must appear before the court because of damage to prison property, where he receives another prison sentence. Again, he rages. Again arrest, bondage – padded cell! A few warders, and yes, even prisoners, the so-called 'reliables', regard themselves as entitled to intensify the prison management's reprisals on their own initiative: brutal mistreatment occurs.

"Finally, the doctor is consulted, who diagnoses high-grade neurasthenia, hysteria, etc. and prescribes sedative and detention in a shared cell and other things. However, implementing this is at the discretion of the prison management. The doctor is completely powerless, and this is especially the case in institutions with a conservative leadership: gentlemen who regard the abolition of medieval means of torture, and therefore newer endeavours by the penal system, as person-

al insults. If the prison management believes it has reasons to oppose the change in lifestyle demanded by the
prisoner, then all the torments described carry on as
previously – until the doctor proposes a transfer to the
lunatic ward. As a rule, this is what then happens, insofar as the station warder does not first find the unfortunate on the clothes hook or with slashed wrists. The
number of suicides, and even more, the number of attempted suicides, is shocking."

The average warders in the "modern German penal system"
do not regard suicide attempts as anything tragic; they do not
appear in official statistics. Every parliamentarian, in his capacity as "representative of the people" is misled when he
asks for information about the suicide rates in jails and prisons. Suicide attempts are simply recorded as deceptions. It is
not disputed that among the thousands of suicide attempts
that the prison management is not even informed about, now
and again one is simulated. But this is not the rule, as they
want us to believe. Crucially, 95% of prisoners often play with
the idea of suicide, and many prisoners constantly inhabit the
border areas that lead to suicide; often, a prisoner takes a
piece of string, a knife, a piece of glass, or something similar in
the hand with suicidal intent, but then lets go of these objects
as a result of inhibitions, only to reach for them again three or
four hours later, in the middle of the night. Suicide attempts
are usually emotional acts. The technical possibilities while in
detention nevertheless require lengthy preparations to carry
out suicide. This situation keeps prisoners who are moving in
the direction of suicide back from following the path to the
bitter end. If the prisoners came into possession of narcotic
drugs or poisons they could easily use, e.g. by turning on the
gas tap, the judiciary would have to create extra funeral
homes for each prison to cope with the number of suicides. A
shocking suicide statistic would be the result.

In view of this fact, it is utterly absurd for Detloff Klatt to
demand in his *Los der Vorbestraften* (The Lot of the Convicted)

that qualified doctors and organs of public social welfare organizations should finally be given a hearing concerning the
sexual problem in penal incarceration.[37] Klatt's intention is
honourable, nevertheless it is telling that it is a pastor who expressed this cry for help. Klatt's demand is quite negative and
at the same time dangerous. For there is not the slightest
doubt that official medical officers would not talk about the
dangerous effects of suppressed lust.

---

[37] Detloff Klatt was for several decades the chaplain at Berlin-Moabit jail. His autobiography *Treffpunkt Moabit* appeared in 1957.

8. Methods proposed by prison officials for the "alleviation of sexual distress"

An assessor once told me, in the course of a conversation, to bear in mind that physical work greatly weakened prisoners' sexual instinct. The Head of Department Dr. Wulffen expressed something similar in the 36th sitting of the Saxon State Parliament of 16 June 1927. He took the view "that prolonged and tiring prison work minimizes sexual instinct". However, the senior legal counsel at the Prussian Ministry of Justice, who gave a lecture on sexual dysfunction among prisoners in December 1928 within the framework of the Central Office for the Prisoners' Welfare, raised Wulffen's thesis to programmatic status.

First of all, it must be said that 95 per cent of prisoners perform no physical work at all in the sense of a healthy workout, whereas a small percentage are forced to overexert themselves physically while having to get by on miserable nourishment. Then, the following should be taken into consideration: comparing physical workouts with sexual functions is a testament to the vulgar view of the meaning and purpose of sexuality itself. The only "compensation" that satisfies the sexual instinct is normal sexual gratification. How wrong it is to say that the sexual instinct can be "compensated" by physical work is well proven by real-life experience. Nowhere is the sexual instinct more developed than precisely where physical labour is performed; nowhere is the instinct more intense, stronger and more primitive. If you consider the sex life of the people in the country, it is to be noted that very lively sexual functions prevail, that rural youth starts with mature sexual activities much earlier than urban youth. One cannot dismiss this in moral terms; rather, sexual powers have a much greater effect and are lived out when rooted in the soil of rude physical health. The conditions in the country are not foreign to me, because I grew up there, so I know the practices.

Moreover, a very strong sexual tendency is noticeable among the field workers in penal institutions; amongst these field workers are also to be found the most "settled relationships", as prisoners from the prisons of Sonnenburg, Brandenburg, Wartenburg, Neustrelitz, Insterburg, Lichten-burg and Luckau consistently told me. Contact with the opposite sex is not the cause of this phenomenon.

Officers of all grades in prison continue to believe that exaggerated sexual tension could be reduced "by means of appropriate regulation of the diet". This precept, which in its effect hinders the body from producing sufficient bodily substances and therefore must bring the body and bodily functions into total disarray, is just as outrageously scandalous as the other; the practical effect of both is that they want to inflict severe punishment of a particularly evil nature on prisoners. Namely, where the diet of human beings is deliberately designed to prevent the production of sexual substances, the engine for producing primary substances is taken away from the human organism, substances that arise in the active cells of the sex organs and intermediary glands and enter the bloodstream from here to build up and maintain the human body.

Hirschfeld writes the following about the influence of human nourishment on the sexual engine in *Geschlechtskunde*:

> "Incidentally, the significance of diet precisely for increasing powers of control should not be overestimated. I have met many people, with both normal and deviant sexual instincts, who have become vegetarians in anticipation of being able to live in sexual abstinence; but abstaining from meat has usually only had a very transient success, if any at all. In this respect it is also worth pointing out the remarkable fact that among the animals, the herbivores are sexually more vivacious and passionate than the carnivores; for example, the bull and the stallion are more sexually active than the lion and the tiger."

In an article in the *Leipziger Volkszeitung* of 26 January 1927, entitled "Sexuality and Punishment" which, I assume, was penned by the former Saxon Minister of Justice Neu, the following applies very much to this side of things:[38]

> "The prisoner is of course still a human being while in prison, whose human organism continues to function in all its constituent parts, including his sexual glands. Most criminal people, both men and women, are in the prime of their life, when their sexual desire is greatest. It goes without saying that they must suffer in the most serious way from the complete lack of sexual relief and erotic tenderness. This is especially true of the many thousands of married people who are used to enjoying periodic sexual intercourse. Internment for months, perhaps years, does not only tear them out of deep-rooted habits, but forces them into sexual abstinence that neither their secretions-organism nor their nervous system has adjusted to. Consequently, either self-gratification is practiced to a large extent and in a way that is particularly dangerous given the prison diet, or the prisoners become perverted and return to freedom as homosexuals, or else the abstinence actually practiced undermines the entire human organism.

> "What actually happens in prisons seems downright infantile by comparison. Sodium carbonate in the food! Of course, that is denied. But it happens, all the same. Just put the prison officials under oath for once, which the investigating committee is authorized to do."

Better still, just ask prisoners to bring along a portion of lunch, with which one can determine the presence of sodium carbonate or other additives in the food simply by means of the naked eye without requiring any chemical examination by a "professional".

---

[38] Karl Alfred Eugen Neu (1871-1969) was a German jurist and politician in Weimar Germany (SPD) and the German Democratic Republic (SED). He was Saxon Minister of Justice from August 1923 to January 1924.

Hirschfeld writes, "Zest for life and the ability to perform influence one another to a significant degree." He continues:

> "The task of a medical professional is not to weigh up which of the two evils is the greater, but to exert the greatest possible hindrance of both. The most appropriate remedy for harmful abstinence is the regulation of sexual life with regard to the sexual intercourse that the sufferer is having to do without."

The distressed sexual conditions of prisoners are also not to be remedied by the "medical proposals" that have been made by the Saxon prison doctors and which have misled the ministerial bureaucracy into specious regulations. The relevant provision reads:

> "Measures in prison to alleviate sex life are lots of daily exercise, exercise in the open air with gymnastics and sports."

95 percent of all prisoners in German prisons and jails have "lots of daily exercise" for just half an hour a day, whereby it is also to be borne in mind that remand prisoners cannot even claim this half an hour. Third level prisoners, who have more than one hour's exercise in "fresh air" and who can do gymnastics and sports account for only one percent of prisoners in each institution. In one, which has 800 prisoners, between 5 and 10 are ranked on the third level; according to ministerial orders, no more should be accepted into the third level. The public is thus deceived with the above-named provision.

There is likewise a total misunderstanding of sexual functions in the assertion that you can compensate for sexual urges by means of "self-discipline" and "cold water". This might be possible in normal life, when sexual instincts can achieve frequent gratification. But in an environment in which all the normal life functions are switched off, the opposite is the case. Cold water can overcome a person's tiredness, it can temporarily refresh body and mind and momentarily turn back the sexual waves; but you cannot see in this compensation for sexual functions. Self-discipline and cold water therefore only mean a dangerous displacement activity. Trying to compensate for sexual instincts with cold water also presents some particular difficulties in prisons. Although no one forbade me cold rinses in detention, I was repeatedly made aware that "the cell cannot be continuously placed under water; how long would the floor last, it would soon rot and need to be renewed every year." If I pointed out that when taking cold rinses, I could not ensure that not a single drop of water falls on the floor, and that perhaps I could be given a larger bowl to prevent it happening, I received an ironic reply: "Certainly, before long every prisoner will also get a bathtub for daily use!" It was as though it was being suggested that I should not bother with the cold rinses at all. Of course, I continued with the cold rinses, but had to swallow all kinds of annoyance and frustration in return. Because such a way of life brings with it the need to ask for fresh water more and often, and to give back dirty water from the cell. There is no water supply in the cells of German prisoners. And whoever wants to become "unpopular" in a prison only needs to occupy the sergeant's time for more than the "usual amount". At any rate, one cannot say that self-discipline grows out of this soil and that one could "compensate" for the sexual instinct with cold water.

Freud, of whom the Christian doctor Maag writes, "It is the enduring merit of the psychoanalytical school, and especially of its founder S. Freud, to have brought light and order into this important field of spiritual life," says what is not sufficiently emphasized and cannot be repeated often enough:

> "It may be asserted that the task of mastering such a powerful impulse as that of the sexual instinct by any other means than satisfying it is one which can call for the whole of a man's forces. Mastering it by sublimation, by deflecting the sexual instinctual forces away from their sexual aim to higher cultural aims, can be achieved by a minority and then only intermittently,

and least easily during the period of ardent and vigorous youth. Most of the rest become neurotic or are harmed in one way or another. Experience shows that the majority of the people who make up our society are constitutionally unfit to face the task of abstinence. Those who would have fallen ill under milder sexual restrictions fall ill all the more readily and more severely before the demands of today's cultural sexual morality, because we know no better protection against the danger to normal sex life through defective facilities or developmental disorders than sexual satisfaction. The more a person is disposed to neurosis, the less can he tolerate abstinence."[39]

[39] Sigmund Freud, "Civilized Sexual Morality and Modern Nervous Illness" (1908).

II. Concerning sexual hypertrophy in solitary confinement

1. General sexual fantasies

Until now we have only learned about one side of sexual self-gratification in detention. Enforced self-gratification has, however, a hundred sides to it. We must put the spotlight on these in their turn. This is all the more necessary because there are also doctors who think prisoners will satisfy their sexual instincts by the shortest available route. This statement, which a medical officer made to me in 1926, shows what is still possible today. I compare it with the scientifically untenable statements that Lumpp made in his lecture at the afore-mentioned forensic-psychiatric association in Heidelberg in 1913. He noted:

> "In the forties and fifties of the last century, when the controversy raged over detention systems and the question was raised as to whether solitary or communal detention was preferable, an objection that was emphasized against solitary confinement was that it favoured masturbation. That is not true, and while it may be admitted that some indulge in this vice in an excessive manner, this may not be as bad as other misconducts that are possible in communal custody. In solitary confinement, an untainted prisoner is not seduced by other debauchees. His imagination is awakened by nothing, it gives him no opportunity to practice fornication of the mind; he sees and reads nothing that stimulates the senses."

We must analyse these things in detail. Medical and narcotic drugs have the effect on those who consume them frequently of making the body accustomed to them. The human organism becomes increasingly resistant to their effects: they demand ever stronger means, more effective stimulation. Similar tendencies occur with substitutional sexual acts. And that is understandable, because they can never quench the thirst of the senses. Sexually, the senses of hearing, sight, smell and taste, and, most of all, the sense of touch want to be satisfied. Since no sensual fulfilment is to be found in the sexual activity of masturbation, the imagination must compensate for this defect. This, however, is a task that it cannot manage. But nor can it defend itself against being assigned tasks that are rooted in other areas of the natural human realm and its organic order. Thus, the imagination is overworked and finally gets into the same state in which the permanently strained nervous system finds itself while in detention. Addiction to sexual self-gratification tends towards the use of methods that have a devastating effect. Hirschfeld says about this in his *Geschlechtskunde*:

> "Such processes have also been referred to as mental onanism, as well as moral onanism (Rohleder), thought onanism or onanism through 'pure mental fornication' (Hammond). It is considered to be especially harmful because of the waste of the nervous substance and the accompanying mental weakening that it causes (Rohleder, *Masturbation* p. 28).

> "Ever since Hufeland said in his famous *Macrobiotics* (or the art of prolonging human life), 'Mental masturbation is possible without all the unchastity of the body, it consists in filling and agitating the brain with wanton images', the notion of mental masturbation meanders through scientific literature, but without it having gained clarity over time. As far as I can see looking through the literature, there are three things that the authors understand under this heading; some regard 'mental fornication' as psychological masturbation, Hufeland also seems to have meant this because he speaks only of the filling and agitating of the brain with wanton images without any hint of the ejaculation caused by it (discharge of semen).

> "But that would be very different from what is commonly understood by masturbation. Others use the

term thought onanism to mean masturbation with specific imaginings, in contrast to mental onanism. This would be the form of self-relief called surrogate onanism, which in and of itself is no more harmful than the one practiced without fantasies. Still others envisage, under the term psychic masturbation, increased sexual excitement through imaginings alone without touching the genitals until ejaculation. But then this is not masturbation *per se*, rather it belongs to the area of sexual hyperesthesia (=hypersensitivity). It would be best to let the term 'psychic masturbation', which Hufeland probably originally meant only metaphorically and figuratively, for instance in the sense of what Ellis later understood to mean sexual daydream or Eulenburg to mean idealistic cohabitation (= sexual intercourse), be completely dropped.

"If brain activity becomes very much to the fore in so-called mental onanism, it is almost completely pushed back in another form, 'unconscious masturbation'."

Thus, the unfulfilled yearning for a natural, sexual form of life in the prisoners creates a state that spans the arc of sexual desires: one sees everything from the perspective of sexual privations and imaginations.

The domination of all thought by sexual fantasies casts a spell over everyone. In this process, downright sexual fantasies unroll as a series of images before the eye, in an almost filmlike way. And these desires, which find no satisfying fulfilment, one way or another create other outlets, i.e. the yearning for the satisfaction of sexual instincts manifests itself in one way here, and in another way there. Here, too, the conceptual world of the prisoner under normal living conditions, the spiritual-moral level on which he is otherwise carried, also plays a role, but in the end it becomes of only secondary importance. The deciding factor in the nature and internal content of the effect of unnatural suppression of the sexual instincts may be the amount of time that the repression takes place or excessive tension persists. Although the effects of the closed down sexual functions may be expressed differently, this does not change the fact that the predicament, with almost mathematical certainty, leads to infantile sexual paths and creates instinctual deviations that are mentally unhelpful in all cases. This both in terms of the imagination and the act itself.

What rolls out before the eyes under the obsessive-compulsive state of sexual images is simply horrifying; it is more extensive and worse than what, for example, Casanova sweated out; it is not at all to be compared with the sexual or love-follies, as Jolanthe Marès shows us in the *Confession of a Bon Vivant*.[40] Sheer, insatiable desires for sexual orgies torment the man as prisoner. Even with Giovanni Boccaccio's *Decameron* it is not possible to come close to expressing what forms "intellectually" under the horizon of despotic sexual repression. The imagination paints pictures that no painter has ever created, that no painter will create and that are impossible to present using any technology, images that even a specialist in pornography can hardly imagine. Having to say this is for me, for whom the erotic stands for something sacred before the eyes, something awful. And these phenomena remained awful even when a prison governor once explained to me: your anxiety, which already resembles a kind of fatalism, seems to me exaggerated and out of place. Emotional distress of this magnitude will disappear once you can live normally again. If it makes you feel any better, it seems to me useful to point out to you that you are more or less likely to find that even people who live in freedom and who are sexually satisfied have fantasies about sexual orgies.

When I mentioned this to others, they said, "That is

---

[40] Jolanthe Marés, one of the pseudonyms used by Selma Reichel (1868-1934), was a German author of novels of manners, including the one referred to, whose main title was *Seine Beichte* ("His Confession").

doubtless the case. People sometimes have the most absurd sexual dreams, painting sexual images that others simply could not imagine, even if they happened before their very eyes."

That may be partly or even completely true and will eventually be confirmed by the Christian doctor Maag. In his book: *Geschlechtsleben und seelische Störungen* he writes: "Of course there are impulses even in the soul of mature personalities that go against the prevailing direction of character."[41] However, if one looks at things individually, then it is at first characteristic and noteworthy that my dream life is very weak and always has been. In my normal life, I have pretty much remained free from dream states. In detention I was also little troubled by so-called deprivation dreams. What was special while in detention at this stage revealed, if I may call it that, the effect of a daydream. In the conscious state, i.e. when I was awake, completely clear in my head and able to see everything, sexual grotesques entered my line of vision. In my imagination I was then in the physical grip of ten, twenty, thirty and more girls. And they stood before me in positions that I cannot describe; in positions that I would need to draw to give them clarity. I could not possibly come up with the things that were constantly playing around in front of my eyes and their ultimate result. When I visualize these conditions today, with the faintest memory, I must think again and again of the words that Jolanthe Marès used in the *Confession of a Bon Vivant* to emphasize his sexual craving. "I pine for pleasure. There is not a fibre in my body, that does not scream for pleasure." Oscar Wilde expressed it thus: "And all, but lust | is turned to dust | in humanity's machine".[42]

Although sexual grotesques may not have been perm-

---

[41] "Sex life and spiritual disorders," in which Maag attempted to reconcile Christian teaching with modern psychoanalysis.

[42] From *The Ballad of Reading Jail*.

anent phenomena to this extent and have no basis in my sexual instinct as it runs along the lines of proper relationships, an over-stimulation of the activity of the senses is not, however, to be underestimated. For I often experienced apparitions in these over-excited states that led me mentally, sometimes even longingly into the arms of two, three or four girls at the same time, whom I then "consumed" with overheated lust and appetite. In this play of appearances, I always saw only female groups in blissful embrace, never the male complement. This fact best expresses the overpowering craving for a woman. That such apparitions only have "specific" individual meaning, from which nothing in general can be abstracted, is not true. In dozens of cases these apparitions, of equal intensity, have been confirmed to me by other prisoners. Statements by Mühsam also confirmed this in his lecture. Mühsam said: "In letters to wives or other women, with whom prisoners had taken up written communication, the imagination revelled in real orgies."

If such fantastic apparitions had already taken hold of me in my normal life, then in the interest of objective research I would not conceal this, or I would have left this chapter unwritten. If we were not dealing with conditions that dev-elop only in an unnatural environment, then there would be no need to talk about them, at least not in the context of observations of prison conditions and the consequences they have in a sexual respect. But these phenomena find their sole cause in the overload of sexual instincts, where healthy gratification of sexual instincts is prevented. Because, "continued over a long time, the effect of such surrogate acts in the imperfection of their nature is usually just as disadvantageous and unsatisfactory as total abstinence; in many cases, this relief by ineffectual means, with regard to which we must also consider our own body, attacks the nervous system even more strongly over time than complete renunciation" (Hirschfeld).

2. Pictorial and verbal forms of expressing sexual hunger

A prisoner, rich in experiences of all sexual deviations in detention, described to me his thoughts on the nature and effects of self-gratification:

"Masturbation only gives you temporary satisfaction. Memories of erotic events form the basis on which the imagination builds further. However, these constructs lose their power over time. The thirsting senses demand more concrete stopping points than imagination provides and can provide without fresh nourishment. The prisoner will try to portray the desired object physically. He draws, paints, models – genitals, nudes, obscene representations, more or less primitively; eventually he brings to it a certain level of 'craftsmanship'. Then he is sought out by less qualified prisoners to produce such replicas; for a fee, of course. In return he must consider the specific wishes of the client. It is precisely these wishes that testify to the often downright horrible moral depravity of the prisoner as a natural consequence of the conditions to which he is subjected. He makes the greatest sacrifices, gives any surplus food away for months, food that is granted only in small quantities, in order to come into possession of such reproductions. Complete seclusion increases this desire and its consequences, masturbation, to phenomenal levels. Mechanically speaking he carries out the required workload, since prison work requires little or no mental agility. Uninterrupted, film-like, erotic scenes roll before his eyes and he works while he hears, constantly whining in his skull: woman – woman – woman – woman – woman; with every beat of the pulse, woman! The weekly book from the prison library is hastily leafed through to find any erotic allusions, the passage that is found is then spun out further on a sheet of paper, all the while masturbating: woman – woman – woman – woman – woman!"

With regard to the *Prisoners' Artistry*, the first chief sergeant at the prison of L. once showed me some pornographic drawings taken from a prisoner and remarked:

> "You see, such smut is painted here. That's how they spend their spare time, if they have permission to draw. No education and modernization of the penal system is of any use against such moral depravity. No, it only provides the basis for further smut. I could show you some quite extraordinary things, but I have nothing here. Perhaps the Governor will show you them."

This chief sergeant, who testified to being well-read, could not do enough to show his moral indignation. A few months later, when he handed me the work of Hans Prinzhorn, I was astonished at the self-assuredness with which he opened the pages in the book, in which hardly exceptional grossly sexual scenes are depicted. And I was outraged by the coarse expressions he used to "highlight" the grossly sexual images and finally announce his opinion: "I cannot imagine how such smut can still be printed, it should quite simply be banned. Just look at the picture: he is taking her from behind, the second is looking on and the third is holding his dick and squirting his semen in her face." We could see for ourselves the grossly sexual acts that the four were performing in the pornographic display; we did not need this sergeant's filthy sexual commentary. If I have reproduced his words literally, it is because I considered it necessary: the public needs to know the milieu if it wants to arrive at tenable conclusions.

Hans Prinzhorn[43] says in his theoretically very good ex-

---

[43] Hans Prinzhorn (1886-1933) was a German psychiatrist and art historian. In 1919 he became assistant at the psychiatric hospital of the University of Heidelberg, where he expanded an earlier collection of art created by the mentally ill and started by Emil Kraepelin. When he left in 1921 the collection had more than 5,000 works. His *Bildnerei der Gefangenen* (Prisoners' Artistry) was published in 1926 by Axel Junker Verlag and contains 176 illustrations. It was republished in 2019.

planations to his *Prisoners' Artistry*: "Of course, there is a group with gross sexually obscene motifs, which extends from the low level of the toilet wall to the realm of grotesque-macabre, where Ensor, Kubin or even Goya are the legitimate rulers."[44]

It would not be futile to spend a little more time with Prinzhorn's book. The scene with an obscene slant in Figure 54 of the work seems to me to express more the business of the pimp than sexual distress in prison. Of course, one must keep in mind that this image was then given a special feature due to the lack of natural sexual objects. Figure 42, which depicts bread-kneading, is more typical, showing a woman with large breasts in the foreground (relief) and a garland of seven smaller women. Prinzhorn remarks on this pictorial representation:

> "If the prisoner deals with the environment with a realistic and objective attitude, envisions it in a purely vivid way and tries to depict it visually, one can say with certainty that he has arrived at an objectivity that is only possible if he has inwardly conquered his personal problems and hardships, the inescapable intrusive compulsion of his environment. Without such an inner conquest, be it defiant self-assertion behind prison walls, be it a repentant bow to convention, law, state power, or a calm acceptance of destiny, no-one can achieve this realistic objectivity ...
>
> "A kind of personal, confessional relationship lives well in all of them, even the pictures that may be termed realistic. It has the feel of the sentimental,

---

[44] Hans Prinzhorn (1886-1933) was a German psychiatrist and art historian. In 1919 he became assistant at the psychiatric hospital of the University of Heidelberg, where he expanded an earlier collection of art created by the mentally ill and started by Emil Kraepelin. When he left in 1921 the collection had more than 5,000 works. His *Bildnerei der Gefangenen* (Prisoners' Artistry) was published in 1926 by Axel Junker Verlag and contains 176 illustrations. It was republished in 2019.

whether it now evokes the memory of the past or turns
to fantasy in wishful thinking."
Prinzhorn describes this state of unburdening very well in a
combination of sexual-biological and psychological terms:

"These are all preformed ramifications, so to speak, of
the prisoner's existence. In this spiritual guise of the institution, the substantial personal qualities of the individual first express themselves, and are therefore only
recognizable, after they have been extracted from that
milieu. So, it is quite possible that the inclination to the
sexual and obscene, often marked by pious shud-
dering and due contempt, is the artefact of the prison
institution, and this would not be significantly less experienced in the event of a trial stay by respectable citizens, even if perhaps less openly expressed. Everyone
can use their experiences of women, stag parties, drinking parties in this direction, if he wants.

"Accordingly, the figurative predominates, which
is usually burdened with tendentious meaning or surrounded by a sentimental glow, but hardly ever objectively depicted. A female body that one imagines, or
implies or represents, is simply a reflection, a sensory
remedy, a substitute for the directly desired sexual object, a graphic cry of lust and distress, and yet almost a
detour, a sublimation, compared with bluntly un-
restrained masturbation without such pictorial extra-
vagance. Numerous inscriptions in all languages easily
prove to the doubter, who should consider this view
too radical, which is, yes, natural enough for the unleashed, socially uprooted, isolated outcast. Of course,
a lot of grossly sexual imagery has been set aside or
quietly collected. Some police museums keep such material in separate drawers in sufficient volumes to scare
sensitive souls with human nature. Curiously by the
way, the reports of Lombroso, Ellis, Petrikovits agree
that female expressions of sexuality, which, though

nevertheless limited to words, are much more shameless and direct even than those of men, who moreover generally show a certain humour in all its earthiness. Even such graphic boldness as is shown in the card game (Figure 74), is mitigated by the fact that a time-honoured concept for division, the playing card laid sideways, almost inconspicuously flavours it."

This is true not only for female, but also for male expressions of the sexual.

In the first section of the group the "Glory of Maria di Medici" is presented in a kitschy, tasteless way. Prinzhorn says about this:

"When strange events are presented, the dissonance between intention and accomplishment is usually even greater. In spite of everything, the inability to attain indulgence in one's own interest teases, or even has something touching and conciliatory about it. If, on the other hand, such an autobiographical basis for mitigation is absent, one is compelled to judge intentions against accomplishments more ruthlessly, the undue claim to pretension, to dismiss meagre achievement as a ridiculous failure. This is particularly the case with tracings from magazine templates, or combinations of these such as for example in Figure 1, 'The Glory of Maria di Medici' by a painter and decorator. The role here played by allegorical association is a matter of complete indifference to the man – for him, what matters is the luxuriant visualization of voluptuous masses of flesh. It is probable that drawings of this kind, which originated in the distress of sexual abstinence and fantasy, are produced much more often, but have been destroyed by the draftsman himself, confiscated by the prison administration, and disposed of privately or by the state."

In ever "new" forms, in ever different forms, the "luxuriant visualization of voluptuous masses of flesh" manifests itself, be it uncovered or emphasized through clothing, be it in an independent form of presentation or in combination, always expressive of the endeavour to place bodily forms before the eyes, to be observed with sexual excitement. Explicable when we call to mind that our thinking is thinking through the eyes. "Any spontaneously created flourish and any scribble would be more productive in this respect," says Prinzhorn, while he says of the scenes depicted with time and deliberation: "These things have only to do with manual skill, not with design and visual expression of the soul. They bear witness to training, not to life." About the difficult conditions under which such typical drawings arise as vital processes, Prinzhorn has this to say:

> "Some renditions are littered with a sombre gothic-romance: they were secretly painted with the prisoners' own blood on small scraps of paper, often torn from newspapers, as clearly any activity was strictly forbidden. Lombroso's Turin collection includes some such renditions, and the worm that dwells in the dusty boxes obviously prefers this animal diet.[45] Incidentally, of course, there are no limits to inventiveness; and one is often enough astonished to what degree folk wisdom is right: where there is a will, there is also a way. Every type of paper and every type of technique appears. Carton, cardboard, wrapping paper, writing and drawing paper, printed book and newspaper paper, pencil, chalk, ink, ink, watercolour, oil paint, squeezed sap, blood, and yes in one case (which is hardly unique) faeces."

An extension to sexual-pictorial representations is tattooing. I do not mean the widespread use in normal life, but the way in which it is typically achieved in situations of constraint, even though obtaining the necessary material is extremely difficult

---

[45] Cesare Lombroso (1835-1909), was an Italian criminologist and physician.

and tattooing is not officially allowed. The prison chaplain Dr. I. Jäger (Amberg in H. Gross' Archive, Volume 18, pages 141-168 and Volume 2i, pages 116-127) describes about 300 such tattoos. He says among other things, "Dirty, lascivious images are found exclusively on pimps, ponces and pederasts, rarely on other categories of criminals", and states further: "It is not uncommon that sex offenders first carve immoral pictures on their skin after incarceration." Actually, this is very typical.

Thus, you can find an expression of everything that a man feels under constant deprivation tattooed on the bodies of detainees. Sexual grotesques, effects of sexual hunger, sexual distress.

In his book, Prinzhorn himself notes the shortcomings of the pictorial material. Outsiders do not get to know this material, do not come into its possession, because the judicial and penal system's bureaucracy even withholds it from scholarship. If science wants to attain success and valuable results, then it would have to send an emissary to the prison for a few years; eight years would not be necessary; one, two years would be enough. This emissary could, however, do his studies inside. I have done such, and seen sexual needs expressed in graphical form that shook me to the core. Were it not for all the emotional impulses and human niceties in me that baulk against it, then I would provide Prinzhorn with a few hundred such drawings that I had right in front of my face during my eight years in prison.

In this chapter I also want to deal with the linguistic forms of expression of sexual hunger. In Berlin I got to know a very likeable person, with a nature that you could not fail to love, whose linguistic treatment of sexual matters was simply enchanting. We were not yet so spiritually impoverished and had not yet fallen to such a moral low point that we used erotic conversations as an engine of lasciviousness. With this man and another prisoner I once discussed the intention of going into communal detention. Then one of them replied: In communal detention? The three of us? I cannot join you. What do you think would become of my erotic self-entertainment? You do not know the verbal expressions that accompany my sexual fantasy in the evening. If I had to give this up and be content with simple self-gratifying strokes, itself perhaps not invisible, as happens in communal detention, then you might as well put me straight into a coffin. For this reason alone, I am obliged to reject communal detention. Such words, so he meant, are not to be heard. And if they were, they would shock the objective observer or listener. If he wanted to hear such verbal accompaniments in the roughest forms to acts of self-gratification for one, two, three, four, five hours' duration, then the listener would have to sneak into the cells secretly and hide himself there. No one remains free from these solitary discussions with a sexual accent. I openly confess that during masturbatory acts I formed and uttered words that did not belong to my usual vocabulary and that made me feel ashamed and depressed after I had pronounced them, or when the masturbatory functions were discontinued. I have certainly suffered and constantly suffer from the milieu in which the sanctity of Eros is profaned, the seriousness of sex is clothed in the language of dirty jokes. But that does not change the fact that within my dark cell, isolated from all human beings, I myself became the victim of this verbal smut; not cynically and frivolously in dealings with fellow human beings, but rather, only with myself. Is this loss of sexual subtleties incomprehensible? The cultured man in particular, with highly developed forms of community, loses his higher ego when he lives isolated from all normal forms of human life for years, sinking back to primitive levels. If, however, something similar happens with the shutting down of the functions of physical organs, they atrophy, finally being crippled into remnants. In normal sexual intercourse the soulful, spiritual person experiences higher, vibrant feelings with the associated partner, but in the desperate hours of self-satisfaction, the same man will enthral himself with the coarsest sexual language, shaping his own base verbal constructs, as I did myself.

Understandably, over time it occurs that the sexual becomes the single axis around which every conversation, every discussion turns. You want to discuss with the Governor, the doctor, an official inspector, a sergeant, any administrative matters that are truly unrelated to sexual matters, but instead you sing erotic recitatives! You do that, although you often do not have the slightest contact with these persons, and yes, even though you regard them with downright hostility. And time and again you decide not to do this again, to avoid dealing with such people as much as possible – but at the next opportunity the game repeats itself. And this condition is usually hardly noticed at the moment. It is only weeks later that you realize that conversations taking place in the past did not deal with the matters you wanted to discuss. Then you feel like you have prostituted yourself and want to give yourself a slap, which you often do.

3. Effects of the overpowering desire for a woman

The word or the concept "woman" plays a devastating role in penal institutions. There is an eternal melody here, sung with the text: "Just to see women."

Just to be able to see women, prisoners become malingerers and vigilantes on the grand scale. With this motivation, prisoners learn to be virtuosos of simulation. It's amazing how far they will go to get into the city, because there they see women, more women than their eyes can take in, so many women that their imagination can feast on them for a while. As one prisoner in the Brandenburg mental asylum once told me:

> "My eyes devour all the women who come here. In the evening, when it gets dark, I undress each of them in turn, and then they live in my imagination, while I satisfy myself at the sight of them. This opportunity to see women is pretty much the only reason that I keep coming to the mental asylum and staying here as long as I can."

As well as the honesty with which this prisoner spoke about what is truly the case, there lived in him an unusual need to show gratitude. He quite frankly explained to me that he would divide any wealth he came by among the girls he had seen during that time; but he would visit many of them after his release, so far as he could do that without risk. In fact, after serving eight years in prison and escaping (he had seven years left), he sought out my wife, to whom he reported and – confessed.

In prison, the prisoners play "sick", or make themselves ill on their own volition, insinuate illness or make themselves sick using dangerous tools and experiments, often having to be transferred to the city hospital. That is the objective. Thus, their longing is satisfied: they "just see women", here they are touched by delicate female hands, and cared for, an experience for which the prisoner will sacrifice, if need be, another year of his freedom. For, in consequence of the yearning, which indeed has its stages, the prisoners are not even afraid, should no other opportunity come to their aid, to commit acts that bring them back before the court.

There, they can "just see women". A prisoner in the mental asylum told me:

> "The view here is not enough for me, so I prefer to be taken out frequently, or insist that I be led to the *Charité*. This gives me the opportunity to see nothing but women for hours on end. They pass before my eyes in regiments. Here, you can finally take them in to the full once again."[46]

Another prisoner, a close friend of mine, was repeatedly brought to the Charité because of an actual illness. When he was back, and I wanted to know what had been diagnosed, he reported to me with such jargon that I felt compelled to ask him if he had been given booze at the Charité. So, he reported on the alleged medical diagnosis with a sentence, then enthused for some considerable time about the "many pretty girls" he had seen, which he followed up with a broken sentence about his illness, before travelling back to the Promised Land of Woman. For three days after such performances, I usually continued to hear nothing else from him except this or that event involving a woman.

In Brandenburg prison huge numbers of prisoners presented themselves for the widest imaginable variety of inspections. The flood swelled ever greater. Most of the prisoners had no idea what they wanted when they stood before an inspection official. In the absence of another reason, they consulted the Civil Code. Of course, in such presentations before the inspectors, the "business" of the prisoners is regulated, but they provided what was most sought after: on this occasion the prisoners had the opportunity to look out to the street and,

---

[46] The Charité was (and still is) Berlin's university hospital.

if they were lucky, could "just see women".

I myself often found amusement in this way and was happy if I was not disturbed during this deepened activity of the senses. "That heart against heart is stopped from turning, no one will learn to still his yearning."

"Just to see women" the prisoners wait for female visits and they also manipulate them. I came across this phenomenon in Brandenburg prison. The riddle solved itself as to why a prisoner served in *kalfaktor* office functions, for which he was entirely unsuited. I once asked him about it, and he explained to me: I get to deal with women almost every day, not only do I see them, but I can also flirt with them. At Wartenburg it is general knowledge that most prisoners volunteer for work outside and in the fields "just to see women".

Typical in this respect is a statement of one of my comrades on the transport from Halle to Neuruppin in the transport wagon. Only members of the Plättner group were present in the vehicle. The transport was accompanied by criminal detectives. We could sit together two by two, alternately. After nearly two years of pre-trial detention, for the first time I had the opportunity to speak to most of the defendants. I was really thinking of matters other than the sexual. On that occasion one of the inmates, who could not manage to sit still on the seat for more than a couple of minutes, said to me:

> "You know, this transport means a certain sexual rebirth for me. I have to keep looking out the window because I'm so keen to see pretty girls. And that is a necessary aid to masturbation. If I do not have these halfway stimulating and fresh memories of a woman's body in my imagination, then it is no longer possible for me to achieve sexual release. So, don't be angry with me if I am so unsettled today."

These words have approximately the same meaning as those in Jolanthe Marès' *Confession of a Bon Vivant:* "This Venus is a dead stone, but here comes to me living beauty, animated by flesh and blood". Now, however, the highly efficient sergeant majors of the "modern" German penal system are supposed to bear down on "vices" with an iron fist. But, "those who watch them are ignorant fools, and those who pay the watchers for such a service are even more stupid, because prohibition must excite the wish to break through such a tyrannical law." (Casanova.)

If a prisoner, after years of isolation from life and from all normal life functions inside a prison, suddenly sees a woman again, he loses his last powers of self-control. He wants to embrace and crush every woman that comes his way with the fullness and elemental nature of his driving force. "Be embraced, millions! This kiss to the entire world!" These were my thoughts when I saw a woman in the prison. I stripped every woman that stepped into my circle of vision out of its last covering and engulfed all forms of the body that can be imagined. [47]

Again, I have a few practical examples of this from my own experiences. I will show this with the help of two poems, which were written immediately after visits or in moments of a similar kind, verses that testify to the power and strength rooted in sexuality, and that it is the very factor that builds life in its foundations. All of my verses – I am not a "poet by profession", and still less a "poetic genius", moreover, I cannot work to order – are a typical expression of inner processes; they all had their inspiration in the divine hour of female magic. I will pick out just one example from such incidents, which are in any case very rare in prison. During an ordinary visit of my wife, I saw joy and bliss in her face, I could see in her eyes that she must have experienced something special. Before she had come to me, she had travelled to a friend of ours, where she had experienced pleasures of a special kind.

---

[47] *Seid umschlungen, Millionen! / Diesen Kuss der ganzen Welt!* These are the first two lines from Schiller's Ode to Joy.

Her joy was so gushing and at the same time so mystical that I too was completely enthralled. I saw in my wife spirits that seemed new to me; I saw them in the kind of rhythm that bursts through all fetters and brings all souls into harmonic unison, under which the dance of the unleashed spirits smooths out all unevenness. She greeted me with the words: I am going to surprise you with something nice today. Guess what! M. has a new lease of life, feels overjoyed, is in a deliciously good mood and casts a spell on all around her. If only you could see her now, she, who finally, after five years of deprivation now has complete fulfilment of all her desires. That would give you strength to continue to sustain the faith and hope in your present vicious life. Come on, this kiss is from her, intertwined with the thousand wishes that she has for you. Quench your thirst in these thoughts. You are glad about this, right?

Yes, I was glad, yes, I quenched my thirst with the thought of this kiss! I turned into a joyful child, went back to my cell, got into a feverish glow and the erotic mind-game circulated though my veins.

Deep Desire!

Wholly engulfed by the gleaming light,
that pierces my heart, illuminates.
On gossamer wings I take flight
and yield to nature's warm embrace.

I cannot see the turbid day
through my exquisite passion.
Delight must hold me in its sway:
Fruit first ripens in the sunshine.

And I will feed on the luscious fruits
of life beneath the sun's brilliance.
I will tell you of the paradise,
in which my love's hot breath did dance.

In passion's strongest, soulful kiss
integrity is born again.
Where blood conceives a noble bliss,
mankind shall never be forlorn.

In yearning's dream, in bright sunshine,
I bathe away my fever's sting.
Reconciled and tender, refined
I hear the airs of early spring.

The bells resound with ample tones
in my bosom, full of happiness
It is only like this, I know
That I can still my fevered thirst.

During the jury trial in Halle, after many years, I once again
saw a childhood friend, for whom I had always expressed
strong interest, but an interest that was uncoloured by sexual
feelings. In the courtroom we exchanged just a few words. My
wife beamed with joy thinking about how I was deeply
touched in this way. I went into my cell and formed in my
stream of consciousness of this experience an

Inflammation

Out, out of the darkness
up to the light:
people are so close to me!
Since I first looked into your eyes
my soul shows a new face.

Girl, O spark of Gods
I kiss your magic splendour
Just one hour of your love
Gives me strength for evermore.

Give my thirsting mouth, to the full
in your shapely form the drink of life

Girl, throw off, throw off the shell,
so I must no longer live in strife.

Now I lay my head in your breast
and drink your passionate blood.
If I could only take my rest
in your burning soulful glow.

But the opportunity "just to see women" is only very infrequent in penal institutions. And, therefore, prisoners look for alternative outlets. In fact, where the institutions do not face onto any outside streets, at least not directly, technical means are devised to give the eyes sexual fields of vision. A prisoner at the penal institution G. told me:

> "Some resourceful prisoners managed to create concave and convex spectacle lenses which, when put together, provided a telescope. This was used in the evening to watch the windows around the institution to observe very intimate family scenes, not least those that were sexually intimate."

I know that similar manipulations went on at Brandenburg prison and they were confirmed to me as taking place at Luckau. I opposed them, I renounced them, for I had, despite all my desire for sexual activity, no mind for snooping, no liking for such contemplation of strangers. When the management of prison G. learned about what was going on, they had the outer windows of the building blinded. In Brandenburg prison the windows facing onto the street were simply bricked up. But you cannot brick up or blind all windows. And if you could, prisoners would find other means "just to see women" again. But even that is not always necessary. I will demonstrate this with an example.

I was a witness to a rather bashful, but on the other hand typical conversation, that many prisoners engaged in while together in a large common room. It concerns a penitentiary surrounded by parks and groves where every imaginable sexual activity or business takes place. From the hospital within the institution's grounds the inmates can see the surroundings by looking out of the windows with the help of tables and chairs. First, they observed "courtship". Most of the couples, however, already seem to be in a rather more "advanced state", rushing straight to their well-known place where they perform their sexual acts. Each prisoner observes this from behind locked doors. Thus, the suppressed sensory burden is stimulated to an unusual degree, the Vesuvius of lust erupts. The sexual intercourse of those out there is accompanied by howling in here, as warders expressed it to me.

It's not just degenerate professional criminals whose eyes gorge themselves on half-naked female bodies, who watch them in wild embrace 50, 100, 150 metres in front of them, it's more the so-called casual criminals and those who commit crimes out of necessity, the prisoners with greater intellect and deeper feelings, who, in here, become infected and deprived of their self-esteem. The senses of young men, often completely untouched by the filth of life, are officially put into demoralizing brood barrels. They only see horrible things here. Released prisoners who had satisfied their senses in this way want to prepare a "delight" for the fellow prisoners and comrades-in-suffering that they have left behind, as they call it. They look for a woman who is willing to provide all services in return for money, come to the vicinity of the institution, get them into a "spread-eagled position" and the locked-up prisoners provide the accompanying music. This is why the hospital is the favourite place of residence in this institution.

It may be that some of these accounts were exaggerated, or "embroidered" to some extent, but even if the story hung completely in the air, stripped to the essentials, it would be typical. However, it does not just hang in the air. The "conversation" of the two prisoners, who did not know I was eavesdropping, was too real for that to be the case. I am of the opinion that these corporate orgies, this profanation of sexuality, this mockery and ridicule of the sensory organs, are much more dangerous in effect than pseudo-homosexual activity. This moral shallowness spreads through disposition, transmission and inheritance. People degenerate. With pseudo-homosexual activity in prisons, this need not always be the case. These are usually just emergency acts that inevitably grow out of circumstances, that are limited to two people, without others being affected or third persons being infected, and the activity becoming the normal lifestyle of entire groups of people. These are, therefore, emergency acts that are entirely explicable and can be approved. Because in the satisfaction of his sexual instinct, man has the need to feel physical forms, not to gratify his instincts on his own, but to satisfy them in harmony with an object of his love. When people of a normal disposition come out of the situation that pushes them into homosexual activity, they usually then return to the forms of sex life that are natural to them. Or we want to assume this is a possibility, at least. Because I want to draw the reader's attention to the following: the main point is that the prisoners be able to stay within the limits of modesty. But prisoners cannot stay within these limits. And this is why moral decay proliferates in closed systems. Because, after all, moral decay is a socially determined condition. If people of inferior disposition are under the influence of great, benevolent people, they can breathe in the air of pure communities; the antisocial roots will then die out of their own accord, because they find no further nourishment.

4. Compensatory means that are withheld; the role of erotic literature and pictures

A certain renewal of the sexual physical feelings can also be achieved in some situations by reading works that have an erotic slant. Fine works of art are to be found in sexual literature. They provide pleasant satisfaction to the reader, especially when sexual functions have been prevented. I have always regarded such reading in detention as a means to gratification, as sexual hygiene. And I have a few experiences of this that I will mention as examples.

The first three volumes of Casanova's memoirs were procured for me during my stay at the Brandenburg prison – but were only handed to me when I was in the mental asylum of the Berlin jail. You might assume that I would have fallen upon it immediately and devoured the content. That is not the case. Although I was aware of their slant, I left the volumes untouched for several months.

I then entered on a period in which I dealt with the whole matter purposefully, scientifically. I then read (among other things) all the works that I have used, and in part quoted, for the present work, including the Casanovas. But I cannot say that I was particularly excited, even sexually excited, by their strongly erotic direction. The intensity of my intellectual instincts drove out all sexual impulses. I was extremely critical of Casanova and came to a negative judgment.

Sexual instincts, while in detention, are ever-changing. I had periods of the strongest intellectual energy, the strongest need for reading scientific material, which often had me so tightly in its grip for months on end that I sat on the stool with my book in my hand from six in the morning until seven or eight in the evening and then falling back to weeks or often months-long sprees in which the need for erotic light reading registered itself. In a period of intense sexual affliction, when it was usually very difficult to achieve satisfaction successfully through masturbation, I read Casanova once more. This time he stimulated me so strongly that I wrote and "composed" paeans of praise to him. The reading matter now provided me with a substitute for woman, a substitute for sexual intercourse. My imagination ran riot with true orgies. Casanova temporarily became my ideal man, although as stated, in terms of an intellectual decision, he meant the very opposite. I raved about Casanova, but even more about his girls. I tried to persuade everyone I encountered to read the books. During this period, I lived at a more leisurely pace, sexually speaking, than in periods when my erotic imagination was, let's say, deaf and blind. I now lived in a world of imaginings that worked wonders; my eyes sparkled with the joy of life. Everyone was surprised by the change in my mood. My energy was inexhaustible: I sat working from five, six, seven o'clock in the morning until 10 in the evening and wrote so intensively that I found no time in the course of five or six hours to roll a cigarette and light up, or I forgot to continue smoking, even though I had a very strong need to smoke. At times, when I took a break and looked around, I was amazed that there was a visitor in my cell, whom I had not noticed coming in.

In such situations, my senses conjured up the voice of a woman, then singing waves penetrated my mind. My sense of smell awoke; I breathed the bewitching scent of a woman, although there was no woman anywhere near me.

These conditions are not to be compared with ordinary horniness, to which I am not disposed, otherwise I would have been able to take my refuge more often in Casanova. How little I did so, despite all sexual distress and despite the lack of natural stimulation is proved by the following fact: my wife brought me volumes 4, 5 and 6 in July 1926 – but I had not yet read them by March 1927. In March 1927, I received volumes 7 and 8; however, I read all these volumes only at a time when I again had no possibility to imagine a woman.

Narrow-minded attitudes could use this observation as an opportunity to deny prisoners any erotic reading. Nothing would be more fatuous. Too much wrong has already been done in this regard, in remand and even more so in the penal system, by coroners, prison directors, teachers and prison chaplains competing in the philistine censorship of books. Although I personally enjoyed preferential "special treatment", I could write a whole book about this murky subject. Sexual satisfaction and hygiene, through serious and appropriate reading, is made illusory here. Only very rarely do prisoners manage to get hold of erotic books. I once had to ask Dr. Lippmann, so what kind of reading material did he actually deem appropriate for prisoners? In this respect he adopted, it must be said, a theoretical position on sexual matters that has some merit. However, what he asserted in theory, he denied in practice. No sooner had he agreed with me that Casanova or better erotic reading could have a regulating effect, as I put it, than he shook his head over the fact that the volumes had even been handed to me and demanded that I promise not to lend the work. He also confiscated books of a political, erotic, scientific or psychiatric nature from other prisoners. So much for book censorship and its sexual-psychological effect. In the above-mentioned article in the *Leipziger Volkszeitung*, "Sexuality and Punishment", it aptly states:

> "It is even more ridiculous when everything that could stir erotic fantasy is cut out from or pasted over in all books, magazines and yes, even daily newspapers. Harmless advertising is cut out from the *Leipziger Illustrirte Zeitung*, which one could hardly accuse of licentiousness. In a novel, a passage, in which it is stated that a girl has an illegitimate child, is carefully crossed out. In a Dresden newspaper, a prettily drawn, but in no way indecent advertising picture is pasted over. By such means they believe it is possible to overcome the most powerful of all human instincts. It is, therefore, no wonder that the prisoners let off steam in their diaries, in their paintings and verses, with which they scribble on table and chair, wall and book. The prisoner soon finds his deliverance, when through such a drawing he

can somehow let his need for love and tenderness extinguish itself, when he can knead from dough the means to engage his soul. You can hear the roar of blood and pounding of the heart in these 'works of art'. And yet, these are just scant substitutional attempts, and one day instinct, suppressed for many a year, breaks through in the most elemental way."[48]

It must be remembered – with horror – that the decision about pictures and cell decoration lies with institutional pastors, who only accept crucifixes and images of saints. In the Luckau prison, the Governor once remarked, after I had been given an edition of *Die Schönheit* magazine (Volume I, Year XIII), that I occupy a large part of my spare time with art. "This illustration on the front page of this magazine is, however, not art; I was therefore in doubt as to whether I should give this to you at all."

In general, however, the prisoners are even deprived of *Uhu* and other similarly plain bourgeois magazine-reading with pictures.[49] Also hanging in my cell was, among other things, a reproduction of Edmund Steppes' *Erika im Rosenhag*.[50] The fine lines of this body, wrapped in a simple red reform dress, delighted me. Spontaneously I kissed the forehead, the

---

[48] The *Illustrirte Zeitung* appeared from 1843 to 1944. It was originally published under licence from the Illustrated London News, the world's first illustrated magazine.

[49] *Uhu* was a monthly magazine published between 1924 and 1934.

[50] Edmund Steppes (1873-1968) was a German painter whose innovative style drew on both impressionist and explicitly conservative influences. Following the birth of his daughter Erika (1904-1993) his artistic style, which at the beginning of his career had followed the conventions of landscape painting, became increasingly individual. Steppes joined the NSDAP in 1932, though his art remained uninfluenced by ideology. Much of his work was destroyed when his studio was bombed on 7 January 1945. The name of the painting referred to draws its inspiration from two classics of German art entitled *Madonna im Rosenhag* ("Madonna in the Rose Bower").

mouth, the eyes of this "Erika", refreshing myself with her facial features and her bodily form. That made me happier, more contented. But I also did something else. In desperate moments of cruel distress, I often stood before this *Erika im Rosenhag*, and assailed her, as if I were entertaining myself in the company of a living being. I often stood in front of this picture, complaining of my pain in soliloquy, and sank into formal melancholy – until a stream of tears spilled out. Then I felt relaxed, inwardly halfway tranquil and well balanced. But prisoners entirely lack such objects with which one can release one's frustration, as stated. That's why I myself had to wage a stubborn fight to keep this *Erika im Rosenhag* in my cell. "We don't have to tolerate it," the Governor in Luckau prison once said to me. And no sooner had he declared this, than he went into other cells and he did an audit, i.e. he tore everything from the prisoners' walls that gave even the most remote expression of eroticism.

If I had to decide whether everything that is in some way consonant with eroticism should be withheld, or if they should be allowed possession of coarsely sensual objects for their contemplation, then I would not only declare myself in favour of the latter, but I would even favour pornographic images. Under the prevailing circumstances that would be the lesser evil for diminishing sexual overcharge. The most proper and healthiest thing would be to give prisoners the right and the opportunity to satisfy their sexual needs in natural ways.

5. The benefits of normal satisfaction of sexual fantasy; the adverse consequences of obstruction

The increasing inclination to masturbate does not arise from seeing women. It is therefore false to conclude that by suppressing the sight of women, sexual instinct can be stilled. The opposite is the case. This stimulation of the imagination lightens activities that will be exercised in any case and which only consume more physical, mental, and spiritual effort if the imagination does not receive any stimulation. I have followed the effects of self-gratification on myself under different conditions: first in the Brandenburg prison, where I seldom received erotic stimulation and was still less able to feel the atmosphere of a woman's proximity, and in the remand jail B., where almost every day I could observe the women coming on visits and therefore the aura of women washed over me. The number of my acts of self-gratification did not increase, but, the goal of masturbation, ejaculation and sexual relief, was easier to achieve and the satisfaction became more intense, even pushing close to the levels of emotional activation and physical sensory satisfaction that you would associate with the normal sexual act.

I achieved the same effect of physical satisfaction of a sexual nature, with greater power, during and after my wife's visits. A soft, physical touch, so far as is possible under the watchful eye of a warder, a fleeting touch on her breasts, a short breath of her womanish fragrance refreshed me both physically and in my imagination. If my wife had been with me for a few hours without supervision, as happened in May 1924 at Brandenburg prison and in March 1927 at Luckau prison, then I did not need four or five hours or even the whole night to finally achieve the long-awaited sexual release; success came in a few minutes. On such visits, I could tell from the slightest physical touch that I did not have any disposition towards impotence, as I had always more than unnecessarily feared. This observation already rooted out my depressed mood. During my wife's visits, when "the coast was clear" for a moment, I burrowed my head into her breasts; my arms embraced her form and held her body tightly in my power. We forgot about our surroundings. Then I explored all areas of sexuality in our conversation in the presence of the supervising warder. I have never been prudish in my life, but I adjusted the conversation to take account of the environment. This peculiarity was lost over my time of imprisonment under the pressure of my urges. I talked recklessly about all sexual phenomena, so I often read indignation in my wife's eyes, which was intended to tell me that there are things that would be better discussed only between ourselves. But when could we be alone together? After five years, during which time we had already been separated for five years.

I was frequently visited by female comrades, with whom I had things to discuss other than the purely sexual. Yet when they were near me, I very often looked at my notes for the subjects to be discussed, but a thousand streams of desire issued forth from the "agenda" and into the zone of the erotic. Ultimately, I toyed with the idea of asking my friends to send me female comrades seven times a week, if possible, so that I could achieve full satisfaction. I was always toying with the idea of undressing these girls who visited me. I could barely manage to give a firm handshake lacking in any erotic overtone, or a kiss of friendship, even though these were quite natural acts in my life outside.

Novorusski, the publisher of comprehensive "Memoirs of an Idealist", does not write much on this subject, but what he does write is rather characteristic. I quote:

> "The presence of women in our circle filled the atmosphere even more with sentiments and brought into them a touch of tenderness that inevitably appears everywhere where there are children and women. Ludmilla Alexandrova Wolkenstein, whose goodness of heart we have all experienced and who is no longer among the living, certainly received many small thoughts from

us in that epoch, related to this rush of emotions – these could not be acted upon, flickering powerlessly in bondage, just as our mind flickered feebly, caged up, deprived of the most elemental means of creative and lively activity.

"They are far off days; you can confess that our feelings for the ladies (!) had a slightly different character to those towards our fellows. We were in a tomb, it is true, but we were still living people. And the living man, especially the young man, is also subjected to the impulses that arise. On the contrary, it would be quite unnatural to be under the same roof all the time, to feel the woman's presence daily and then to remain as cold as a corpse and callous as a wooden dummy at the sight of her."

When I received a visit from a female friend, for whom I had feelings and also knew that she was aware of my situation, I came very close to losing control, pulling the girl into my arms, and throwing the sergeant out of the cell. Because he saw what I was going through and was sensible enough to turn his back, I should have been able to slate my erotic thirst. But I was so sexually overcharged that out of shyness I did not even properly reach her mouth to give her a kiss with the full force of love. So awkward was I that my hands whirled helplessly in the air, not reaching her breasts, which were the object of my desire. Such nervous ecstasies cannot be explained by the natural shyness that dominates people when they are courting. We were not reciprocally soliciting love. But then I never got to know this form of courtship in my natural life. What took place in this case was no longer a natural and powerful solicitation, but a statement of greedy sexual hunger, without regard to the surroundings, and without asking whether the process was agreeable to the other party or not.

In the first three months of my presence at the Luckau prison in 1926, I had never come into contact with any female body. My sexual difficulties were so intense that they were barely describable. An experience shall illustrate the point: In the first period, every fortnight, or three weeks, or sometimes after eight days, if I was lucky and did not miss the opportunity, I briefly glimpsed a girl in the gatehouse for a few seconds. To do so, I had to look through a narrow gap. So as not to miss the opportunity, I lurked there for the moment that the gate opened. If I managed to see the girl, I wanted to start singing. She was hardly even a beauty. The urge to see the girl was often so strong that I was ready to stand at the gate and just explain: I'm standing here because I want to see a girl, and I stand here until I have stilled my desire. Yes, I was often about to run through the gate to force the girl into my arms; like it or not, try holding me back from violent acts by means of violence. Such urges did not let go of me. The fact that they did not get the upper hand in practice was due to self-reflection at the "last moment".

When I once talked to a prison inspector about the effects of sexual repression and isolation from anything feminine, I did not expect approval, but I heard an admission that completely stunned me. The official said:

> "During the war I noticed the same effects on myself and others. When I arrived at the German border on leave after more than a year of service at the front and saw the first girls, I was simply no longer master of my feelings, my clear self-awareness disappeared and my sexual desire made itself noticeable. I was on the point of jumping off the train."

I heard the same thing from a number of prison sergeants who were honest about themselves and others.

In appreciation of the facts drawn from experience, I will answer the question that I myself asked: was this always so, have I ever, some day and somehow, possibly played with the idea of using force against desirable girls, or any girls whatsoever, in order to have sexual intercourse, in order to gain possession of their bodies? I can only give one answer to that question: not once, under the effect of psychological impulses (to speak in Maag's terms) have I ever attempted anything of the kind in my normal life.

In Turkey, for years, there has been a relentless struggle against the veil. Exposing yourself, showing your genitals in the event of any kind of physical itch is no more offensive there than when someone here puts their hand to their face. Yet in Turkey, raising the veil is condemned as immoral. The struggle against the wearing of the veil has ultimately led to the threat of the death penalty for repeated violation of the veil regulations. A female journalist asked the dictator Kemal Pasha about the reasons for the abolition of the requirement for Turkish women to wear the veil. She received the following reply:

> "Criminal wrongdoings are often hidden behind the veil."

Further:

> "The veil excites sensuality too much. It has been observed that in areas where men have never had a chance to see a woman's face, sex attacks have occurred much more frequently than, for example, in Constantinople, where numerous Christian women never wear veils on their faces." (*Leipziger Volkszeitung* Nr. 40, 1927.)

Translated into the language of a sexologist, this means, to paraphrase a topic Hirschfeld used in a lecture to workers in Leipzig: "People's bye-laws must be brought into harmony with nature."

Before the day I was due to be released from prison I had an indescribable anxiety. I was afraid that I would force the first woman I encountered in the street into my arms and become a so-called sex offender. As a precaution I sent for my wife, but I was released a few hours before she arrived. As soon as I stood on the street, everything settled down. The sight of women seemed quite normal to me; there was not even a hint of increased sexual covetousness.

The dangerous direction in which I was heading sexually

while in Luckau prison, both in criminal and in moral respects, weakened as soon as I could mix more often in the company of a woman. At first, I formed a close relationship with an inspector whose office overlooked the street. I often spent hours in this office, entangled in a stimulating exchange of ideas, while my eyes feasted on the passing girls. When I witnessed this for the first time, I spontaneously exclaimed: "Look, there is Venus cleaning the windows!" The official, overcome by the power at work in my soul, stood up and said: "Then I will give you Venus apples, and you will have perfection!" [51] He gave me two apples, which I looked after, until a few days later I handed them over to my wife with a formal hymn to Venus. I felt the throb in my wife's chest, which lay happily in my arms as I squeezed the "Venus apples" of her breasts.

I then arrived at a favourable sexual accommodation, for after the leaves had fallen from the trees, I had a narrow unimpeded view. The daily sightings and observations of the representatives of the female sex worked wonders. The worst afflictions of sexual hunger disappeared. In every situation of a sexual nature, regulatory effects occurred. I was soon exceptionally stimulated, and just as soon distracted again. This effect was even stronger when observing pregnant women. Every time I saw one, I slid into compensatory sexual thoughts, with the consequence that sexual abstinence became easier to bear.

A prisoner told me, casually:

"But in truth, masturbation is no remedy for me either. I also feel that; yes, it brings me into a state of even greater depression. I only achieve success with masturbation when, in my imagination, a female body enters my vision, one which has moved me, or at least stimu-

---

[51]So called after the legend of the Judgment of Paris, who awarded Venus the golden apple. Portrayed in Bertel Thorvaldsen's erotic sculpture, *Venus with the Apple*.

lated me. If this image is absent, I often go months on end enduring sexual urges yet unable to find any release, until I once again have the opportunity to come into the orbit of a woman."

These circumstances are well known to the organs of the penal system. Therefore, they "guard" against them. The penal system has recently "evolved" to such an extent that, occasionally, it holds a concert within its institutions, so that the public should recognize the "humanity" of its new approach. Even though this is not much more than pomp, a sham, a total pretence, outward formality and duplicity, typical dungeon-masters are already rebelling against it, because they see in it the "undermining of correctional norms".

Although they prefer that so far as possible no female staff participate at such events, this is sometimes unavoidable. For example, at a concert in Brandenburg jail, a few female members of the ensemble participated in the programme. This circumstance prompted the Governor to leave the prisoners in their cells during the concert; the row doors were open, but meticulous care was taken to ensure that none of the prisoners stuck his head outside their cell door. I was spontaneously driven to leave my cell – not because of the female members of the ensemble who were taking part in in the programme, of which I at first knew nothing – but as a result of a natural impulse that prompts people to see performers, or to see them while listening. The Governor, who surprised me in the "transgression" of this order, explained to me with a certain bashfulness:

> "It is certainly not good that this event takes place with such a technical defect, but it cannot be otherwise: there are some female artists involved; and to pull the rug from any possible disturbances, I had to arrange things in this way. The sight of a female person can have an undesirable effect on one prisoner or another who can no longer control himself. We cannot be sure, but we have to protect ourselves against that and preferably

prevent it in the first place. You will understand, won't you? On the other hand, I did not want to let this concert take place in the church, because it is quite inappropriate for such events. Because that is an old type of architecture from the Middle Ages."

For sure, the Governor's fears were exaggerated. On such occasions, the primary objective is not "the sight of the beautiful woman as a magic instrument," but the fullness of the sonorous voices snatched from the instrument, the concert that captures the senses. The Governor's decree would also not have been able to prevent undesirable releases of sexual urges, if the preconditions had otherwise been met, because the cell doors were open. But the fact that there were fears demonstrates that the committees of the penal system are well aware of where the suppression of sexual instincts can lead. There are no more effective testimonies than such events. A second concert event in jail B. bears witness to how "undesirable releases" are artificially and arbitrarily induced. This time, the prisoners were left behind closed doors while the strings of the instruments sounded outside. Having been deprived of the sight for sore eyes they were longing for during the presence of a woman, the prisoners became rebellious; they drummed against the doors and the event was cancelled. It was quite understandable that the prisoners rebelled, because they were rebelling against a stupidity. That they called off the event was not understandable.

Once I suggested to the Governor that he should get a girl to sing songs accompanied by the lute; I wanted to set up the programme and make sure that a lute singer would be provided for the institution at no cost. The Governor, horrified, remarked, "For God's sake, not a female lute singer, that would make people completely love-crazed. It would be much better to let a man sing songs to the lute." I answered that in this way all the enthusiasm and enchantment would be destroyed, for only a girl could sing songs to the lute with charm and grace.[52] The director refused, but he was shocked again when I told him that at the Brandenburg prison, female performers sat barely two metres away from the prisoners, female performers with whom they could have fallen in love. Many would have done so too, but only in the sense of an expression of desire that would have an effect on their minds and imagination; it could not have driven them to take any action in this respect.

---

[52] Consciously or unconsciously, Plättner may well have had in mind here the work of the Leipzig-born artist of the orientalist school, F.M. Bredt (1860-1921), which often portrayed a woman playing the lute in harems and other erotic settings.

6. Exhibitionism

Situations of sexual distress also create conditions activating the urge to expose oneself. Sexually charged kassiber and later actions on the outside are also related to this phenomenon.[53] One day a prisoner explained to me why inmates feel the urge to expose themselves to those standing outside, remarking:

> "In everyday life it is normal for hungry eyes to graze on the beautiful lines of the body; it is normal that thirsty eyes drink in the sight of shapely female legs as a symptom of the inner delight over this apparition. In the absence of normal impressions of this kind, however, one grows beyond these everyday occurrences: one no longer falls in love with girls' legs, but one gobbles them down, the way the famished devours his meal."

The Medical Health Officer Lumpp says that "it is exceptional that a prisoner exposes himself at the cell window, from which he can see people working in the field in the distance." He has seen this only once in 25 years.

This doctor must be very naïve in assuming that prisoners only put their many forms of sexual release into action when a doctor or another prison official happens to be passing the cell window. And if Lumpp has only witnessed exhibitionism once in 25 years of service, it cannot yet be concluded from this that sexual release of this nature is an isolated incident. So, I will now let a prisoner speak with one example on behalf of many and I do not hold back from declaring that I myself have been on the edge of such dangers. The prisoner tells me this about the penal institution W.:

> "On the North Wing, the path goes past the Governor's garden. The path is surrounded by bushes. On one occasion, a woman was relieving herself in the bushes. A

---

[53] *Kassiber:* a secret language with Hebrew and Yiddish roots, used to send coded messages.

prisoner watched this: he then placed his table at the window, climbed upon it, and started to masturbate. An extraordinary relationship now developed between the two. The woman came regularly, positioned herself in such a position between the bushes that she could be seen, pulled up her skirts and exhibited herself in various teasing positions. Finally, this activity was discovered. The prisoner was transferred to the South Wing as a *kalfaktor*. He himself told me about this long-distance intercourse. I often saw this woman myself when urinating, and at first I was always amazed at how often she showed herself."

Later I was repeatedly the witness to similar goings-on.

However, such events should not be considered merely accidental as they appear to be in the above example. This long-distance sex is a more or less organized activity. I base these assertions on events that I observed in Luckau prison. From my window I could look over the streets and the immediate vicinity of the location. I repeatedly saw, in the rather empty street that stretches in front of the prison, female persons promenading, apparently by appointment, and keeping in touch with some prisoner or other, as evidenced by their movements. I also have evidence that such long-distance sex is known about, because shortly afterwards a prison sergeant lingered in the street. I had already been observing for some time a female who strolled up and down the street, but always within sight of the prison.

A few weeks later I once again noticed a female strolling outside. After half an hour or so, I returned to my work. Two hours or so later I went over once more to the window and saw, in the alleyway, a female person who, so long as nobody came by, alternately revealed her breasts and her lower body. It was the same female that I had noticed strolling up and down two hours earlier. The game lasted a good half hour; during this time the girl went away for a few minutes, then came back to the alleyway and repeated her teasing acts, until the light faded. A few weeks later I once again noticed similar activity by another female person. I tend towards the opinion that this involved the wives of prisoners, who stooped to these acts in order to satisfy their husbands in prison.

These examples are charges to be laid against the cruelty of conditions that afflict not only prisoners but also their partners in sexual intercourse. Many break down under the burden of sexual misery.

Exhibitionism is widespread among female prisoners, too – everywhere they come into contact with male prisoners, even if it is only face-to-face. I registered an observation of this kind myself.

One day while in a remand jail I noticed two female prisoners cleaning the windows on the top storey, where the doctor's surgery was to be found. I had done a couple of circuits of the yard when one of the girls blew me a kiss, to which I did not react. After I had done another two circuits the two of them positioned themselves at the window in such a brash manner that I could see right up to the thigh, if I looked up. Finally, one of the girls unbuttoned her blouse and showed me her breasts. I called up: "Mind you don't get caught!" Now the woman thought she had made contact. She exposed her breasts still further, held her breasts up and called her friend over. She came, but went away again immediately, probably with the intention, I assumed, to check that the coast was clear. The girl then started to undress completely, and then reappeared in the window. After a while the second girl came over and replaced the first; she too began to expose herself in a similar fashion to the first, continuing the game until she also stood there quite naked. The second girl then called to me: "Are you aroused? Show it to me!" I did not do as she asked; the necessary conditions were lacking, both in terms of how I was feeling and the physical environment. I would have had to come to the other side of the wall, and thus directly in front of the windows of the administration room, for the girls to have been able to see me in a naked position. I tried to scare off the girls, but that only made them get together as partners and perform same-sex acts in front of my eyes. When the sergeant, who had gone away during my exercise hour, came back again, the two girls had finished their game. They went on cleaning windows, and I saw that in the meantime a female warder had appeared.

This example allows of no definitive conclusion; I cannot be sure from which social milieu these two girls came. But one conclusion that can be drawn from this event is that the girls felt a wanton sexual passion and were willing and able to let off steam.

III. The flight of famished sexual fantasy into the domain of instrumental self-gratification

1. Fornication with animals

"Generally speaking, it can be said that life in a cell puts a stop to sexual excitement," says Lumpp. Let's also reduce this statement *ad absurdum*.

We have already examined the tendency to sexual self-gratification at various levels and in various guises, shining a light into the bottomless pit of sexual misery. One might imagine that we have exhausted the topic. But that is not the case. The erotic play of thoughts also breaks through the "usual constraints" and contemplates unlimited possibilities.

In penal institutions that have their own farms you can usually find prohibition signs in front of the animal stalls with the following message: "Prisoners are allowed to enter the stalls only in the presence of a warder." The naive reader might ask why that is so. The expert in these matters, however, knows that in penal institutions that have livestock "much bestial fornication" occurs, as the penal bureaucracy calls it. For this reason, it also guards against any self-management by the prisoners, because it knows that the prohibition signs are without any practical significance. Yet prisoners who are in direct contact with cattle cannot be placed under permanent supervision if they are to work. And other prisoners manage to get access to the stalls in one way or another, if they have "good relationships" or have some "means of payment".

What plays out in the animal pens is horrifying. Prisoners, who certainly have no pathological sexual disposition, are grateful to the animals if they can somehow relieve their urges on their sexual organs. They are even happy just to be able to see and feel the sexual organs of animals. A prisoner who spent three years as the "pig-pen keeper" at Sonnenburg prison told me that he had witnessed at least 100 prisoners having sex with animals.[54] He knew of many who were no longer content to stick their member in the vagina or anus of pigs, goats, horses and oxen, but were so sexually hungry that they use their arms and drill their heads into the orifice. These acts were generally accompanied by highly charged sexual language. I learned from another prisoner that a large number of inmates who look after animals get into sexual ecstasies when they are able to beat them.

Prisoners who are already sexually out of whack do not even refrain from using poultry. Pigeons and geese are used and literally abused to death after having previously served as an object to subdue the need for physical affection. Cats are also not safe if they can be caught somewhere. Lumpp and other medical health officers admit this but maintain that these are exceptional cases. I am willing to concede this point, but the question then arises, why are these exceptions? Well, the prisoners who sit behind bars are isolated from all nature, so obviously they have no opportunity to catch cats. This means they seek other outlets, driving them onto the gruesome path of instrumental sexual acts.

---

[54] Sonnenburg, now Słońsk in Poland. It was one of Germany's toughest prisons, for serious criminals. During the Nazi period the prison was used as a concentration camp, mostly holding political prisoners.

2. Pillows, blankets, mattresses, modelled bread and meat as sex instruments

Everything that came into my hand at some time or other became a "sex tool" in my imagination. I could be picking up my plate or my bowl, I could be receiving a piece of bread or grabbing my drinking glass. In the morning or at another time of the day, I might be getting my soap and my sponge out of the cupboard to wash myself, I might be making my bed or using a wipe, receiving fruit or my extra sickness allowance; I could be looking at my medicine or the container with pine-needle extract, or feeling the hand-brush to sweep my cell, or touching and looking at any other object; again and again while doing these things the idea came to me: you have "sex tools", you have genitals in your hands! If I looked at the grating in the window, it whispered to me: yes indeed, in an emergency I can also be transformed into a woman's body! If I was standing in front of the radiator, the thought surfaced: could this radiator not mutate into a woman? I looked at my typewriter box and heard a voice: find all the blankets and soft objects in your cell, fill me with them, and you'll see, I'll provide you with the same services as a woman does in normal life! The mere process of picking up a tin of canned fruit only gives scope to the question: how is it possible to make a vagina out of this object? After I had let down my bed in the evening, the thought flew into my head: three mattress parts, a pillow and various blankets – it must be possible to create a female body from these items! I heard the whisper from all corners: Yes, you can, give it a try! I did not try it, I defended myself against the voices and apparitions that tormented me, but I could not defeat them. If I "overcame" them one day and they attacked me again the next, in a different way and a different form: they could not be overcome. I was so dismayed, contrite and listless over these apparitions that I thought: there is no way out of this desolate situation, other than suicide!

The situation was all the more depressing because, despite some knowledge and experience of matters sexual, I had heard nothing of such phenomena, let alone experienced them myself. Of course, I knew something about homosexuality, which I abhorred, because I had a false idea of what defines it, but I knew that there were fetishistic sexual tendencies, perverse forms of sexual gratification, of which I was also horrified – but I did not know any more about this area. I knew that women resort to mechanical forms of masturbation, using instruments that mimic the male member, and had also heard that they construct devices for masturbation. Whereas I knew nothing of men using instrumental means of self-gratification, when the object of natural love was absent; I only learned about this later. This ignorance could have been dangerous to me and led to my suicide, because I could not manage to explain the nature of these apparitions as an urge for release. I only learned about these forms of self-gratification through Hirschfeld's book *Geschlechtskunde*, in which it states on this subject:

> "The technical term for artificial imitation of the male member, made of rubber, leather, wax, horn, wood, metal, etc., is: godemiché.
>
> "The word, already used in the Middle Ages, is said to be composed of the Latin *gaude mihi* (= enjoy myself). Other names in the catalogues of the 'Paris Rubber Goods Industry' include: consolateurs and *bijoux indiscrets* (= indiscreet toys). Bloch, in his 'English moral history', published under the pseudonym E. Dühren (Berlin 1903, Bd. 1, p. 282-290) provides detailed, historical-literary records about godemichés. He reports here that they already appeared on ancient Babylonian sculptures, in Egypt and in the Mimiamboi of Herondas (3rd century BC), and have been used since ancient times in East Asia, where the Spaniards encountered them in the Philippines. Especially well known are the artificial wax phalluses of Balinese

women. In Europe, as early as the twelfth century, Bishop Burchard of Worms lashed out against artificial male members, and especially in the Renaissance their use became general and the production techniques increasingly refined. The peak, in this respect, was reached in 18th century France. No less a person than Mirabeau, the famous French politician, already described such an artificial phallus in his erotic novel, *Le redeau levé ou l'Education de Laure*. In our sexual science archive there is a collection of such apparatuses used by women for the purposes of masturbation; they range from simple, smooth wooden cylinders of Chinese origin to a condom stuffed with cotton, in the centre of which is a rigid rod, to the lifelike replica of the male member made of rubber with an imitation of the scrotum providing the ability to fill this apparatus with warm milk, and the highly artistic horn phallus imitations, which originate from Japan and are used both directly for masturbatory purposes as well as when strengthened by specially made stimulus rings. In this collection, which through the diversity of the countries of origin gives a clear picture of the similarity of the phenomena despite the diversity of people's ideas, there are also the kind of metal spheres which are inserted for masturbatory purposes in the vagina to awaken lustful feelings in the body through agitation. Photographs from Dresden Criminal Museum show a masturbatory machine to be found there which was confiscated from a masseuse; it consists of a phallus mounted on a rack which is set in motion by the feet via a treadle, in the nature of a sewing machine, while a woman sits in front."

I found out what this means in practice in the lunatic ward in Berlin, where the principle of isolation was also disrupted in my case. I was given the opportunity to study prisoners, which I was unable to do to the same extent while in prison.

When I became friends with a prisoner and talked to him about all these manifestations of sexual need, he told me, after a little hesitation:

"Ah, these apparitions are nothing out of the ordinary; I have had them and have them still, I have had them all the time since the fourth year of my imprisonment; they are to be encountered in a more or less strongly developed form in every prisoner, even to a frightening extent in the form of actions of this kind. I came across many cases of people trying to fashion female genitalia in order to fake nature. They built the shape of a female body from mattresses, and the slit between the mattresses had to serve as the vagina. They lubricated it with Vaseline or, if this was lacking, used their monthly fat ration. I myself also tried this, but the surrogate was of too little use to me. I was unable to deceive myself. I also found out from the catering staff at prison G, that raw meat was also used for this purpose if it could be stolen – at the prisoners' expense, of course."

If I found a certain amount of reassurance through this confession, the thought ran angrily through my head: People, what have you turned people into? Or, to use, with Hirschfeld, the words of Shakespeare's King Lear: "Why dost thou lash that whore? Strip thine own back."

Another prisoner reported the following:

"I fell deeper and deeper into sexual despair and confusion, because I wanted gratification for my basic drives, and could no longer achieve this through masturbation. I once had a piece of bacon. It occupied my thoughts for a fortnight without pause, before the strength of my urge overcame the shame of attempting to see if this means could be used for self-gratification. In a quite awful moment, as I confronted the choice: Suicide or self-gratification, I hollowed out the piece of bacon – then put it aside again. Once again, my shame was stronger than the desire for self-gratification. But these were only brief moments that held me in check, until the unsatisfied impulse drove me into a vague sexual frenzy. I wedged the bacon between the mattresses and now totally lost control of the situation. I no longer recognized any limits; time and time again my desire burst into flames. I probably ejaculated 15 times that night; eventually I thought that a never-ending sexual river was flowing out of my member. I no longer knew what was actually happening to me. Over the next four weeks I used the same means without keeping to sensible limits, or being able to keep to sensible limits: I had also lost the last powers of self-control and was only ruled by the thought, they could identify the device I was using, or it would rot; at any rate, I wanted to take maximum advantage of it while I could. During this time, I spent about five or six weeks working out so much that I had at least five or six ejaculations per night. Sleeping was out of the question. If I wanted to prevent anything even more harmful happening during the day, I had to do my daily work; I was not human anymore. Then this means also became dulled. My shame once again became stronger than my sex drive, and I eventually had to throw it away, because it was becoming putrid. I now entered a period in which I would have liked to run away from myself. In particular, I became aware of the implications of what I did and how I did it: on the first night of this sexual perversion, the frenzy was so strong that I would probably have killed the object if it had been alive."

One can easily imagine that such confessions require extraordinary trust. I am incapable of describing the agony that strangled this man, so long as he wrestled with himself in deciding whether or not he should offer me this confession, and which did not let go of him after he had testified. But he begged me not to reveal his name.

I could provide numerous examples of this sort. Another

man who made models, that is, kneaded figures from bread dough, told me the following:

"In this art I am very handy, perhaps even 'artistic'. From time to time, I literally make a female abdomen from bread dough and mould a vagina for myself on it. In this way I get closer to 'natural' conditions. That is to say, when the bread dough is kneaded and brought into shape, the whole takes on a certain hardness, but still retains a certain elasticity, so that the correctly moulded vagina yields only as much as is necessary. With Vaseline or fat, I moisten the vagina, and, in this way, I have certainly invented the most effective of all the surrogates that I use. This has the advantage that I do not need to hide it: I generally remodel it after this particular use, so it does not occur to anyone that a sexual imitation is hidden behind this disguise. With other types of surrogate, you are always living with the danger that they will be confiscated after a search. Reproductions of vaginas made from meat are of course better, but for one thing they quickly rot, and secondly, they are very difficult to come by, if at all. The means that I use here has only one victim, namely, many bread rations. Because I usually build the apparatus on a large scale, I also need large quantities of bread-mix. And that means I also have to go without bread for many days."

In the procurement of sexual instruments, prisoners develop a virtuoso resourcefulness. And the unsuspecting warders imagine that everything is as it looks: the prisoners are observing the "prescribed order".

Hirschfeld writes about this in *Geschlechtskunde:*

"But there are also apparatuses for male instrumental masturbation, such as upholstered pillows with an opening framed by horsehair as a vaginal substitute, or, in one special case, a life-size doll in women's clothing, in the middle of which a vagina-like rubber tube has been inserted; the original, which is in the Berlin Crime

Museum, was found in the possession of a convicted prisoner. It bears eloquent testimony to the strength of human sexual hunger that other artificially fashioned abdomens, made of material, oakum and wood were confiscated in POW camps. Irrigators and similar hygienic devices are also used, especially by women, for the same purposes."

You might be inclined to attribute such "degenerate activities" to spiritually primitive and "morally depraved subjects"; prison doctors speak of "debauchees". The opposite is the truth; we are dealing here with people who, for example, put me in the shadow both in intellectual terms and also in terms of their practical experience of life. The instruments are often original, refined constructions that require a certain genius, exuberance in erotic imagination. Primitive people do not even find these "ingenious" ways to escape from their oppressive sexual needs. They take recourse to same-sex intercourse, without having homosexual inclinations.

Another prisoner commented to me regarding masturbation in detention in this way:

"Masturbation has different types and grades, but all of these are expressions of typical sexual activity in prison. One of these prisoners, known to me as an otherwise normally sensitive person, drives objects into the anal orifice while masturbating. Only then does he obtain the desired, required and necessary release. If he were a homosexual by nature, he could exercise homosexuality here as needed and to his heart's content. Others excite themselves through self-inflicted bleeding on their own bodies. The feeling of pain gives them a pleasurable sensation: they are not by nature sadists or masochists, rather, they are first turned to these practices in detention."

This statement did not entirely convince me, above all I assumed that the prisoner was generalizing. I therefore asked him if he had observed this phenomenon multiple times. He replied to me that in his six years of incarceration he had made the acquaintance of at least 30 prisoners in four institutions who sought gratification in the way he had described. And it is of importance what Medical Health Officer Lumpp, who more or less belongs to the "guild", declares (in "Notes for Jail Patrons"):

"The adolescent, mentally limited prisoner had already inflicted a mass of cuts on the chest and abdomen while in pre-trial detention, whose scars were still visible at the time of admission; he said they originated from a suicide attempt. In the first few months of his sentence, he was reported because of nosebleeds; there were traces of blood in his cell and on his handkerchiefs. The extremely pale man then came to my attention during the cell visit; I arranged for him to undress and found even more scars on him, including one on the back of the penis, which had not yet completely healed; the left nipple was missing, it was cut out, also the navel was missing. The prisoner did not say anything about the cause of this pointless carving, but it was clear the cause could not be a suicide attempt. He came to the hospital, everything was taken away from him that could be used to hurt himself; then he bit his upper arm, so deep that it was bleeding profusely and now he shyly admitted to me, after intense interrogation, that this gave him carnal sensations, which caused him to ejaculate from time to time. As I found out from him, he had very wrong, outlandish ideas about sex life. He has since been released, has married, and lives peacefully and withdrawn in his home parish."

I met with some fellow prisoners who were close to me in discussions following up on these reports and experiences, which kept us busy for weeks. I made all kinds of ob-servations, explained some aesthetic terms, and finally declared that modesty must remain the master in all predicaments, to which one said:

"Modesty is a nice idea, where it can be practised. In here the precondition is illusory and therefore the term itself is empty of content, indeed it often seems stupid. Modesty is an expression of aesthetic feelings and only a partial aspect of personality in general. Personality traits, however, are dependent on one's ability to bring willpower to bear. Because of this, the exercise of aesthetic feelings founders when in prison. In any case, so long as I am prevented from giving full rein to my natural inclinations, I will use the forms of satisfaction that at least halfway satisfy me and above all prevent me from getting into the kinds of states that you have gotten yourself into, and others who have gotten into even worse states, as I know from ample experience. If I am to offer you advice, then it is not to let yourself be driven into dire situations, and perhaps even driven to death, as a result of relative notions of aesthetics and modesty. Inner inhibitions, when they disturb natural functions, are there to be overcome. Incidentally, I myself have also gone through this stage of inhibition, but then, whether you like it or not, you move onto another stage in which you overrule your own will through your own actions, over which you no longer have any possibility to make decisions."

Who could call a person who can express such thoughts mentally primitive, let alone call him a "morally depraved subject"? The only people who could do so are those who want to hide the things of which they themselves are really ashamed.

With regard to the instrumental masturbation of women, who can more easily help themselves than men, I received the following information:

"In autumn 1923 I was in the grip of prison psychosis and in January 1924 I was transferred to the lunatic ward in Breslau. Again here, the same conditions prevailed. There was a female ward in the jail with perhaps 200 or 300 inmates. I had become a *kalfaktor* in the lunatic ward and once listened to a conversation be-tween warders about female self-gratification. After-wards, during a search, the matron of the women's prison had found a multitude of objects that served for self-gratification. Women were not allowed, for exam-ple, to be given full sausage rations there; the sausages were always cut up into small pieces, because other-wise there was no guarantee that the sausage was being consumed for its intended purpose. Neverthe-less, en-tire sausage portions were found that served a different purpose. The women had somehow managed to pro-cure them.

"In addition, the women use pieces of wood that they wrap around with rags, broom and brush handles, candles, bottles, knives, fork and spoon handles, rubber rollers, and other items that could serve as an inferior substitute for a man. The matron complained that eve-ry search, which was undertaken on a monthly basis, repeatedly found such items, and she was unable to identify and block the source of such aids. And by the way, the warders emphasized that homosexuality be-came more prevalent among women than men, when-ever they could find no normal release."

3. The escape from my situation of sexual distress at this point

I already quoted the Christian doctor Paul Maag, who asserts that "there are even impulses in the soul of mature personalities, which are in opposition to the prevailing direction of character – inopportune or instinctual urges that are opposed to the moral norm". But they are held down, Maag says, they are not chosen and fade away more and more as the character matures. He adds:

> "The situation is different where disposition is close to normal and does not show such defects. Since instinctual life can be held in dependence on the psyche, it can be controlled with proper education, i.e. brought into the correct relationship to the will. An instinctual urge signifies no more than a stimulation, an appeal to the consciousness for satisfaction. Where the situation has not gone askew, sex drive is also easy to hold down, easier even than any other. The normal operation of sexual drive, that is to say in the appropriate service of the whole, confirms the mastery of the psyche. But if the impulse is confirmed against the objection of conscience, which cannot be sufficiently acknowledged as guardian and guide, then it takes on a dangerous aspect. It now becomes autocratic and disturbs and destroys the equilibrium of life movement."

Emphasis must be placed on the preliminary thought: "Where the situation has not gone askew." But the situation *is* askew in detention; so much askew that the conscience, as guardian guide, i.e. as the sum of all volitional attributes, is almost completely eliminated, if not in its entirety then otherwise to a great extent.

In fact, after gaining the enlightenment described in the previous chapter, I came to the very edge of attempting an instrumental means of self-gratification. But inhibitions, anchored in my conscience, and the ability to govern myself through willpower prevented me from crossing over that line. The decisive factor, however, was probably that I was psychologically and sexually not in the most distressed situation while in the lunatic ward in Berlin and the temptations arose more out of a curiosity to find out, by trying in practice, if any such experimental means of self-satisfaction were viable.

I was indeed pushed over the edge of such temptations, prompted by psychological impulses, when, back in the penitentiary itself, I went for about three months in a row without seeing a solitary female form, hearing a female voice, or imbibing the scent of a female body. I therefore tried my first "sexual experiment" with "simple forms of sexual intercourse". Unsuccessfully. I tried it with blankets, mattresses and pillows. Without success; it did not work. Mental inhibitions were stronger than psychological impulses. I tried filling a large glass container with kneaded bread dough, allowed the whole to dry out, then hollowed out a vagina inside, using blankets and pillows to replicate the female body. But that didn't work either. With my sexual hunger I stood helplessly before this artifice and a voice inside of me cried out, should you use this object to regulate the functioning of sexual secretions, to relax, to satisfy one of the most delicious desires in human life? No, stupid idea, three times no, stop or I will kill myself, so you can no longer play your sacrilegious tricks on me!

Yet, despite the inner inhibitions, I made frequent further attempts. I allowed myself to be tormented, hunted and whipped by double-dealing. From one corner of my cell I wandered to the other; I crept into the darkest corner with my sex aid – but I did not yet try out any sexual activity. Attempts never really got out of the starting blocks but that did not mean I gave them up. Finally, I lay for hours and nights on end beside such surrogate instruments, trapped and bound, without salvation. I only got out of the abyss of experimental sexual activity once I was again able to see female figures from my window more often.

In my sixth year of imprisonment, however, I did cross over the line with my experiments. I stood before the decision: either I could turn to more effective forms of sexual relief, or I would take my own life. Once again, I got hold of a glass, filled it with bread dough, hollowed out an opening, greased it, and wondered if I could risk it. I was seized with anger when I noticed that the warders had made the spyhole see-through again, when I had only just blocked it. Finally, this inhibition also disappeared; I did not care if I was watched at night or not: I used the sex aid. And while I normally prac-tised the masturbatory act by hand, usually every night, once every 14 days I indulged in self-relief with the aforementioned artifice, which was enough.

As difficult as it has been for me to make this confession, it seemed necessary to me in the interest of enlightenment.

4. Individual self-control over sex drive, and phenomena when self-control breaks down

While in detention I still remained capable, under difficult circumstances, to stay in control of my sexual urges, to exercise self-discipline, even to avoid opportunities for normal sexual intercourse. The events described below testify to this, further providing an opinion on the extent and depth of women's sexual distress in custody.

On several occasions I had received mouldy bread and one day I went to the administration offices to draw attention to this. I did not meet the jail's Governor, so I went to another office to find a secretary. The latter had, so I was told, gone to the bank. The duty sergeant was dealing with a female warden and was completing the last processes that are necessary before a prisoner is released. He took several documents from the files and directed me into a room adjoining the Governor's office from which I came, which he did not know, as he also did not know that the Governor was absent. Finally, he said: the secretary will be back soon. With that, he left the office without a care to allow the prisoner to be taken to the gate, and then to do other things, as evidenced by taking documents from the files. So, I stood alone in the office with the female warden, who did not really know what to do with me. Finally, she saw the piece of bread in my hand, took it from me, and engaged me in a conversation about "the bread". But something else was going on between us, emotionally. Knowing that she felt strongly sympathetic towards me, I am justified in speaking of an inward sexual contact that existed between us. So it happened that in the space of 20 minutes the piece of bread passed between my hand and hers. Presently she held the bread in her hands in such a way that, if I wanted to take it back and look at it again, I must unintentionally touch her lap; then she held it mechanically, pressed against her breast. Now I had to take the bread in my hand again, and I touched her breast softly. Inside, I immediately felt a whoop

at this, and we chatted for a long time about quite other subjects and events, while the piece of bread passed mechanically
back and forth. I was almost about to say: Listen, you loveliest
of all women, I am now experiencing the most beautiful moments not only of my incarceration, but of my entire life. For
your sake I would gladly go to prison for ten years, if I could
first indulge in your blessed paradise. Come, take me in your
arms, I have never in my life had such strong physical feelings
as I do now, when your eyes light up before me – tonight you
will come to my cell and enlighten my soul!

While this was going on, I was surprised as the secretary
and duty sergeant both came back, and we now spoke "officially" about the mouldy bread, which the female warder still
held in her hands. I was happy that she had it, for now I had
to take it from her, with my hand once again reaching hers, at
least her fingertips, and coming close to her breast, whose
form I was feeling in my thoughts, and which I would have
liked to enjoy – I had become so sexually excited.

In five minutes the mouldy bread has been examined on
all sides, about which she gave explanations that I had already
heard a dozen times from her lips. But I was simply happy to
be able to hear her voice. It may be that in this respect I was
dominated by a certain fiction that went beyond reality. But it
is of no consequence, not even the possible insinuation, that I
was completely under the spell of a sexually charged fiction.
Decisive is solely the fact that I was alone with this woman for
more than 20 minutes, that I combined an erotic contact with
her in feeling and in my thoughts, and that I nevertheless be-
haved myself. After six years' incarceration that would no
longer have been possible. One has to compare this behaviour
with that disastrous symptom, as I presented earlier in this
section.

Another occurrence of this kind: It was during the war,
in the winter of 1917/18. I returned from an interrogation
with the examining magistrate and had to wait in the so-called
processing room connecting the prison to the court. This pro-

cessing room was full of people who were to be brought in or taken away. On this occasion, a young girl, not at all ugly in nature and appearance, grabbed my hand, pressed it, and finally led it to her body in a way that was invisible to the others present. I was so stunned and surprised that at first I seized up to some extent, but pulled back my hand when the girl led it to her genitals. She whispered into my ear: "No one can see us." Once again, she grabbed at my hand, and once again I pulled it back, and made it clear that I was not sympathetic to this kind of behaviour. I tried to remove myself to another position. The girl realized what I was doing and deftly brought her whole body into contact with mine, finally positioning herself so that I had to stare at her breasts, which she handled to make them even more pronounced. The situation I found myself in became increasingly uncomfortable, as I was unable to say anything to the girl without denouncing her. I did not want that either, nor could I, even though at the time I was somewhat prudish, at least I did not have the elasticity in the assessment of sexual phenomena that I possess today. I was glad when the clerk asked, who was ready to be taken away. The clerk first processed the girl, then me, leaving the girl, and then me, outside of the processing room, mechanically giving the official in the main office the usual sign that people were returning, and then closing the door to the processing room without giving it a thought. At the same time, the girl, who was on the other side of the corridor, stayed put, finally saying: "Come over here, I'm dying for a fondle. We are all alone here and undisturbed, you can quickly make love to me here." It would be clear to every psychologist that this could, indeed must happen in the position we were in, only for me it was not clear and above all not self-evident. And before I could have said another word to her, the girl had revealed her breasts. And so, defeated by pity for her yearning, half pitying, half disgusted, I uttered the words: "Listen, dear girl, I really have no feeling for this kind of caper and, what's more, at the moment I have no desire for caresses of this kind.

I am really sorry for you, but with all the will in the world, I cannot help you. Don't you think about what you are doing here: you're almost throwing yourself away; don't you have any self-awareness, any self-control? You will get us into a very difficult situation here if I willingly do what you want. What do you think they will do with us if they catch us out?" But the girl had already exposed her lower body. This action held me spellbound and prevented me from continuing. She whispered to me with a ringing voice, which really appealed to me:

> "You are so polite, as I now see, but I can't help it, I am so besotted with you. I am totally in love with you. Come on, there's no one who can catch us and watch us. Look, the officer is not even in the main office, he seems to have left, and the inspector is busy. We can lie down here on the floor, and then the officer in the main office won't be able to see us when he comes back; he will know nothing about it, and the clerk in the processing room won't be able to see us, if he is admitting someone. I have done that before, and it worked, even though I did not like the man. Come on, we'll soon be finished, before someone comes by. It will make me so happy and you'll enjoy it too."

That surprised me, because I had not suspected that the girl was so intelligent. I then said: If I am to talk to you for a while, you have to lower your skirts and button up your blouse, otherwise I am off. The girl followed; with this, I had gone to the other side of the room so as not to have to speak too loudly if we wanted to speak to one another. Although I had no intention of having sexual intercourse, and for that very reason, not least because the necessary preconditions were absent after I had been with the examining magistrate for nearly six hours and a mass of thoughts were swimming about in my head; I had spent a good hour of heated discussions with him and his secretary. Nonetheless, after the hither and thither, the girl had aroused a certain interest in me. Because, despite everything of a sexual nature, something refined sounded from her soul. And that attracted me. I said: Girl, be sensible, control yourself, it is impossible to make love here. The mood is not right. Come on, are you a prostitute? At these words, she embraced me and relaxed noticeably, rubbing her body against mine, showering me in a flood of kisses, accompanied by the words:

> "No, I am not a prostitute, and what's more I am in no position to become one. But I am a girl with sexual feelings, that were only awakened while in jail. I will go mad if I cannot get natural satisfaction once again; I can't hold out any longer. You're not at all nice. How can you be so hard on a woman? A girl cannot live on sermons. The opportunity is so favourable right now, we could have been finished long ago, while you were going on about moods and dangers to me. Look, maybe there's an empty cell here we can go to. Then we'll be completely undisturbed, because they cannot miss us by chance."

The girl calmed down a little. Now she told me that she used to indulge in sexual activity with a fellow prisoner from time to time. But there was not much opportunity to do so, and she did not like it much. Apart from that she masturbated, but without getting any satisfaction in this way. Then she tried to pull me over. She grabbed my member while fiddling with her genitals. I forcibly freed myself from her embrace; she shook and trembled, fell into crying fits and finally said: "I will start screaming if you do not satisfy me." At the same time, she had thrown herself on the floor; she had become completely the victim of impulse. I assured her that I wanted to satisfy her, if I could just find an empty cell. This gave me the opportunity to get out of the situation without having to do anything that would have become an emotional burden.

I left the girl lying in an exposed state; she continued with her masturbatory movements and sobbed inconsolably. I reached the central office in the rotunda and was able to convince myself that the duty sergeant was not present. I looked around again for that girl and saw that the clerk was back, processing another man's admission. I was worried about the girl, who was only now in danger of being caught. But she was not caught: the officer discharged the man from the processing room, just as mechanically as he had discharged us earlier, without paying attention to whether the officer was present in the main office or not. What I had not done with the girl was done by the man who was admitted after me from the processing room, apparently without any hesitation, as he stumbled over the woman's body, which was still there on the floor, leant over it and then mounted it. While this was going on the sergeant appeared in the main office in the rotunda, so I had to proceed. I looked round once more and could see, to my relief, that the "lovers" could hardly be noticed. I don't know how this scene concluded, as I was put in my cell and had to suffer all kinds of oppressive thoughts in connection with this experience.

The key point that matters is this: at that time, I was able to pass up on such an opportunity to have normal sexual intercourse while in jail.

Another incident of a similar kind happened to me in the summer of 1922, also while I was remanded in custody. After an interview with the jail's superintendent, I collided with a woman who embraced me without any foreplay, kissing and performing other sexual body movements. Before I could even be sure what was going on, she had gone to the extreme, so I had to use force to free myself from her embrace. For I found this behaviour at one and the same time shameless, hurtful and offensive; on the other hand, I also had to reckon with the likelihood that the superintendent or some other officer might turn up at any moment. And before I could even say a word to the woman, she whispered to me, in broken sentences: Ah, that was nice! I'm already done, that was a much better orgasm. Come on, let's go into that room over there, it's free, we can really get off in there and then you can also have fun.

With these words, she really did take me away with her for a few yards. I managed to control myself, pushed her back again after a second attempt and went, to avoid more, to the secretary's office and talked to him for a while, finally asking him to unlock the door to the prison building. He did so, and I went to my cell, thinking about this incident, shaking my head, but then I shoved the whole affair into my memory storage, that's to say I did not devote much time to explaining the causes of such events, or why they came about, or the innocence of victims of such incidents.

A year later I experienced a further, similar incident, in the same remand jail. While I was doing my monotonous circuit during the exercise hour and was lost in my thoughts, a female warder and *kalfaktor* came into the yard to cut soup vegetables. The stooping posture of the *kalfaktor* made it possible to have a close look at her breasts, although I was not following any intention to do so. But the *kalfaktor* apparently did not want to cover up her alluring charm, rather she wanted to give it free play as far as possible, which she achieved through the necessary positions and movements. The warder then went inside the work-shed, leaving me virtually alone with the *kalfaktor*. She immediately took this opportunity to make her breasts even more alluring. Then I noticed that she was fumbling with her blouse and baring her breasts. I was not unsympathetic towards this game, my eyes drank in the luscious shapes, I toyed with the idea of going to her and giving her a kiss before pressing my cheek to her breasts. By now she had gone to a place where she could not be seen directly. Now she spoke to me, asked if I was enjoying myself, to which I replied with a nod of the head. This admission excited her; she went into a shallow ventilation shaft, fully revealed her breasts and beckoned me to come over and feel them. Since she was very close to me, it was possible, so I did it too; I offered her my head, which she covered with kisses and then pressed into her breasts. I pulled back again, went on with my circuit, wondering how the situation might possibly develop further, and whether I would remain master of the situation. When I came within reach again, she had freed her lower body and now said just one word: "Come!" But I did not go. On my next lap I found her lying on her back; she whispered to me, that there was no harm in coming over to her, to "make love to her" quickly. I whispered back that with the best will in the world, we could be surprised and caught. At this, she said to me: Not going to happen; the warder has got stuck in the shed with the sergeant; you'll see that that it's ages before she remembers me again. You need not worry about getting caught. I whispered back: but the sergeant will remember me, if he does not hear my steps, or someone can come out of the jail's back door to go to the work shed. It's too risky a business for me.

> "Well, of course," she retorted, "if you are just going to philosophize for half an hour, then it will be too late. And even if we get caught, what does it matter? So long as they don't catch us too soon. But they won't catch us. I not only know my warder's ways, but also those of the sergeant; the two of them always spend ages chatting with each other. Just come here quick; I have a stone and if I bash it against the wall, that will sound like footsteps."

The girl interested me more and more; I stood at the extreme edge of a decision to go over to her, hearing only the words: shall I, or shall I not? This refrain accompanied me through the entire exercise hour, which had actually overrun the allotted time. I had already been outside for three-quarters of an hour, although the so-called exercise hour normally only lasted half an hour. That often happened, when the time was up, I saw nothing unusual in it. In the end I was ruled by the strongest self-consciousness that is possible in such situations: I decided, not do to it. The *kalfaktor* climbed out of the ventilation shaft again, a little flustered, and then said: "Your fiery love eyes delighted me, made me hope they would light my fire. How you can practice so much self-restraint in such circumstances, I simply cannot understand; you are not lifeless, but you are a puzzle to me." Then she carried on cutting her vegetables. But not for long. She soon stood up again so that she faced me within easy reach. She then grabbed my hand and took it to her breasts, while she clamped my body between her legs and pressed her genital area against my flesh. We stopped in that state for a moment, and I might have stopped there for ten days if she had not repeated the "idiocy" of trying to bring it to a soulless act of intercourse. I immediately freed myself from this embrace while she now began to masturbate.

So even in this situation, where I was being thrown off balance one way and the other, I remained in control of my urges, even though anyone will grant that I brought an almost inhuman willpower to bear, which is far from a daily occurrence. And I can assure you: in the sixth year of my detention I would not have been capable of such self-restraint if such opportunities for normal sex had presented themselves.

In this connection, what Mühsam told me gains a certain poignancy. He mentioned that in Niederschönenfeld his cell was cleaned by female *kalfaktors* for a while. This offered, now and again, a moment alone with one woman or another. Conversations immediately took on a sexually charged nature, and the subject of maybe engaging in a natural sexual act came up. The remarkable thing about these cases, Mühsam told me, was that all women were pursuing the same objective, whether it was a proletarian woman or a doctor, a prostitute or an actress.

IV. "Sex life" in shared cells

1. Skin contact by others as an expression of sexual sublimation

So far, we have looked at conditions that no one sees, conditions that are unique in solitary confinement and are mainly played out in isolation, i.e. isolated from what is happening in shared cells and thus away from the eyes of others. The prisoner cannot, however, even under the strictest isolation, always be separated from every other living being. What must be taken into account here is the fact that masturbatory forms of sexual gratification, which, as we have seen, no longer satisfy over time, turn to instrumental activity and lead to mutual forms of gratification.

Anyone who observes everything that goes on between prisoners in penal institutions can only conclude that events which seem to be self-evident are transformed into substitutional acts of sexual sublimation. Shaving and haircutting lead to sexual frontier areas. It may be that one or the other prisoner shaves his head for health reasons; there may also be a whole series of prisoners who have their neck shaved out of vanity. They want to sport an English hairstyle, or whatever the language of fashion might call it these days. But head and neck shaving is, on the contrary, nothing but sexual sublimation for a considerable percentage of prisoners. Wherever we are dealing with such sublimations, prisoners are not content with simple shaving, i.e. they are not satisfied with shaving of the head and neck. Head, neck, face offer so many ways that enable the so-called "beautician" to extend his functions for hours.

The explanation for what happens here is to be found in the need to find some way of venting strong bodily feelings, which demand their satisfaction in one way or another. It may seem exaggerated, but it is nothing but legalized sexual activity, so to speak, that goes on under the watchful eye of the prison warders. I do not assert anything that is not plausible, but substantiate my claims with general experiences, and in places, my own. My heart certainly beats for women, and in my normal life I never stray from the path of natural sex, I know no deviation from healthy sexual feelings and forms of satisfaction. This powerful attachment to the feminine nature of sexuality, which is so strong that even in impulsive moments it is hard for me to give a man the so-called friendship kiss, has kept me clear of any temptation towards same-sex relations. Even in times of bitter sexual distress, in which I felt my willpower waning and temptation was gnawing into my flesh like an artful fox, I defeated every temptation and overcame it even when faced with people who had magnificent physiques and facial features. For all that, I often enjoyed a pleasantly satisfying physical sensation through a simple shave in custody, even though the barbers in the prisons are often recruited from rather unsympathetic people. Under normal living conditions in freedom, the functions of a barber are utterly inconsequential to me, but in prison I yearned for them, because a certain satisfaction was involved. But not satisfaction in the sense that I found a sexual-psychological sex satisfaction as the barber went about his business, the sort that one longs for, one seeks. The whole business was nothing more than bodily satisfaction. In normal life, this demand of nature is met with "simple" caresses, for which there is ample scope in the interaction between man and woman, without thereby thinking of the specific bodily stimulus areas and functions: the whole process of sexual intercourse. The yearning for bodily feelings, this caressing of some body parts, has nothing to do with infantile-sexual functions, but is a natural phenomenon as old as humanity itself.

Prisoners try to obtain these physical satisfactions for their feelings by other means. For a long time, I had been unable to grasp the reasons why prisoners who did no work and were by no means dirty received several baths a week and had their backs scrubbed. I said to myself: back-washing can serve a purpose for people doing dirty, greasy and dusty work that makes them sweat so that the dirt sticks. But even in such cases it is not absolutely necessary to have your back scrubbed; this is especially unnecessary if you can lie in hot water in a bathtub and have enough time to let the dirt soften. In addition, with every normal person, your arms grow long enough to be able to reach just about any part of the body, if that's what you want to do. In pursuit of my assumptions I once again concluded that sexual sublimation is also going on in this case. Of course, these actions are generally outside of sufficiently specific admissions or even confessions. But that does not make any difference to the fact itself. There are also prisoners who freely and openly confess that getting their backs washed has an almost sexual satisfaction. In several cases I was told that back-washing, in conjunction with the hot water lapping the body's sexual organs is the only way the prisoner is able to achieve ejaculation, whereas all other attempts failed. One prisoner who told me this was a sensitive person, who otherwise felt sexually normal, but could not achieve any satisfaction at all, even though his sexual urges demanded satisfaction. He was embarrassed by the process, and those who washed his back did not know he had ejaculated. This prisoner was not prescribed spa treatment or baths; he had the opportunity to go to the prison hospital to bathe thanks to his own ingenuity. This ingenuity does lead down paths that can end up with a punishment of solitary confinement. This prisoner led a sexually hellish existence before he got opportunities to ejaculate. He had to pay dearly for these opportunities; he not only gave up his weekly rations, but also his monthly purchase, so he had to eat dry bread if he wanted to keep his bathing appointments. The *kalfaktors*, who are the potentates in prisons, are insatiable in their demands.

These are a few examples of the better type of forced sexual hygiene. I know that some are trying to refute such claims, which I am grouping around these phenomena, with the remark that these observations are eccentric. Well, what some want to refute, without being able to come up with empirical facts, others whose judgement is more reliable can confirm. Here too Mühsam, in his lecture to the Institute for Sexual Science about "The Penal System and Sex", puts his finger on the keyword. He emphasises:

> "In the Niederschönenfeld fortress, about 30 to 40 men between the ages of 17 and 60 depended on one another in a narrow space for years. Attractions and rejections arose, close relations and jealousies. The need, not so much for sexual activity as for physical closeness, for tenderness, was insurmountable. People who had always felt normal fell under the spell of impulsive deviations they had never noticed."

The report of this lecture in *Vorwärts* very rightly remarked: "The prisoner material of Niederschönenfeld fortress was somewhat different to that in jails and prisons. Nevertheless, what he reported and confessed, gives rise to gruesome conclusions about the sex life of the inmates in prisons and the psychological torture that the people there endure." One also thinks of the case described in the following example by Wilhelm Pinnecke (from Honnef) in a newspaper article in the Cologne *Sozialistische Republik*:

> "As I had to hear, to my amazement, this poor woman sought and found her sexual satisfaction on the way by periodically reporting to the prison doctor, claiming that she was suffering from abdominal pain, so that she could gain satisfaction during the medical examination at the touch of her private parts by the physician."

2. Pseudo-homosexual forms of gratification in the dormitories

According to prison regulations, each prisoner can only be held in solitary confinement for up to three years; after this it is only with his agreement. Or so it says on paper, which in practice does not mean much. However, in the light of the regulations the administration of a penal institution must, for good or for ill, first allow the prisoner into communal custody after three years, if the prisoner in question claims this right. The word "first" inserted here should refer to the exceptions which the prison administration may make in special cases, namely when the placement of one or more detainees in communal custody appears to endanger them. However, this measure is very limited, because with a population of 800 or more prisoners, there are usually no more than 50 to 100 cells in prisons, so for this reason alone the prison administration cannot pursue either the one principle or the other in a linear fashion. The power of circumstance thus forces the prisoners into communal detention, even against their will. Communal detention is necessary, and solitary confinement in cells is the exception that comes into effect when there is "danger ahead" because of the refractory behaviour of one prisoner or another, or in order to grant an exceptional privilege which is not granted to prisoners in communal detention. But most prisoners also want to be in communal custody, because the individual cell, which is too short, too narrow and too low to be able to stay in it constantly, depresses the prisoners to an intolerable extent and kindles psychoses of all kinds. This oppression intensifies where the windows are closed; the windowpanes are often completely opaque, but generally speaking opaque for half of the casement, inhibiting any view. (Looking out is forbidden and punishable with isolation.) Of course, sexual torment must increase further in such a cage.

For this reason, the prisoners perceive communal detention, given the prevailing circumstances, as the lesser evil; a communal detention in which a hotchpotch of different human species comes together. Prisoners who are highly sensitive are held here together with those of a gross or raw nature, men who are not restrained by even the most elementary moral concepts, while others have moral ideas and try to assert these sensitively and even hyper-sensitively.

Concessions of all sorts are unavoidable, also in areas where they become a burden on the conscience or destroy the inner self. A prisoner who has studied this milieu better than I could personally, gave me the following information on the topic:

"I was strengthened in my conclusions by the behaviour of former children in care establishments, who are almost invariably in the deepest swamp of moral neglect. I've really looked into some abyss, I've wallowed in the swamp right up to my neck, so I had hardly expected to encounter anything new. But I did encounter it. The care children fall into the hands of bigots, perverts and sadistic teachers and clergymen during their adolescence, are guided without the slightest attention to their individual psyche and naturally fall into all vices. The descriptions of lifestyles in educational institutions for neglected children that I have heard would be regarded as exaggerated or entirely fictitious by any outsider. But I believe them, and moreover the reason I don't doubt them is that my daily observations confirm them. The sixteen to twenty-year-olds escape from these institutions or are dismissed as 'reformed' and then almost invariably fall into the hands of homosexual elements. Craving for material pleasures completely rules them; the necessary funds are procured using unscrupulous methods. They land in prison and set the tone here as a compact group. In spite of their corruption, they are the least in conflict with the house laws – a consequence of the hypocrisy stirred in them since their earliest youth, which, through completely false views on good and evil, only preserves the appearance of external modesty, whereas the inner man decomposes more and more. This is the true product of the education system of 'correctional facilities' and prisons."

In this milieu, sexual functions are not suppressed, but they are performed in all their forms under the gaze of others. Some perform them while others watch. Society, however, is surprised at the corruption of people, outraged by this "fornication" and takes a moralizing delight in this hideous object of reflection. This moralizing is more hideous than the "fornication", because no other option is available to its subjects. For none of these moral guardians cares about how prisoners, who are held incessantly for years in such "communities" without having the chance to be alone for a single second, are supposed to "satisfy" their sexual instincts. However, some prisoners sometimes find ways out of their oppressive situation. They intentionally commit acts that result in punishment in arrest cells or other forms of isolation. Or they behave in such a way that communal detention is disrupted and so-called "order and discipline" can no longer be maintained. Then they go into solitary confinement and here they at least find, at first, the hour that they have been longing for after years in despair and ambivalence. But only a few seek and find this way out, because such prisoners do not generally regard it as a way out. Some are afraid of the brutal nature of punishment, while others cannot tolerate the isolation. He who is isolated stays isolated; he is completely prevented from dealing with other prisoners, and he finds himself buried alive in the grave of his narrow cell.

Just as one recognises a bird by its feathers, you can recognize from prisoners' language whether they have a congenital disposition or are acting under a certain compulsion. There is a phrase that is very frequently used by the inmates of penal institutions: "Just get yourself a sweetheart with two balls!" Anyone can recognize from this sentence that it is not the language of a truly homosexual person, but the language of people who, in their basic nature, have no predilections for homosexual intercourse unless they are prevented from having sexual contact with the natural objects of their desire and affection.

No homosexual sees a figure of fun when he imagines the object of his satisfaction; rather, he sees an object which in his own way, he not only does not profane, but also puts on show. No homosexual talks of a "sweetheart with two balls"! In the judgement of such things one can assume: Ordinary people constantly turn the sexual into a verbal dung heap; one can easily fall into the world of dirty jokes, which draws on everything sexual, one can go there where two rough individuals converse in filthy *double entendres* and yet cannot find any explanation for the words: "Just get yourself a sweetheart with two balls!" Mühsam said the following about the sexual problem in prison in his lecture to the Institute for Sexual Science:

> "In various groups of prisoners, who found each other according to their predilections, dirty jokes became the most popular topic of conversation. Even those with the most chaste natures could not resist this infection. Their sense of shame was lost. The most intimate things were shamelessly revealed."

During my investigations I found out that in Sonnenburg prison there is a hall called the "brothel room". But that did not begin to explain things to me, because it is such a generalized phraseological expression that the outsider cannot properly imagine anything at all. I tried to get some positive information about the "brothel room". Unsuccessfully. I only knew that Sonnenburg prison, along with other pretty furnishings, also had a "brothel room". I tried to investigate what went on at Sonnenburg prison through a later acquaintance with a prisoner who had come from there. The prisoner said: I did not sleep in that room; I slept in the dormitory next door; it did not look any different here than in the brothel room, because everything looks pretty much the same in all prison dormitories. Everywhere I've been, you get the same picture.

In the further course of our acquaintance, I then received the following comprehensive written report about the goings on in Sonnenburg prison with regard to the sexual functions in certain milieus:

"The prisoner is admitted to communal detention. His way of life is radically different here. He sees and hears men talking, he is spoken to, he answers, he breathes out. Soon this becomes home, insofar as this term applies here, and he soon finds his 'friend'. A harmless conversation ends, almost without exception, with the question: 'Where are you sleeping?' 'Dormitory 2!', Well, that suits me, that's where I sleep!' Of course, the newcomer is so enthusiastic about so much friendliness on the part of an old 'lag' and he looks for a place as close as possible to the newly won friend in the dorm.

"The arrangement of the dormitory differs from one prison to the next. However, it is done in such a way that most of the beds can be viewed by the warders. If there are more than 10 prisoners in a single dorm, the light is left burning through the night. A large part of the sex life of the prisoners now plays out in these dorms. The attentive observer will find truly shocking examples of how the prisoner seeks to free himself from his miseries. I will pick out a few from a huge number.

"Around 7:30 in the evening the dorms are locked, and the prisoners are left to themselves. More or less lively conversations take place. The day's events within the prison are discussed – but the main topic of conversation, which is inexhaustible, is women. The tone of the conversation is in accordance with the moral level of the majority of prisoners. Gradually it gets quieter, here and there prisoners whisper mysteriously. I observed two prisoners, one of whom was sitting on the edge of the bed in which the other was lying. It seemed as though they were busy discussing a book that they were holding. At the same time, the hand of the sitter was under the blanket, whose rhythmic rise and fall allowed me to guess what the hand was up to. After this the active participant went to his own bed. This scene is repeated every 5 to 6 days.

"A bed is creaking somewhere. Unobtrusively, I observe. My neighbour, two beds down, is lying on his stomach and making movements as though engaged in coitus. His partner is the mattress.

"Over there is a prisoner who proves his abilities every night as a masseur. On request he massages arms, legs, chest, back, shoulder. This happens also in the workroom under the eyes of the warders, seems perfectly proper and all the more so, as the people being massaged also include those who need to rub in medically prescribed ointments for rheumatic complaints. Upon cautious questioning, the 'masseur' admits that this touch provokes a feeling of pleasure and brings gratification. His 'regular customers' partly admit to feeling and achieving the same gratification; others deny it.

"At one time structural changes were being made to the dormitories in Sonnenburg prison. Beds were therefore temporarily moved to one large room under the roof. Here I witnessed goings on that shocked me to the core. The prisoners were in possession of women's clothes, underwear etc.; items that they sought out from the rags, sometimes in a completely dirty state, sometimes in the condition that a woman normally has under her shirt and trousers. Almost every evening a 'tarts' ball' took place. Some dressed in the aforementioned underwear, stockings etc.: Apache dances[55]

---

[55] The Apache dance had nothing to do with the native American tribe; rather, it comes from turn-of-the-century popular Parisian culture and was thought of as an

and the like took place, then with the help of bed-clothes, alcoves were fashioned where inflamed passions could be given full rein. Despite my permissive attitude, I felt disgusted because all of these actions lacked the discreet and natural note that is characteristic of the pronounced homosexual predisposition; but on the contrary, this was a conscious surrogate, which the violated instinct simply demanded, and which degenerated in the restricted atmosphere of this milieu. This clearly demonstrated the way in which prisoners are infected. Prisoners who at first held back or were indignant soon relaxed, took a liking to these activities, and in no time were in the thick of things, to be the first to take part on evenings that followed. Sucking of the penis seems to most prisoners to be the most harmless way to satisfy sexual instinct. After I had already served three years in prison, I persuaded a younger prisoner, formerly a child in care, to grant me this 'courtesy'. It then happened immediately on the toilet, but it awoke in me no desire for repetition whatsoever. In return, I paid him my monthly lard ration of about 80g. After three days, I realized that the obliging prisoner had already given 'blow jobs' to most of the nearly 100-man strong station. And these included people who otherwise shunned all company. But the opportunity was too good to forego.

"The couples seek and find, despite all the measures taken by the prison management, ways and means of 'union'. Entering the toilet in twos is prohibited, yet despite the warders' attention, I have met many a couple in the 'most intimate' embrace. But you also find things out by other means. Thus, I observed a case where the partners slept in solitary confinement and

---

enactment of a violent discussion between a pimp and a prostitute.

only met in the workroom. The warder kept watch over the toilet in order to catch any 'smokers', but he missed the other thing; he had not even been briefed on this. Even in this environment the prisoner knows how to help himself. One sat at the table, apparently working, while the other kneeled under the table and performed the reciprocally satisfying 'courtesy'. In this respect I want to emphasize that sleeping in solitary confinement, or in bunks, whereby every bed is encircled with a partition, does not succeed in keeping this curse under control. There is no lack of resourcefulness on the part of the 'rogues' as one official once complained.

"Here I am describing another, particularly peculiar situation that, however, does not lack a comical aspect. One night I am sitting on my bed reading, when I am called. Someone is asking for my help. I go and see that the person concerned has introduced the handle of a hand brush about 20 cm long into his anus and was now making futile efforts to remove it. After some experimentation I succeed and as cause of the problem I find a rag, which is tied down onto the handle. This later turned out to be a woman's trouser legging."

The so-called bunks in the large dormitories have the purpose of isolating prisoners. Apart from the fact that it is simply brutal to force people to get into a coffin from 6:30 p.m. to 7 a.m., this isolation provides absolutely no protection against substitutional sexual activities. Prisoners find ways around this – even if they have to perform them directly under the eyes of the warders. But even inside the bunk-house acts of sexual compulsion and substitute functions are by no means prevented. A prisoner provides me the following account in this regard:

"In Luckau the dormitories were divided into so-called bunks, so that everything was directed towards masturbation. That was only how it seemed, however. The prisoners bored holes in the bunk frames, through which they could stick their members. In this way so-called blowjobs could be performed. This could only happen if the partner slept in the neighbouring bunk. But generally speaking this is easily arranged."

When I came to Luckau a few months later, I found that these statements were true. Prisoners unfasten the wire in the bunk and then go to their partner; others open the lock to the bunk door and can then get out of the bunk by quite "legal" means.

In a conversation with a fellow inmate, I incidentally learned that the wing with the cells was once again home to a number of "grooms", some of whom were already under isolation arrest. This news stunned me all the more as I had previously had no sexually oriented conversation with this prisoner.

An inmate reports from penal institution W.:

"When I take a leak at the urine bucket in the night, someone asks me over the shoulder in whispered tones: 'You! Let me hold it!' When I asked why, he gave no answer, but went to his bed. The next day he said to me: he only wanted to have fun, if I wanted to do him a favour, he would give me his weekly supplementary allowance."

Every type of sexual activity that goes on, which I am not able to enumerate exhaustively here, is "paid for" with fat, margarine, cheese, sausage and similar items. Anyone who has monetary or other equivalents pays and thus obtains the opportunity for a kind of "special right" to be able to make requests of a "more valuable" kind, so to speak.

In penal institution G. a prisoner told me:

"In the dormitories, 'music' and 'dance' were commonplace in the evenings; other games, such as *schinkenklopfen*, [56] U-boat, trains etc., were popular and had a more or less sexual element. The invention of

---

[56] *Schinkenklopfen*, which translates as ham-knocking, was a children's game, which involved guessing which of your friends had smacked you on the bottom.

new games knows no limits, but there is a certain sexual release in all of them."

Games involving movement, as in our example, are variations of dances, and run along the same lines. And when one looks at the *schinkenklopfen* game played by prisoners in the large dormitories, one involuntarily compares it to spanking pedagogues, for whom caning children brings sexual release and relaxation.

The other types of games in such communities ensure a certain level of mutual bodily contact of the body to work off sexual tension in a manipulative fashion, as I showed in the first chapter of this section, that is to say disguised substitutional acts for the satisfaction of the sexual instinct.

In view of this way of life among the prisoners, is it really tenable to maintain that prisoners bring all of these sexual forms of activity with them into penal institutions; is this voluntary homosexual activity, that does not grow out of enforced sexual denial? We have already established how unjustified such a hypothesis must be, without dwelling on the subject. We always relied only on more or less abstract assertions, which of course could not provide a final verdict. Let's now make up for that.

A prisoner, who had a great deal of experience behind him, without being embarrassed to recall it, gives me the following description:

"I entered into these relationships without ever having learned about this kind of sexuality; I could not get used to it. Three young people, who came to the dormitory with me almost at the same time, fell into homosexuality. The dorm had a complement of about 80 men. Among these there were perhaps five genuine homosexuals and 60 who practised homosexuality only under duress, as I established based on subsequent observations. Almost all long-term inmates had a 'hot streak', as homosexuality is referred to in its various forms. In the cell I have struggled to come to terms with such sexuality by thinking things through, but I have not progressed any further and I have now spent seven years in detention. If I had not become an onanist, I do not know what could have happened – nevertheless I have no disposition towards homosexuality. But that alone does not provide protection, as I saw later, because young people who are disgusted at attempts by others to seduce them through homosexual advances (which in most cases is to some extent violent) have in many cases become prostitutes. They sought to capitalize on their shame and their fall.

"These forced homosexuals do not hate women; on the contrary: they yearn for female company. The character of these people's morality is shown by the following: two of my associates were from Charlottenburg. They already knew each other on the outside. One had been a prisoner for three years, the other seven. Here in prison they had formed a habit of homosexual intercourse and were often together at night. Their relationship came to light in their conversations. Both were engaged at the time of their arrest and received letters from their fiancées. The two of them excited themselves about the preferences of the fiancées, often debated and got into arguments over this, read the letters together and yet were – 'homosexual'. If they talked about being faithful, they admitted that they could not be expected to live in abstinence, but woe betide if they were to learn such things: 'Then it's over!'

"From July 1923 onwards, I went back into communal detention. There were five of us. Here again there were two men who practised homosexuality under duress, who also lived together. One was married and the other had a close lady friend."

Moreover, the withdrawal of all stimulants, such as tobacco etc., as well as the shortage of food for a number of prisoners, creates the basis for sexual coercion, as an inmate from the penal establishment St. testified with the following report:

> "In May 1923 I came to Luckau and was accommodated in communal detention. The cots still existed, despite repeated riots aimed at getting rid of them. In one dormitory I met a man who could be had by anyone regardless, young or old; all that mattered was that he was paid well (tobacco and food rations). Even though he had become 'homosexual' only under duress, he now exploited the homosexuals in the most ruthless manner. Toilets, corridors etc. were used for these acts. His nickname was 'Trumpeter Hans'."

Another prisoner shared the following with me:

> "In one dormitory it was so bad that 'sweethearts' were mutually exchanged. I myself saw a young person wander through four beds in one night."

The outsider is unaware of the extent of the pseudo-homosexual intercourse among female prisoners. Here, too, after years of deprivation and attempts to repress urges, the participants are no longer content with simple forms of pseudo-homosexual intercourse. According to the reports that I have received, women get together in groups of five, eight, ten persons and find satisfaction only in the most unusual orgies. If they are beyond this stage, then they also resort to instrumental aids in large communal detention. They make artificial penises, strap them onto their body and thus offer the partner a substitute for a man. Even this form of intercourse does not only take place between two partners, but also sometimes with voyeurs present or as group sex. A prisoner told me about a woman who after a while could only get satisfaction when she was being taken in the vagina and the anus with artificial penises by two women simultaneously, while she herself satisfied others with her hands and mouth. When this group is finished, the artificial penis is passed on to another group and the acts of sexual gratification carry on from group to group.

Unless you have very limited horizons you will already

realize that this business is not entirely without problems. The ructions that have already become usual are no more than "quick-fire justice" between prisoners. There are outbreaks of jealousy or insulted shame. In this penal system the following applies: one does not think about the prisoners' human dignity and self-esteem; one does not consider the sum of unspeakable suffering that is stacked up here. After all, prisoners who are still governed by ethical powers have a right to be isolated from an environment that robs them of moral breath. You cannot forever be content to breathe in a foul stench when you need fresh air. Of course, even in freedom, nobody is fully protected against harassment or insults from sick or degenerate people. But you can avoid them; you do not necessarily have to live with them. What's more, such conditions are lost in the mass of the population; they are more rampant in dens of iniquity, which no one is obliged to enter. By contrast in penal institutions such degeneracy, nourished by impossible living conditions, is concentrated within a limited circle of persons and is played out in confined spaces; it cannot be overlooked with even the most short-sighted eyes. Prisoners are forced to live in this environment; they then bear the costs of explosive mental states when they can no longer endure the outbursts of people who have been brought out of equilibrium.

I know that proper medical health officers will stand up and 'confirm' that they know nothing about the fighting among the prisoners being in itself a result of sexual repression. It would only be possible to rebuke them definitively for this if they were to be reluctant to grasp, theoretically, the interdependencies. If you do not hear about these goings on, that's understandable. No prisoner betrays the real causes of such brawls; their strong mistrust towards the doctors, which they cannot put to one side, prevents this. I will allow prisoners to speak up about their own experiences:
The first report of this nature:
"In autumn 1920, I was taken into communal detention

for a short time and got to know the worst effect of enforced asceticism, which is: enforced homosexuality. I was young, and in good physical shape, and as a result I had to endure all sorts of requests, the last of which led to an attempted assault at night while I slept. Because I was physically fit and had excellent strength, I was able to defend myself. I mauled one so much that he needed to be treated in the prison hospital. After this I had peace and quiet. I had earned respect. The horror of these conditions, however, caused me to go back into solitary confinement."

The second report:

"It was only possible to prevent real rape thanks to the intervention of some level-headed people. I know that this often comes to the attention of prison management. Inquiries are then ordered but mostly do not lead to any result. People keep quiet, and any informers would suffer unpleasant consequences."

I myself once had to intervene to prevent such acts of downright rape, that they were trying to inflict on a sixty-year-old man, who had been repeatedly been caught in masturbatory acts, which he often indulged in without having the proper opportunity for this. The man became the object of coarse ridicule and mockery.

The third testimony of another prisoner finished with the words:

"You must, however, not assume that prisoners condone these situations. There are often enough complaints. On the whole, however, the situation is tolerated, or else it would otherwise lead to hatred and malice, and to fights. These men who practice homosexual acts under duress are capable of anything, if they get bothered over long periods. In 1920, while in G., I experienced a case in which a strong and lusty homosexual, who was otherwise peaceful, stabbed himself three times in the lower abdomen because his sweetheart refused to sleep with him. The reason for the act was kept secret by the partners."

Here is a fourth description of these situations:

"The pairs who find themselves, and whose relationships often last years, do not tolerate infidelities by their partners. Thus, such a relationship once had a tragic conclusion. A young prisoner, whose business was very profitable, had extended this business to the 'sweetheart' of a 'lover' who was known to have a violent temper. The latter stabbed him in the chest, which brought him to within a whisker of losing his life."

That this milieu also creates dangers of a criminal nature was confirmed to me by a prisoner with the following case:

"There is, for example, a prisoner, an exceptionally strong person, whom I already knew well in freedom, where he had not the slightest inclination towards homosexuality and only had a very limited sex life with women. Here, however, he incurred two punishments of six months for assault. Motive: Jealousy! He himself expressed the opinion that the sexual instinct, which hardly touched him in freedom, put him under a lot of strain in prison; then he looked for a pretty boy and 'to hell with anyone' who got in his way."

3. Functional fetishism

There is some fetishism in every person. One has a special love for his wife's hair, another her eyes, another is enraptured by her breasts, and yet another by the shape of her legs; one man likes to see her in an apron, another in sandals or high heels, one man is spellbound by her mouth, the other by the shape of her ears, this man likes free-flowing long hair, that man prefers pony tails, and that man over there is enchanted by bobbed hair. These are all varieties of fetishistic inclinations and everything depends on the way they are activated. But the situation is entirely different with the kind of fetishism under discussion here, which produces the well-known linguistic dirt in the large dormitories, doing much mischief among prisoners. Prisoners who were unfamiliar with such things and who did not even suspect that they existed, and who brought no disposition towards fetishism with them, learn about such business in practice in prison. This fetishism is in no respect spiritually constructive, but only destructive; people in its grip degenerate. It has nothing to do with the harmless mild forms of fetishism, which are an expression of falling in love with parts of the object of one's desire, a fetishism that does no harm to anyone. But protecting people against the degenerative fetishism practised in penal institutions is a matter of moral cleanliness and for public policy.

I first learned about the way the fetishists operate in communal detention or in the dormitories from a short note:

> "When receiving a visit from his bride a fetishist always had her deposit a urine-scented handkerchief with him. Another possessed some of his wife's pubic hair, a third had a piece of cotton wool soaked with his wife's menstrual blood. Another, in order to achieve some sexual satisfaction, got his wife to send him soap, with which she had already washed; and yet another possessed, as a 'holy relic', his bride's lacy underwear."

That's the point of view of a prisoner. Prisoners have more and more items with which they satisfy their sexual urges.

Speaking to a prisoner, I mentioned things that I had learned so far about what fetishists get up to in the dormitories, whereupon he remarked:

> "Oh, there's really nothing special about that. They are just boring everyday events. If you want more material on the subject, I can give it to you in such abundance that you simply could not handle it. But I want to tell you something particularly unusual. In penal institution L. I learned the following: In a state of totally overcharged sexuality, a prisoner persuades his wife to bring him chewing tobacco, which she should first put in her vagina. The woman does just that, marks this chewing tobacco, and packs it up specially. The prisoner comes back from the visiting hour and starts dancing around in the large dormitory. Although he still had other chewing tobacco, he gives a stick of this especially 'prepared' tobacco to another prisoner, to a second and a third; he draws the three of them into his 'trust', i.e. he reveals the secret to them. That has the effect of a burst of lightning; it gets lively and before long the entire company of this dormitory is chewing the especially 'prepared' chewing tobacco. The prisoner had cut and given away five sticks of tobacco in a matter of minutes, doing the very opposite of what every real fetishist would have done with this stuff: namely, using it himself in a fetishistic fashion."

When I remarked that people who do not practise any sexual deviations would also be unable to relate to such stories about chewing tobacco, he clarified things to me in this way:

> "Prisoners who had not chewed chewing tobacco in their entire lives were the most intent on getting this kind of stuff, and prisoners who, to my certain knowledge, had practised no kind of sexually perverted deviations in their normal life were the most voracious in

their greed for this tobacco. This action shows us once again that we are not dealing with natural fetishists. For no true fetishist dirties the objects of his sexual gratification, as happened in this case, nor does he show it off before the eyes of others. I myself picked up a few fetishistic tendencies in prison, perhaps I had them in my normal life, but they never actually surfaced. In a situation of imprisonment, in which my hunger for sex was so unlimited that in my thoughts I literally gobbled up my wife's genitals with my mouth, I tormented myself unsuccessfully with the attempts to bring my member into my mouth, in the effort to still my sexual hunger, at least to some extent. This lack of success then drove me to get a bundle of my wife's pubic hair, which I've owned for years now, and that no one has ever seen nor will ever see, and which I worship like no other thing in the world. Because it gives me a certain amount of satisfaction. You are the first that I have told about this and will probably remain the only person with whom I speak on the subject without holding things back. What always disgusts me about the whole business of the fetishists is their vulgar profanation."

Infection is the darkest chapter of all. It is well known to the administrative organs of the penal system. Some of them, in dealing with the things that go on, refer to the structural defects of penal institutions. Most, however, make the mistake of championing rigid isolation policies. They do so because prisoners in solitary confinement are, of course, easier to handle and govern than prisoners in large dormitories, where the one leads the other astray.

The following testimony from a prisoner illustrates a typical example of such risks of infection:

"When being transported I was accommodated with several prisoners at the police headquarters in H. and stayed there for several days before the transport proceeded. At first, I was in solitary confinement and had the opportunity here to speak with a woman who was responsible for cleaning the corridors and stairwells during her detention. We often chatted through the cell door. Naturally, we soon came to the subject of sexual frustration. I moaned, the woman moaned even more and then exclaimed, among other things: 'It's worse for us in the end, but we can certainly do more to help ourselves than men, and we do just that.' She then went into details, which astonished me.

"In H. I myself had a secret love, who had meanwhile learned of my presence, came to visit and brought me copious amounts of food and delicacies. As I went up the stairs from below, the woman came to meet me with the tenderest caresses. The moment of our remaining unattended was too short for us to be able to progress from caresses to actual sexual intercourse; the duty sergeant came, and I was now admitted into a communal cell. There, I was of course welcomed with a loud hallo. And whereas today I can sit in the biggest communal detention with a huge food package without giving much of it away, I did not manage to do so at the time: I still had a sense of solidarity and compassion. So, I sat in front of my food package and cut a large sausage into slices. Suddenly, this spectacle presented itself to me: all 10 or 12 prisoners crowded over to the 'spyhole', whose disc had been removed. I saw a finger pushed through from the outside but ignored this because I assumed the prisoners were pushing something out or otherwise joking. Finally, I was done with my sausage-cutting, got up and unconsciously went to the spyhole. Only now did I realize what was going on. The prisoners were taking turns to suck on the finger of that girl I already mentioned. I regarded this as a quite harmless game and way of passing the time and finally also joined in, quite automatically, and sucked the finger. Only now did I notice what was happening: the girl first stuck her finger in her vagina before she pushed it through the spyhole. The smell and taste confirmed this. I realized that all of them got into a certain ecstasy just after tasting the 'sample': one of them ousted the other, a very bad situation arose, which almost ended up with a brawl."

I objected that it was impossible to hold imprisonment responsible for this behaviour. I received the following answer to my objection:

"Listen, I'm well-read in this area, was involved in many investigations against sexual criminals. What's more, I can correctly judge what happened here, because I also pushed around in pimp circles and got to know the life of the pimp – at least I lived with whores and therefore I do not only know a lot of sexually abnormal phenomena and goings on but pretty much all of them. As far as what was going on here is concerned, that was certainly due to imprisonment. Because the critical fact here is that everyone took the finger in his mouth and sucked on it. It would have to be a very strange coincidence if it is to be assumed that this random motley crew of 12 men in a cell had already practised such sexual acts by nature. You cannot assume this; the opposite has to be true. For you see, hear and feel such things; especially when such sexual acts have been practised before, as happened here. In not one single case was this normal practice. I assert that of all the prisoners who gave themselves to the game with the girl, not a single one of them had previously indulged in these sorts of sexual activities. It is noteworthy that a prisoner of about sixty years, who had served nearly 12 years in prison, started this. Everyone got a certain gratification; at this moment, the prostitute was for us the most lovable girl that had ever come our way."

I will provide another example to show the power with which prisoners' sex drive erupts after years of oppression or being led astray. A political prisoner related the following to me from his prison:

"The prison also housed a steam laundry that washed not only the prisoners' clothes but also those of the officers and their families. The ladies' underwear caused strong sexual excitement among the prisoners in the laundry. They gathered all the hair from every single item of unwashed laundry, such as shirts, trousers, stockings, and bound together into small curls. Other prisoners then secretly engaged in a lively trade in these curls of hair. Snuff, chewing and rolling tobacco, bread and other foodstuffs were the exchange currency. The demand for these locks of hair was so great that some 10 to 20 packets of snuff were exchanged for them. Prisoners who got hold of the locks did all sorts of things with them. A few cases were reported to me about prisoners who put these hairs in their mouths while in bed in the evening, achieving the most intense sexual ecstasies in this way.

"One prisoner had especially fallen in love with the underwear of a daughter of one of the prison's officers. He rhapsodized about the unknown girl day and night, even though he had never even seen her. One day he wrote a long gushing love letter, which he then put in the ironed and folded laundry. The daughter showed the letter to her father, who then raised a complaint with the prison governor. The 'sinner' was punished with isolation arrest. This brought the matter to the attention of the Attorney General, who decreed that women's lingerie should no longer be washed in the prison laundry."

The Medical Health Officer Lumpp writes in the prison officers' newsletter, *Blätter für Gefängniskunde*:

> "I once observed fetishism in the way that prisoners send each other their pubic hair with corresponding drawings."

4. Sexual acts during collective transport

The concentration of highly charged sexual feelings often explodes in prisoner transport vehicles, which are generally overloaded. Doors remain unlocked, but the prisoners are chained up. Female prisoners are allowed to place themselves in the middle row of the van, make friends here and make themselves available as sex objects. They are ready for anything, either to satisfy their own needs or out of pity for the prisoners. A prisoner writes this to me on the subject:

"In August 1919 I was transferred to G. in the transport van. In Berlin the transports were brought together at the police headquarters. Ten to twelve men and women were accommodated in the police vans that we had to use. I got a seat between two women who were being transferred to S. One was about 30, the other 19 years old, and I was 23. I was attracted to the 19-year-old. Her horror and regret at the length of my sentence was quite genuine. It is probably not surprising that this mutual sympathy, as a result of long abstinence, turned into sexual excitement. We touched and felt each other; more was not possible because of the others. The women had found a lover for each of the four of them. In the prison transport train carriage, the women were accommodated in the corridor because the cells were needed for the men. They went from cell to cell making contact. The 19-year-old was in front of my cell most of the time. It was open, though I was still in chains. We could join hands through the gap etc. When we parted in S. she had tears in her eyes. The last thing she said was: 'The punishment would be easier for me if I could stay with you.' Since punishment means vegetating as a result of the lack of experiences, such events stay with you for all time and create certain excitement in their remembrance."

However, it also comes to actual sex acts. A prisoner who was sentenced to eight years in prison and who served the sentence to the last day, gave me this report:

"In February 1922, I was taken to K. in a transport van and had to spend the night in the police jailhouse M. I entered a cell that was already occupied by three inmates. The cell was the usual small single overnighting cell and was dark. The police jail made a depressing impression on me. There were only a few rooms and they were all overcrowded. Noise came from all of the rooms. We sat on a straw sack that was lying on a bunk because there were no stools available and the cell was too small to move around in it. We were telling each other our news when suddenly the door opened, and a female person was admitted to us. A warder said: We want to put you in here as they are the quietest and also seem to be the most sensible!

"The woman was Polish. She spoke broken German and was drunk. We greeted her with a hallo and received her. It was dark. The lantern in the courtyard only let in a faint glimmer of light through small, high-up windows. However, even the smallest cell has room enough for the greatest sexual sorrow! Sexual intercourse then took place between the four men and this one woman."

Here we have shown an open wound, a running sore which must necessarily infect the people who are forced to live in such an environment. Chastity, moral taste and such things are quite dubious concepts here. If necessary, people with a serene nature may be prevented from getting involved in such degeneration, but those with less strength of personality are subjected to such temptations and must be subjected to the worst sexual distress in the prevailing circumstances. Everything is understandable, everything forgivable. What is unforgivable is that the preconditions for this situation are due to officialdom. A warder, whom I informed about this incident, said that such incidents are not a daily occurrence. That is a very dubious excuse. Is it necessary that the venting of sexual frustrations must always take place in the ways that it has taken place here? There are a hundred ways that it can take effect. If, in the present form, it really does not turn out to be a daily occurrence, then it is a question of a special occurrence, the effect of which is also not annulled by putting a fig leaf on it. After all, the question is: can this form of release of sexual frustration become effective as a kind of daily occurrence? That would require prisoners constantly to have the opportunity for it.

Of course, in most cases sexual release takes place in other forms. Just imagine yourself in the predicament of a prisoner who has an intense sexual drive, who has already spent more than five years in prison, and who then suddenly finds the opportunity to perform a normal sexual act. He will do it and will not even shrink from doing it when it must take place in front of the eyes of strangers and in an ugly form.

With regard to sexual pairing I am weighed down by a few inhibitions, I have already shown with a few examples that I was inclined and disposed to exercise discipline over my urges in the most trying circumstances; I am also of the opinion that the physical act of love of two people does not tolerate the gaze of onlookers, of spectators. Nevertheless, it is at least doubtful to me whether, after six years of dissatisfaction in my sexual desire, I would have succeeded in remaining sexually passive if, after such a long time, I had been offered such an opportunity to have normal sexual intercourse. Self-control, aesthetic sense, entrenched morality and such qualities become a house of cards in the face of the wild storm of sexual lust as it assaults a person detained in custody.

Another transport experience was conveyed to me in the following description by a prisoner who had already served 15 years:

"I got to know a woman on a transport, with whom I enjoyed real orgies. She came to my door, the usual questions were posed and answered, until she learned the length of my sentence. Sexual contact was made immediately; she initiated it herself, without coming across as unsympathetic. I feel and touch her, she likes it; however, I want more than simple caresses. But how could it be done, where everything was to be reached through a gap in the doorway about 5 cm wide? And then the surroundings: behind me sat a prisoner who had already become a beast in prison. He had already made his presence felt with the words: 'Carry on, I see nothing, I'm asleep'. Our actions were being reflected, so they could be observed in other cells. Apart from this, the woman was situated directly within view of the warders. Now, as I could not reach the objective any other way, she turned her back towards the crack in the door so that I could pass my hand through the back of her dress and touch her vagina. She stayed in this position for about an hour, during which time she came three times. My girl liked this game, but I could take no further pleasure in this way; I wanted to see something while the girl wanted to satisfy me in turn. But how? I racked my brains. Finally, I found the following solution: I proposed to the girl that she go to the lavatory and turn the dress around so that the slit was at the front. The girl did that, and pulled her knickers down, so that I could reach all parts of her body from a more comfortable position. We now took turns satisfying each other in the hours from 3 in the afternoon to 1 o'clock in the morning. I managed to ejaculate around ten times, the girl came more than 15 times. My fellow inmate, who sat behind me and had uttered: 'Carry on, I see nothing, I'm asleep', was not asleep though, but rather hustled over after a while and declared, categorically: 'Now I want a turn.' And he got on with it. I myself was exhausted; the girl, who was out of her wits, did not even notice the change. If the transport had not ended, I would have broken down the door and fallen on the girl: no officer could have stopped me. For weeks after this experience, I was completely exhausted and mentally not of sound mind."

I told the prisoner that such debauchery is not typical in detention, but common among some people. This statement caused him to tell me more about his married life, which also showed him in a different light. He told me:

"My God, I know what I am and what I did when I could live normally. I lay in bed with my wife, we teased each other like children, we performed headstands in bed and got up to all sorts of high jinks, without any sexual emphasis, for months we carried on with these high jinks, without joining together sexually. What I did here in the transport van was a consequence of detention. For once I was overwhelmed by a very cold calculation that told me: now you have the opportunity – use it! You don't know if such an opportunity will present itself again in the next 15 years. But then: what else are you going to do from morning until evening in such a meat wagon? I would imagine that I would have hanged myself in the cell if sexual distraction had not offered itself."

I expressed the opinion that such goings-on would be impossible, given that the girls are segregated, and the doors are locked. He rightly answered me:

"The first cannot be applied at all, because the transports are usually overcrowded, the second cannot be strictly applied, because otherwise any collective transport would turn into a ruckus. Acts of violence would be on the agenda, the sergeants would be constantly harassed, so that they would not get any peace at all and would deviate from the rules, even if strictly forbidden. They would adhere to the regulation for eight, maybe fourteen days, then break it and put the doors back behind chains. If, instead, the female prisoners were to be completely isolated from the males and locked in separate cells in the transport vans, then the cells would have to be repaired after every transport that carried females: the male prisoners would drill or carve holes in the wall, they would remove the boards in the side walls, if they knew women were present, and they notice soon enough if female prisoners are sitting in the next cell. It would only provide much more convenient opportunities to engage in sexual intercourse, because under these conditions it would be possible, and the majority of women would in most cases get pregnant.

"However, the transport attendants have no interest in such a rough situation: some leave the female transport prisoners outside, because they want to flirt in some form with them – it may also come to further activities; others leave them outside, because they secretly observe the goings-on; a third set leave them outside because they are aware of the sexual needs of the prisoners and do not want to make gratification any more difficult."

I have received a whole lot of descriptions of sexual activities in collective transport vehicles. Let me provide just one example of this sort. It concerns the story of the prisoner who refused to take part in sexual intercourse on his first transport and did not do it because "others were present". But after many years in prison he was able to do so, despite the presence of others. He reports:

"In 1921, I went by transport to H., spent about eight days in Berlin police headquarters and then went on. Here, I got to know the film actress H.V. She was on the aisle of the transport van with another two women. Since the doors were open (on chains), the women could talk to everyone. H.V. Must have liked me, because she conversed with me and after an hour, I knew her fate. She had been in custody for nine months, a sensual girl, and soon she turned to the subject of sexual deprivation. When she heard about my sentence, of which I had served two years, she exclaimed in horror: oh, she would go crazy, no one can endure such a long period! Then she was so sweet to me, out of pity, that I was stimulated and felt her through the crack whilst she pressed against me. It caught the transport leader's attention; he came to look, because he could see nothing from there. Of course, he could not notice anything further, as I had seen him coming. But from now on he stayed close, spoke to us and suddenly said quite impulsively: Kids, if it were up to me, I would put you together in a cell. I can understand how you feel but I cannot allow it; it could get me into hot water! Nevertheless, we managed to touch each other again and again: the excitement was strong. My cellmate, a prisoner on remand, looked out of the window as soon as he noticed our closeness; he had plenty of tact and understanding. Time flew by for me and H. V. and we were in H. much too early. And now came the most exquisite thing of all. As it happened, a vehicle with shared seating took over transport to the prison. The women got on board first and I followed as the first man, then the others, but in such numbers that we had to sit close together. It was dark, and in order to find room, H.V. sat down on my lap. When my excitement was so strong that she felt it, she went into action. We performed the act, which satisfied both of us fully, without the others noticing. This first natural release of sexual arousal during detention gave me a physical and mental refreshment that lasted for months."

The remark, "without others noticing" is certainly a "white lie", an expression of some self-consciousness and shame. He cannot possibly seriously imagine that he could have sex in a shared transport with the woman, without the others noticing that, according to his own information, one was on top of the other.

4. "Sex offenders" in prison

I will illuminate with just two examples how the State, as an alleged law enforcer, drives people to despair and into a moral quagmire.

I have taken the following factual statement from *Vorwärts* of 31 January 1926: A 32-year-old man, intelligent and hard-working, spent half of his life behind jail and prison walls as a result of the effect of his sexually abnormal predisposition. As a child he was severely beaten by a "pedagogue"; at the age of fifteen, he was punished for the first time with a year in prison. The first link in his chain of destiny was forged here, which is to say: If this man had spent half of his life behind bars by the age of 32, his time in freedom as an adult was very short. In each new case that brought him before the law, he asked to be examined by a sexology researcher. This request was not granted in one single case. With the following letter, which I took from *Vorwärts*, he finally turned for help, in his deepest desperation, to the Reichstag deputy Löbe.[57]

> "It is impossible for me to keep sexual urges under control. I know perfectly well that if I fall again, I'll be punished with a long prison sentence; I fight these urges desperately, I do not want to do it, but then comes the hour when I lose all energy and unwillingly surrender to my unfortunate animal instincts. I feel that all good will, all moral awareness, all fear of prison disappears; I am dominated only by the thought of satisfaction. I know that I am sick, I know that my condition is contrary to nature, and for this reason I feel innocent of the crime that I will be charged with in the upcoming trial. I deeply regret that I committed the crime, and I also regret that I am in the world at all, because I live only for myself and am a burden on the whole world. My

---

[57] Paul Löbe (1875-1967) was an SPD deputy and later President of the Reichstag.

nature makes me so unhappy that I have been thinking for a long time about putting an end to my life."
An actual suicide attempt failed but brought things into flux. Dr. Magnus Hirschfeld, who had previously been denied access to the prisoner, was now able to visit him. The prisoner was considering castration. Dr. Hirschfeld, who only rarely gives his consent for this, decided, in consideration of the circumstances, in favour of a surgical intervention; a ray of hope for the prisoner. But he had to wait. Even before the trial, the chairman of the court, a district court judge, brusquely stated that the prisoner would first have to serve his sentence before he could be operated on.

Thus, a person commits acts as a consequence of his sickness, which the law then punishes with imprisonment. After fateful experiences he arrives at the conviction that he can escape his agony only by means of castration. He demands it. The castration is not carried out. The unfortunate man is condemned and, with the pathological predisposition against which the law and judges allegedly want to protect the people, is moved to prison, where the illness may continue to grow and may take on worse forms than it would in normal circumstances. When one day another catastrophe occurs, the man will once again stand before the court; the fact that his unnatural urge is now directed in prison against male objects will not protect him from a new punishment. One almost wants to believe this is a piece of satirical whimsy, but it is the picture of a tragedy, this abduction of human beings, which is cynically carried out as an expression of so-called law and order. What matters here is not punishment but rather the power of nurturing and healing. We should never punish people for their sickness; no sickness can be healed with "punishments". I know that citizens, especially those with a rigidly conservative mentality, who see absolute meanings in "morality" arising from the supposed "character of their social life" are already very upset at the thought. But this does not help, in fact it is irrelevant, unworthy of further consideration, because there is no rational argument that can be used against official hypocrisy. We know, however, that moral precepts are also changeable, just as everything can change in the evolution of the cosmos and that these moral precepts undergo their transformation for clear reasons.

The sexual deviant cannot be made responsible for his illness; certainly not if he is sent into prison, where he must certainly suffer and become "guilty" once again.

That such a person, whose letter shows that he has moral ideas and such a high sense of responsibility towards his victims and humanity, had to be castrated, is a terrible indictment of society.

The typical circumstances of the Gerth trial shall provide us with a further basis for scrutinizing the current state of things.

Gerth, a police officer with the Berlin *Schupo*, had murdered two women in the heat of sexual passion and had to answer for the crime before the jury court in Berlin.[58] Before the case came to trial, the defence had requested lengthy observation in a public mental asylum. However, the two court doctors, Professor Strassmann and Dr. med. Störmer, declared the accused to be of sound mind and that a longer period of observation in a mental asylum was unnecessary. Nevertheless, at the first hearing the court decided to place the accused in a public mental asylum. In the second hearing, several official and private doctors unanimously declared the defendant to be of unsound mind. In his plea, the state prosecutor treated the psychiatric reports extremely lightly, according to *Vorwärts*. He used the unscientific term "senseless drunkenness", wanting thereby to disprove the scientifically based assessment of Berlin's most renowned doctors. He explained that the experts are victims of the mischief of psychological empathy and a

---

[58] The *Schupo* (Schutzpolizei) was the uniformed police of most cities and large towns.

cheap sentimental attitude towards even the most vicious crimes; he appealed to the sovereignty and sound common sense of the judges. No expert is required to judge the gravity of a crime committed in a state of intoxication, he maintained; one's own life exper-ience suffices.

On the proceedings the day before, this prosecutor quoted Goethe: "All theory is grey, dear friend, but the golden tree of life springs forever green". He considered the accused to be sane and demanded recognition of his criminal responsibility. According to this logic, he should have been found guilty of murder.

The prosecutor nevertheless qualified the double killing as a double manslaughter: "The general public will not understand it if the court succumbs to the temptations of pity and, contrary to genuine German feeling, does not refer to manslaughter as manslaughter. Internment in a mental asylum affords no protection to society. The defendant himself demands atonement. Twelve years in prison, taking into consideration two years and three months pre-trial custody, and ten years of loss of civil rights would be enough to atone for the wrong done." The attorney Dr. Frey then began his plea with the words: "The prosecutor's speech was legally outstanding, while outdated in terms of criminal policy, and judicially brilliant, while wrong for Gerth."

The court withdrew to take counsel and announced the following verdict: Gerth had committed his crime in a semiconscious state and was to be acquitted. However, as a mentally ill person who presented a danger to the public, he was to be handed over to the local police for internment in an asylum.

Why did I describe these things in such detail? Because if the court had not followed the advice of the medical and psychiatric experts, but rather the direction of the prosecutor, then Gerth would have been sentenced to 12 years in prison. And if it had pronounced the death sentence, then Gerth would not have been beheaded as things stood, but the sentence would have been commuted to lifelong imprisonment. By doing so they would have sent the seed for moral weeds to grow in the prison, where they multiply, shoot up, expand in their extent, and put down deep roots; thus, *ex officio*, they would have sent the living germs of mental illness into prison, thereby believing that they had fulfilled their humanitarian mission to the full.

According to the Reich's Statistical Yearbook, there are around 7,000 so-called "sex offenders", i.e. people who have been convicted of sodomy, rape, etc. in German prisons, of which there are around 1,000 adolescents alone.

No one who seeks to judge things properly, and to evaluate events objectively, will hold the prison system responsible for conditions over which it has no control. But as long as society unconscionably adheres to harsh laws and never even undertakes the possible reordering of things, so long as it is too malicious and misanthropic to be able to undertake a change of principle, it is to be held responsible for the effect and spread of all pathological states, especially where this concerns people with a healthy and normal sex drive who are sent to places of incarceration. Does the penal system want to bear responsibility for the fact that these people, who are not separated, and cannot be separated, establish objectionable relationships with other prisoners and maintain these for years on end? Simply because there are not enough cells, those prisoners who are still halfway sexually healthy must witness sexually abnormal obsessions; the reciprocal interaction of this milieu must create a substructure built on the duress of sexual misery suffered by prisoners, a substructure which then supports every sexual abnormality known to the science of sexology. One must think through the consequences when we have people before us, who at the age of 20 or 30, that is to say, in the prime of their lives, are put away in prisons for years. You cannot simply put this off for business as usual with a light shrug of the shoulders and words that show cold misanthropic incomprehension: "They will satisfy their urges by the easiest means!"

You can only understand the horror in all its consequences if you have experienced how 30, 40 or 50 prisoners, or ultimately the entire prison personnel, witness and become intimately acquainted with all the goings-on between homosexuals. "Love letters," which such prisoners write to each other, become the reading matter for all prisoners.

In the penal institution W., the so-called head cook, who ruled in the kitchen, allegedly covered his member with butter, which he then had licked off. I am weighed down by a sense of responsibility and do not like to publish things where it is necessary to write: "allegedly"! That said, there is plenty that should be spoken about openly, and nowhere more so than in prisons. Moreover, in this case it concerns a prisoner who was sentenced for the crime of rape. And although I go about my work in a scrupulous manner, the word "allegedly" gains importance in this respect. In addition, a prisoner once said to me: "Even if there is much talk in prisons and the most distorted travesties of the truth arise and defamation is a popular pastime, in my experience rumoured information on sexual activities is mostly factual."

The situation with the head cook, who, as a convicted rapist, was placed in a position where he could become "well provided for" naturally opened up dangerous perspectives given the prevailing circumstances.

If there are two, three, four, five or more sex offenders in the prison, they chat about their "offences", they revel in the enjoyment of "memories" in connection with the events that three, four or five years previously brought them, finally, to prison. They wallow in their own degradation, incest and child abduction; the "exchange of ideas" between sex offenders takes place in the presence of whole groups of prisoners who are in the worst sexual distress, who are already on the way to committing crimes of rape and greedy for the "experiences" described and abnormal pursuits.

I once entered the bathroom of Brandenburg prison and

met the *kalfaktor*, who was holding a "conversation" with five other prisoners there. In all salaciousness and down to the last detail he was describing how he had raped girls aged 7, 13 and 19 years old. Wanting to eavesdrop on the conversation, I went out to the corridor of the prison hospital. What I heard in the next ten minutes or so shook me to the core. When I opened the door, I surprised the six, who were engaged in sexual acts that they never even stopped when I entered the bathroom. Finally, I forced an interruption. They wanted to bribe me with foodstuffs so that I kept quiet about the incident. When I was then left alone in the bathroom with the *kalfaktor*, he produced a large number of drawings showing men having sex with children. I later found out that the five prisoners mentioned had been convicted of rape, child molestation, etc.

5. The impact of the repression of sex life during the World War

"As a psychiatrist I am totally unaware of the psychoses occurring during the war being attributable to the sexual abstinence of combatants and prisoners of war. I have read nothing about this, nor have I heard or seen anything about it. This is a very vulgar assumption of conventional medicine."

The reader will probably assume that these words were composed by a typical prison chaplain who set himself the task of rebutting prisoners' sensory desires from the prison pulpit. But that is not the case. These words were spoken by a district doctor who served in an official capacity as a medical counsellor. This outrageous assertion by a psychiatric doctor, which has no basis in science, is of such stupid ignorance that it can only be understood when you know for certain that this is a deliberate lie emanating from officialdom and an arti-ficially constructed "sexual science" that does not stand up to any serious scrutiny.

This district doctor said that he had learnt about psychoses, but that these were so-called war psychoses rather than sexual psychoses.

If we are examining these utterances by the district doctor, we are doing so first and foremost for the following reason: they provide a basis to draw parallels, comparisons. For the circumstances under which wartime servicemen were forced to practice sexual abstinence or grossly control their sexual urges with massive force can be compared with the circumstances under which convicts have to cope with their sexual impulses.

Let's pose a couple of questions. During the war, was there no so-called hinterland, back home, in which all kinds of sexual psychoses appeared? How does this medical official explain, in its entirety, the situation of the women and girls who were not at the front – and yet were undermined by psy-

choses? Do these also come under the heading of war psychoses? Is the whole sexual-moral decline during the war in the
hinterland not a typical symptom, and a massive indictment,
of these sexual psychoses? Did every man with feral impulses
not find in the sex-hungry women and girls willing and cheap
and weak creatures during the war, in whose mind and body
there was just one motive force: Sexual satisfaction! Oh yes,
they were all satisfied – and how!

Is the percentage increase of prostitution during the war
just a testimony to material distress, even if a downright terrifying one? Or is it not at the same time a testimony to sexual
distress? The criminal inspector Gotthardt Lehnerdt writes in
Dr. Ludwig Levy-Lenz's *Sexualkatastrophen:*[59]

> "The World War brought a surge of the noblest feel-
> ings, of devotion and sacrifice, but it also brought into
> the daylight, like the gliding wave of the sea, the ani-
> mals of the deep. Misery and sorrow stood defenceless
> against rapacious lust and rampant pursuit of pleasure.
> The excitement of the senses awakened drives that
> were hidden and dammed up. The more ferocious the
> drumbeat of 'death', the more piercingly screamed out
> the cry of: Life! Life!
>
> "Thus, the vaunted 'purification by steel'[60] became
> the furnace of the senses, and as always in times like
> this, since time immemorial, sex drive has risen abrupt-
> ly. Misery broke iron, and gold broke misery.
>
> "Prostitution opened its doors and took millions of
> women and girls from all countries into its sultry gar-
> dens, where an army of crazed men greedily waited."

---

[59] *Sexual-Katastrophen: Bilder aus dem modernen Geschlechts- und Eheleben.* Leipzig
1926. Dr. Ludwig Levy-Lenz was an early pioneer in sexual science and a close
collaborator with Hirschfeld.

[60] In conservative circles the term *Stahlbad* (literally, steel bath) signified
purification and strengthening of the state through warfare.

The army of "crazed men" was composed of men on leave, who, often separated from their wives and children for more than a year, were let loose, with the manners of the front, on people in the hinterland, together with the army of those unfit for service.

Are all the marital tragedies that occurred during the war, as bloody evidence of sexual breakdowns, therefore manifestations of high spirits, or are they manifestations of psychoses? Anyone who dares to object that he does not recognize the causes of psychoses when an entire army of degenerate children exists as living witnesses to sexual distress and the psychoses associated with it, not only offends people in their distress, but offends the human race in its entirety, wreathing it with a crown of thorns in ridicule. And anyone who has not recognized, even in the theatres of war themselves, sexual distress as a cause of psychoses, and in particular among prisoners of war, has wandered deaf and blind through the world and has forfeited his receptiveness and ability to absorb impressions in the knacker's yard of official lies. Does it not seem simultaneously monstrous and yet altogether typical, when a combatant writes to Hirschfeld: "Previously my wife was my right hand, now my right hand has taken the place of my wife?" Truly, experiences and events that occurred during the war, in which millions of people, who practised none of the functions that give life meaning while in the very prime of life, and who were caught up in the organization of moral degeneracy and the determination to destroy human life, all of which was decorated with medals and "badges of honour" and otherwise bore the stamp of every formal protocol, these experiences horrify, and will horrify forever; they have only one explanation: they are only products of psychoses whose cause was sexual distress.

Also horrifying are the innumerable cases of prisoners who sat behind barbed wire and wire fences but saw the free play of clouds, the heavenly canopy, as the roof over their heads. By this I mean prisoners of war, who, despite everything, were ruled by the strongest psychoses, even though they otherwise had relative freedom of movement and some possibilities for satisfying at least the most elementary necessities of life. They were shut off from the world behind a fence that constricted them and trimmed their wings; they were constantly looking down the barrel of a rifle or at pointed bayonets – but they could still carry on with the most vital functions. Above all, they could associate with other people. For, "everyone will admit that man is a social being. We see this in his dislike of solitude, and in his wish for society beyond that of his own family" (Darwin).

Of course, prisoners of war had all of that. They were able, amid the deepest grief that can ever oppress man, to associate with others who were also suffering, thus achieving some relief from their own pain. But the fact that they could not satisfy their sexual drive naturally made all the alternatives fatuous, made them physically ill and weakened their nerves, turning them into highly strung beings reduced to the existence of mere creatures. The massive violence turned against sexual urges, the constant suppression of healthy sensual lust necessarily led, in this climate, to the destruction of everything characteristic and noble in humanity, to the destruction of normal human aesthetics. For "the hopelessness of all attempts by the ascetics follows from the fact that one cannot separate man from the rest of the organic world, without him ceasing to exist as a human being. But in the living world, the very phenomena of sexual life form the axis around which life as a whole revolves" (Nemilow). But even more is known: the concrete form taken by phenomena of a sexual life that has been turned off. The violence done over many years to natural human functions and the body's organic circulation, and the suppression of man's strongest instincts over many years, did not create the soil for the accumulation and storage of a spiritual force; desire did not throb in the ardour of hope that fulfilment could be found if not today, then tomorrow or the day after, it did not succeed in creating the soil for cultivating and intensifying proclivities that would find their fulfilment in human love – in the form of sexual acts, by means of which two separate beings mutually impart spirit, well-being and beauty to impregnate and pro-create; rather, it created the soil in which all degenerate kinds of perversions formed and grew as catastrophic "natural phe-nomena", i.e. commonplace daily phenomena, clumped to-gether, which turned the very source of feminine aura into a puddle of decay, drowning out all the delicate tones of female symphonies with the timpani and trumpet sound of shrill brass music. Nothing remained of that steadfast and unbreak-able soulful devotion that is governed by the natural law of the sexual instinct, which fulfils everything, begets everything and extinguishes the fire of lust, which kisses dry the fever of sexual ardour and turns humans into the marvellous creations who move mountains.

The suppressed lust of years flowed into the swamp-life of the military base during the war. This is the context within which sexual repression enveloped itself in the garb of "poet-ry", in which perversions took shape and form. The orgies in this swamp gave the "poetry" of those perversions their tone. And the snake in this swamp, with its filthy poison, not only rules the "uneducated and unpolished" recruits, the ordinary riflemen, but, to a much greater extent, that privileged layer, according to whose snarling jargon human beings only begin with the officer class. As far as the lower strata of the squad were concerned, they were not injecting powerful primal mat-ter but poison into female bodies, bodies which meant no more to them than a lifeless, fleshy mass bedded on straw. Admittedly, the degenerate noble in officer's uniform, who lived like a wild dog transplanted onto the plush upholstery of official and private harems, did not have to stoop to such manners.

The officer literally hacked his way through female flesh, but he did this out of view. Those who want to look behind the scenes can read Wandt's *Etappe Gent*, the book that is an unsurpassable mirror illuminating the inner life of the "cream of society". Hardly any wonder that Wandt later had to serve a term in prison for this exposé.[61] Meanwhile, this reflection has been given further depth with the publication of Hans Otto Henel's *Eros im Stacheldraht* (Freidenker-Verlag GmbH, Leipzig-Lindenau). In this book Henel publishes some 17 résumés of life and love in the course of 236 pages. Only 17! These 17 could easily be turned into 700,000. But these 17 stories of life and love suffice to illuminate the impact of repressed sensual lust. He who does not want to recognize any sexual psychoses when presented with these wartime reports must logically regard everything that flowed from a seemingly insatiable sexual hunger as quite normal phenomena, including all the abominations. But these are far from normal phenomena. For under normal conditions, this extent of sexual hunger is unlikely to appear even in places noted for the dance of degenerate orgies; in the palaces of Chicago, for example, where girls who have not yet reached maturity are raped and forced into prostitution by millionaires, or in the night clubs in Berlin, where respectable provincial uncles practice their "naturism", as they call it.

When Poincaré sent his band of soldiers to the Ruhr, he could not put the infantryman's female partner in his rucksack.[62] He therefore attached – figuratively speaking – a sut-

---

[61] Heinrich Wandt (1890-1965), author and publicist, became Clara Zetkin's private secretary at the age of 19. Wounded early in the First World War he was transferred to desk duties with the field headquarters of the Ghent section of the Western Front. He kept a diary, extracts of which were published by the left-wing *Freie Presse* in Berlin. This earned him six months in prison, allegedly due to a confusion of names, but at the same time all of Wandt's experiences were published in *Etappe Gent*. The book became a best-seller in Belgium and Holland as well as Germany. The second volume, *Erotik und Spionage in der Etappe Gent* became famous for its "self-censored" dust jacket by John Heartfield. 1928 Wandt was charged with high treason and imprisoned in what was termed Germany's Dreyfus Affair, but was later released under pressure from the Belgian public.

[62] Raymond Poincaré (1860-1934) was the French Prime Minister who ordered the occupation of the Ruhr to force German payment of reparations in 1923.

ler's wagon to every regiment equipped with its own openly sexual apparatus. This is indeed an example that shows the moral level of bourgeois society, but it is also an example that cannot be bettered, and, there is no way to prettify this: it shows the importance that even the authorities assign to human sexual functions. In the Ruhr district, the regimental staffs of the Zouave army transformed these mobile brothels into well-supported, militarily protected, state-licensed, sociologically conditioned and ideologically encouraged sex shops. I am tempted to encourage the Prussian Ministry of Welfare, which is fully in the know, to publish an exposé over this business, if it has the courage to do so. The prostitutes, who were unable to control the business arrangements, got to know the strange ways of Eros, some of them perhaps even halfway original, though it is safe to assume that they were not entirely inexperienced in this field.

But the goings-on in these military brothels were the consequences of excess sexual tensions that were seeking relief, and these found their way into the forms that the situation allowed *faute de mieux*: relief was just induced in the mechanical nature of the camp brothel, driven on by the military machine.

It is no reproach to Poincaré and all of those, both here and there, who are ideologically identical, because what we observe here are the reflexive effects of bourgeois ideas of life, basic aspects of bourgeois life, which are incapable of organizing people more ethically and leading them to a higher moral order. But the leaders of the Ruhr occupation certainly did not intend to idealize the brothel or stir up the waves of sexual degeneration as a matter of principle, to threaten and coarsen forms of sexual gratification; rather, they considered the quasi-militarized brothel as perhaps the lesser evil compared with the incalculable dangers that flow from the forceful repression of sexual instincts.

And what did the German army command do during the imperialist world war?

"NCOs and units that want to visit the brothel in Havremont Castle must always contact me. Visits always take place by brigade." (Henel, *Eros im Stacheldraht*.)

That was during the imperialist war in the French zone. The sergeant was a German sergeant, the column was a train transport from Germany's "glorious legions". A printed order of the German High Command read as follows:

The following fees apply for sexual intercourse:

In the soldiers' brothel:

2 Marks (2.50 frcs) to the girl

I Mark (1.25 frcs) to the Madam

In the officers' brothel:

4 Marks (5 frcs) to the girl

2 Marks (2.50 frcs) to the Madam

I quote a life and love story taken from Henel's *Eros im Stacheldraht*:

"The thought of 'women' and simultaneously, escape from danger for a few hours, was enough to inflame our stupid brains and to ignite our blood, which had otherwise long since become indifferent. I scarcely heard any smutty jokes that evening and during the night, but I certainly heard words of such abysmal bestiality, compared with which even a Rabelais would seem like a cooing parlour dandy. When shame has become a redundant emotion, and the mind has been killed by the insanity of the battles at the front, sex drive remains purely anatomical and is not even ennobled by sensuality. It is reduced to a means to satisfy a need.

"The next morning, we marched, twenty-five strong, led by three NCOs, to the half-ruined Havremont mansion, where the front brothel was housed. There was fairly lively traffic in front of the house, and I think there must have been about fifty soldiers there.

"'So how many cows are inside?' our sergeant asked one of the group.

"'Ten of them!'

"We had to present ourselves individually to a medical officer in the basement, who examined each one of us for venereal diseases and handed us a tube with protective ointment ...

"We were expecting to find a brothel like in the big cities, where you can choose the girl that suits you in the salon. But that was out of the question here. After receiving the instruction that no woman should be made use of for more than ten minutes, we had to wait in a room, and from time to time the cry was heard: Next!

"After three-quarters of an hour waiting, it was my turn. 'Room number 61' the NCO called to me, and I stumbled up the stairs."

In view of these facts, it does no service to the German High Command and gives them a resounding slap in their face, when medical officers, usually an adjunct to militarism, still declare: Nature does not dictate that the sex drive requires satisfaction! It would imply that the German High Command was frivolous and cynical, and with all the full-bloodedness of a military-official unscrupulousness encouraged the shamelessness that spurred on soldiers and gave them the opportunity to do something that has nothing to do with natural health and purity. But this is how contrasts emerge in an ideology and worldview that has no logical bases and in which the most natural relationships are torn asunder. With a disgust that cannot be surpassed, I followed in Henel's *Eros im Stacheldraht* the dialogue that took place between the first mayor of a city in the lower Rhine and a messenger of the Belgian military command. The messenger from the Belgian occupying authorities delivered, in writing, the commanding general's request to the mayor, saying that "the city should immediately set up a designated house, currently inhabited by a patrician family, as a brothel for the occupying forces." According to Henel, the mayor was fuming after he had read the order. In his anger, he hoarsely screamed:

> "I will not shake hands on this even if I am held prisoner. The morality of our women and girls is already endangered enough by the constant presence of predatory soldiers. Shall we now deliver the strongest and perhaps final blow to German morality by opening a house of ill-repute for today's fortuitous military victor?"

In view of all this arrogance and ignorance on the part of a German mayor, the sergeant preserved his dignity and answered, with a superior smile:

> "You probably wanted to say, a house of joy. And, in any case, Mr Mayor, after this house has been opened, the morality of its women and girls will be less subject to temptations. Soldiers have needs like all other men. If the soldier sometimes has to get satisfaction by means that are less beautiful than those available to the civilian, it is only the special circumstances that are unfortunately to blame."

Mayor:

> "No, and twice no! Tell the General that I would sooner go to jail before I allow the morality of our city to be placed in the gravest danger as a result of a military dictate."

The sergeant coolly and objectively raised the question of where the mayor was during the war, and with pride and pathos the mayor declared: I was civil governor of one of the departments conquered by our victorious armies in France!

> The messenger:
>
> "Tell me honestly, Mr. Mayor, when you were there, in the enemy's country, did you ensure that the morality of the population was not violated by the then victorious German soldiers?"

"I believe so – and in any case – the war was on at the time –," answered the mayor. The Belgian messenger underlined his embarrassment by making a logical point:

"Given that we are occupying your country, that is still the case today, even if it now has a different name. At any rate, there were soldiers who had need of women and who got, in the way that soldiers do, what they needed."

The mayor slammed his fist on the table: "God knows, we were as humane as was possible. Germans are culturally so elevated that they cannot be other than humane. And again – I refuse to comply with this scandalous order."

That the German is so culturally so elevated that he cannot be anything but humane, is banal. Or should I quote all 236 pages of *Eros im Stacheldraht*, should I tell you about the sergeant or sergeants who violated delicate children in Galician villages and locked up those who wanted to prevent such atrocities in the fortress? They called these children "young meat" and claimed a right to this "young meat, that they would have paid for", and furiously took the children, who whimpered in their pain, before passing the objects of their lust to the next man with the words: Changing of the guard! Is this still culture that is expressed in the words: "We'll talk later. If you want to amuse yourself – the dirty minx is lying there. By the way, she's terribly stupid. *Bon appétit!*" Shall I describe that Bacchanalian lustfulness from the Café Leonidas in the main town of the sector, where a student corps in officers' uniforms came together in boozing and whoring?

If we already felt the need to be fair about other nations, we should also be fair towards German militarism; perhaps it would be more accurate to say: we want to act in a good-natured and objective way, considering both the one example and the other as they are: typical! If we make an effort, under the most extreme compulsion, to gain some sympathy for the forms of sexual satisfaction that German military personnel used under duress during the most abysmal genocide in conditions of desperate sexual distress and psychoses, then it is clearly only fair for us to say, like that Belgian messenger: soldiers have needs, like all other men. If he sometimes has to get satisfaction by means that are less beautiful than those available to the civilian, only the special circumstances are unfortunately to blame. And for the protection of the "German soldier in enemy country" the words that the Belgian messenger used in his defence take on an especially valuable meaning: at any rate, there were soldiers who had need of women and who got, in the way that soldiers do, what they needed. And if the mayor of that city in the lower Rhine then thinks, "after years of the unavoidable, we have to let morality and human civilization return in honour", then this is only typical for those deluded layers of society who see the mote in the eye of another, but not the beam in their own. As far as the sexual aspect is concerned in this connection, one thinks of all the "normal" capitalist dung pits that proliferate, "flourish" and "prosper" permanently: the capitalist brothels, capitalist alcohol, the capital that brings alcohol into consumption, namely the downright disgusting capitalist entertainment establishments of all kinds. Bourgeois ideology leaves no or very limited space for the creation of pedagogical institutes, educational homes, meaningful places of joy for the care of the worldly spirit and noble humanity, places of art, true work homes and social rest homes, because these produce no profit according to the typical bourgeois motto: Get rich! Only personal self-interest stimulates the "joy of creation"! Thus, where the meanest passions are disposed and organized, there is no healthy state that refines the instinctual life in man and awakens the yearning for cultural pleasures.

V. The interacting torments penalizing the convicted and the non-convicted

1. An observation

If I am not mistaken, the Chief Executive of the Plötzensee remand prison, Polenz, who is now an official in the Prussian Ministry of Justice, once uttered the following words: "Punishment does not affect the perpetrator in the least, but in most cases the unfortunate relatives, the women and children who are deprived of their breadwinners."[63] Polenz was regarded as a progressive element, who, as an official, makes up his own mind about what is going on behind prison walls, and who knows exactly how our current forms of detention affect prisoners. It is therefore incomprehensible to me how this prison governor can come to such a one-sided and flat judgement. Of course, in the case where man and wife are only united by power and the laws of money; there, where the wife only values her marriage as a safe port in the storm, where she will be well provided for, in that case it is *perhaps* the woman who is hit hardest by the punishment. She wants to be well provided for, whatever the circumstances. But this harshness is of less significance than the harshness felt by women who are inwardly at one with their husbands. I believe that in the overwhelming majority of cases, in which the wife has no inner relationship with the man with whom she lives, she is the one least affected by the perpetrator's punishment. Because it is easy for her to find ways around the situation and she is not burdened with inhibitions. She severs the external relationship with the man who can no longer provide for her. There is nothing else to keep them together. However, there are still some other difficulties that must be

---

[63] Plötzensee was a men's prison in Berlin's Charlottenburg-Nord district and a place of execution by beheading. In the Nazi era approximately 3,000 executions took place there, including many members of the communist resistance.

faced with such practical decisions; these turn on the question of whether the conditions are such that the woman can quickly land in another port as a "loyal partner in life". The time in which we live is inimical to this, but nothing more. Since this is simply an intimation of the basic tendency, we need not concern ourselves with the whole course of these circumstances.

The bourgeois social order, in which the machinery of law moves back and forth, makes the matter very plain and simple. Namely, in accordance with convenience and shallowness, it creates legal provisions that allow bourgeois marital arrangements to be broken in the chasm that is opened up by prison. But that is only an external form, not much more; it is a vulgar regulation of the one side of things that does not solve the problem itself, because it disregards all psychological aspects and bypasses those marital relationships or partnerships that are supported by a deep-rooted psychological and spiritual foundation. I am only highlighting a well-known fact, when I stress that most civil marriages are ruined when one half is punished with a custodial sentence. The bourgeoisie, however, fundamentally supports the view that monogamous marriage is sacrosanct. Or at least, so it declares. I do not want to critically dissect this point of view any further, as it practically dissolves into atoms and, in the most favourable cases, is little more than a paradox that provides cover for lies. But what is the wife of a prisoner, who is bound internally and externally to monogamous forms of sexual life, supposed to do if her husband is forcibly separated from her for many years? She can get a divorce and, logically, she must divorce if she is once again to be free to exercise her natural sexual functions in the context of the laws governing monogamy. But there are a couple of hitches here, firstly, because the wife of a man condemned to prison does not have the opportunity to get a divorce. A mere prison sentence is not sufficient grounds for divorce because § 1568 of the German civil code allows a divorce action only if the other spouse has caused such a profound disintegration of the marital relationship through dishonourable or immoral behaviour that the plaintiff cannot be expected to continue the marriage. A jail or even a prison sentence is, however, not synonymous in the legal sense with "dishonourable or immoral behaviour." Secondly, however, the wife of a convict who has grown together with her husband and who forms with him the kind of harmonious unity and togetherness that only death can put asunder will not be able to divorce, and she will not be divorced. A source of torment begins to flow here and expands into a stream of pain. But this only goes to show that the psychological aspect in such considerations cannot be simply turned off. And where one disregards essential laws and shoves everything down the slide of mere formality, this only reveals the psychoanalytical shallowness of bourgeois ideologies. And not only that: the entire edifice of dishonesty is set in concrete here; the victims of a diabolical social order have their inner being ripped out and polluted in a pointless manner. And now one thinks in this connection of the commandments issued by the Catholic church. Of course, Roman Catholics can get divorced in Germany, especially if they are subjects of the German Reich. However, this right, guaranteed by civil law, can be made illusory by the spiritual court that they turn to with regard to the sacrament of marriage. In Italy, Austria and Spain Catholics cannot get divorced at all. In Catholic jargon the following applies: what God has joined together, only "He" can put asunder! But it was not God, this phantom, who put these two people together, not at all; rather, it was a piece of tradition, a manifestation of the natural urge, indeed, a biological law whose forms change with the needs and growing maturity of human beings. It may be that the Catholic formula no longer has any meaning other than that of an absurd form of words; in general, it never had any other meaning than that of a brazen hypocrisy. But with all this, it is not entirely pointless to look at things from the perspective of those who take them very seriously. Catholics cannot really divorce. Where they do divorce, it has practically no meaning, and it should have practically no meaning, because the partners are only legally separated – "from table and bed", as German common parlance has it. They commit "a sin against God's commandment"; they pollute their moral code, prostitute their ideas, and ultimately take their "world-view" *ad absurdum* when they do the opposite and follow the necessities of physiological laws outside of their married life or their formal marriage. Now in theory Catholicism does not make friends with physiology and regards every physiological phenomenon as the irreconcilable enemy of the Church, because physiological phenomena are the keys to knowledge. The Church cannot tolerate knowledge, because knowledge spells its doom. However, that in no way changes the fact that physiological laws cannot be ignored. Biological science has already sufficiently researched the human race to recognize the physiological interplay in the human organism as a whole. But it simply cannot be belied that the human organism includes the sexual organs. And the regular functioning of the sexual organs with all their agencies makes the incomplete human complete. The psychic satisfaction of elementary sexual desire, however, means more to the woman than to the man, for "the organism of the sexually mature woman keeps a permanent balance between psychology and pathology, with a constant increase in the latter". (Nemilow.)

In this regard one reconsiders the entire complex of female characteristics and idiosyncrasies, looks into the deep source of all the complexities, thinks of the many processes of a special kind that fully concern the female. Nemilow speaks of a reflex mechanism of the brain, which is temporarily out of whack in such processes:

> "Translating this from the language of physiology into the language of everyday life means that all of a woman's actions in this period are different from those over the intervening years. The weakening and impermanence of the reflexes and their increased inhibition

at the time of menstruation means that the simplest habitual actions of the woman at this time bear the character of bondage and occur with a certain inhibition." (Nemilow.)

The quintessence: both suffer mentally and physically, but the prisoner more so, because his life is destroyed. He has to endure the loss of his freedom in addition to the physical and mental hardships and he has to come to terms with the everyday strains inflicted on him beyond the main punishment. The spouse of a strong partnership who continues to live in freedom can eventually defend herself (or himself) against the approaching elements of destruction, if (s)he is otherwise internally strong enough to do so. The prisoner cannot do this; he is rendered defenceless against the forces of destruction, even if he can mobilize such strong internal willpower.

2. Scenes of jealousy, marital tragedies and suffering in the visitor rooms

It seems that there are some prisoners who not only ask their wives, who remain in freedom, to practice sexual abstinence, as long as they are themselves in prison, but who actually imagine that their wives are abstinent because they say they are. In reality, the prisoners do not believe it, or else they at least live in a state of ambivalence, but they use various means of self-deception as a kind of narcotic to numb their brighter consciousness. I disregard such exceptional cases in which sexual abstinence is based on honest reciprocity, because both partners have weak or even the weakest instinctual tendencies of a sexual nature or else because there are other specific circumstances. Many moments play a role in giving people a certain sexual sensitivity, such as bad experiences, disappointments, moods and resentments. I have often had periods of subdued morale, in which I yearned for exclusivity and wanted to withdraw myself into a shell with my wife, so that the terrible disappointments people inflict on others should not continue to annoy us and disturb our peace. There may also be other cases in which the woman struggles with her instincts without seeking sexual satisfaction; for one reason or another she does not depart from the monogamous form of sex life. She wants to protect herself from "social ostracism", knowing that gossips can make life hell for the best of people.

I also regard such cases as belonging to the realm of exceptions. Experience has shown that they are so rare that they can under no circumstances bear the stamp of normal sexual life. Of course, such experiences are not numerically captured and pedantically recorded; even the Reich Statistical Office can give no information about it. Information about such matters is shared only individually and anecdotally.

In such cases as I have mentioned above, the preconditions for the aforementioned self-deception by prisoners are entirely lacking. But the environment from which I drew the exceptional cases is also very different.

Illusions, however, bring prisoners more or less out of moods that would otherwise devour them. They have the effect of preventing or at least reducing excesses in penal institutions. One should always consider, in this respect, the average and below-average human material in penal institutions. Remember, too, that the pronounced jealousy-instinct in these people is especially well-nourished in prison. Woe-betide the prison governors, the judicial bureaucracy and the legislatures if this self-deception, this illusion on the part of prisoners in penal institutions did not exist! It would no longer be possible to uphold so-called order in prisons, unless you put three policemen next to each prisoner! A game that would be far from cheap but would have to be practised and financed to bring the raging beast of jealousy among prisoners under control. What that means is well-known to the authorities, because they know that excesses can easily be unleashed in penal institutions. If the prisoners' self-deception did not exist, this self-deception in the face of regular experiences to the contrary, then the sexual functions of prisoners would have been long-since regulated.

If the wives, as dependants of prisoners, were actually to live in abstinence until the barred gates to freedom were once again sprung open, then – and I am also quite convinced of this – they would storm the jails and prisons. The insistence that you are being "faithful", living monogamously and mortifying yourself for years on end is a dishonesty. And it remains so, even if it is stated with full conviction. In reality the wives of incarcerated men, and the husbands of incarcerated women, have natural sexual intercourse in 95 out of 100 cases, which as a rule they keep quiet about or else totally deny. When you just look at these men in prison, it really is worth it. Because sex drives imperiously demand their rights, they will be satisfied, one way or another. And in this way sex drives are safely channelled, which makes it unnecessary finally to grant sexual intercourse to the prisoners.

However, in viewing these things I distinguish between deliberate lying on principle and the forced "white lie" to which women resort because they find it disturbing and unpleasant to communicate such things; moreover, and in most cases, they also suffer from the lack of an erotic vocabulary. In seeking a way out of such a dilemma, they become "diplomatic", they burden their conscience and then finally collapse under this burden, which is imposed upon them from the ivory tower of a far-flung and misanthropic bureaucracy.

I often get into a certain state of harmless satisfaction in conversations of a sexual nature, which I frequently conducted with prisoners unintentionally, often with a certain feeling of *schadenfreude*. Namely, when I could convince myself from such conversations, as was usual: the woman does not practice sexual abstinence, is unwilling and unable to live in a situation of murderous austerity, but the man assumes this to be the case and deceives himself into believing in this sexual abstinence. What you can observe in this way is outrageous. Men of raw violence, tyrants and despots *en miniature*, arrogantly take for granted all the rights that they do not allow women. These men want to be lied to, they must be lied to, and they are lied to if the women keep silent about their sexual activities and even deliberately deny them. What I say here applies to the average prisoner. I have even met prisoners of a political mentality, dressed in a "revolutionary garb", who turned out to be terrifying Apaches when it came to the erotic. These men, of whom I knew for certain that in their sexual life they were neither mentally nor morally bound to more precious inhibitions and limitations, embodied in this respect the self-righteous mania of wicked slave-owners.

The husbands get the shock of their lives when a woman begins to free herself from all the massive oppressions and is no longer able to be treated as a lifeless commercial object. However, the sexual revolutionizing of women will follow hot on the heels of the social and political revolution. Only then will womankind come to that beautiful dignity, which is today defiled by the raw property rights of men. To some extent women already confess with complete openness and honesty to a new sexual ethics, which takes into account their needs and biological requirements. The unhealthy, unnatural, inadequate and imperfect nature of our contemporary sexual ethics is clearly demonstrated by the catastrophic increase in marital tragedies of all sorts. Alongside marital tragedies that become public, countless so-called latent tragedies rage beneath the surface in their veiled ugliness.

These observations were necessary in order to win over certain personal groupings. Because it cannot be denied that one should make the life functions of inferior people easier, and for sure, one should not arbitrarily make them even more difficult. But a certain proportion of prisoners are inferior people. This is shown by the fact that on the one hand, they desire the regulation of sexual functions in prisons and refer to the withholding of sex as barbarism, but on the other hand, they pursue the same barbarism against their women when they ask them to practice "abstinence" during their detention, i.e. to abstain from any normal sexual life. If these prisoners were generous of spirit, they would have to draw the only conclusion from the torments of their own unsatisfied sexual needs, which is that they should not impose these torments on their wives. Moreover, prisoners who enter prison with higher intrinsic values soon lose them when in custody, sliding down to a certain inferiority of character. One can therefore say without exaggeration that every prisoner deviates from his better qualities over time.

After these preliminary remarks, come with me into the visiting room of a jail or prison. What plays out here is absolutely tragic; but it is also often on the borderline of breaking through any normal behaviour. These are symptoms of marital tragedies, which are already brought into prisons from the start, and where they are nourished by prison conditions, ultimately leading to catastrophes. This is the root cause of murder and manslaughter.

The outsider cannot judge what is going on here as he does not know the true circumstances. The supervising officers, who must be witnesses to these scenes, are able to pass judgement. Many are only forced to be witnesses against their will, whereas others are excited by such scenes; they even enjoy watching such visits. They sate themselves with the pain of the women and the vulnerability of the prisoners, who are thrown off balance and behave accordingly. In some cases, the woman travels to the jail where she gets a few mental slaps, and sometimes even a real beating. When I once casually asked the first chief sergeant at the penal institution L., why his room was divided by a grille, he replied to me with the following:

> "That too is necessary, because if the husband wants to hit his wife and it comes to physical assaults during visits, then I can shove the man through the door and protect the woman in this way. The visits do not always proceed smoothly and it certainly gives us no pleasure when we have to be present during such confrontations."

Shouldn't prisoners of such types be given the opportunity to be alone with their wives? The prisoner, overwrought and driven to the highest nervous ecstasies, experiences in the whole unworthy nature of prison visits all the conditions of a charged atmosphere. Under the circumstances, he feels embarrassed, confined and mentally disturbed by his wife. All that is needed is a harsh or ill-considered word from the woman, who is herself off balance, and the presence of the supervising warder, to provide the spark that causes the powder keg to explode. This is all the more so when the warder is of the type that I refer to in an example.

It is not a rare thing for the prison officials even to make fun of the pain and anguish of the prisoners. I mention here an incident that took place in penal institution L. between a prisoner and an inspector in a question and answer game. I am providing the dialogue word-for-word as it was given to me in writing:

> Insp: "So, what do you want?"
>
> Prisoner: "I would like to ask the inspector for a special letter form."
>
> Insp: "Who do you want to write to?"
>
> Prisoner: "To my babe."
>
> Insp: "Has she got anything going for her?"
>
> Prisoner: "She still has."
>
> Insp: "Man, she's got nothing going in front of her and nothing behind. Do you really want to write to the old frump? I bet she is shacked up with another."
>
> Prisoner: "Maybe she has more going for her than your old dear."
>
> Insp: "I doubt it."
>
> Prisoner: "She has though."
>
> Insp: (In an official tone) "All right, you can have a letter form."
>
> Prisoner: "Thanks and good morning to you."

Such dialogues do not occur every day, but they do happen, and they reveal what falls within the realms of possibility in this atmosphere. Although the prison officials were very careful and restrained in my presence when making such utterances, they often displayed such cynicism, and came out with such smutty thoughts, that I had to ask them to leave my cell or talk to me in other ways. I read this dialogue to a few warders, without saying who was involved, and then asked them who they thought might have taken part in the dialogue. They correctly named the warder involved on every occasion. The warder in question was an official with the *Stahlhelm* mentality, who spoke a lot about "populist racial ethics" and otherwise felt called upon to "clean up public life" and "renew" Germany.[64]

---

[64] The *Stahlhelm* ("steel helmet"), also known as the League of Front Soldiers, was effectively the paramilitary wing of the national conservative party (DNVP) after the First World War and a rallying point for reactionary and antisemitic forces. After the Nazi seizure of power, it merged with the SA.

Prisons have specially fitted facilities in which visits take place. The prisoners call these facilities cattle pens. They consist of a large, bare room without any kind of decoration, divided up into little shacks by partitions. The prisoner is shut into such a shack while his wife faces him at some considerable distance. It is therefore impossible for them to hold hands or give each other a kiss. The prisoner appears like an animal on display in a zoo. The situation becomes completely unbearable if several visits take place simultaneously in this "visitor room", this "cattle pen". It is quite obvious that you cannot speak out, you cannot communicate anything in this environment. When I was first shut into the "cattle pen" in the Brandenburg penal institution, on the occasion of a visit by a female comrade I broke down; I was incapable of looking into the eyes of the comrade facing me.

In penal institution H. the situation for visits is even more undignified. Here, the prisoner is entirely separated from his visiting friends and relatives. Both parties sit in a locked room, which is connected by a small window, and which is also fitted with a close-meshed wire grille. It is therefore hardly possible to recognize the person sitting opposite. Given that this situation is unbearable for prisoners, they try to ingratiate themselves with the prison chaplain who supervises their visits, because that provides the only opportunity to be led not into the "official visit room" but rather into the room of the prison chaplain himself. This is a not insignificant reason for the prisoners expressing a "need for spiritual guidance" and thus prostituting their character and disposition. On the whole, you can see prisoners forced into ambivalent attitudes time and again in virtually all their dealings by this oppressive situation.

Although I had categorically told the Governor of Brandenburg prison, shortly before my wife's first visit, that I would not allow myself to be locked up in such a cage during visits under any circumstances, and that I would rather forego the visits altogether, and the Governor ordered that I should not be locked in the cage during visits, despite my protest the first chief sergeant locked me in the shack until I hinted that I would throw my files in the face, so that he would then have an excuse to lock me up in the arrest cell. Even though I made him aware of the Governor's order, he simply grinned at me mockingly. I declared after about two minutes that he should consider the visit ended, so he had to let me out. This gave me the opportunity to go to the officer in charge, who then supervised the visit in his office and expressed his displeasure to the chief sergeant.

While on remand I experienced something even worse. When I was arrested, my wife was about to give birth. For more than six months, they had held her in the jail of "Red Saxony".[65] On 3 February 1922 I was arrested, on 6 March 1922 she gave birth, an event which was for her perhaps the most important of her life. In the days in bed following the delivery she observed, as though in a wonderland, the witness to the creation from the power of the community. To let me be the first to see the child was for her a heartfelt need. Her friends had trouble preventing her from travelling from Leipzig to Halle as soon as possible after the puerperium, in winter, which would have been detrimental to both mother and child. After six weeks she then appeared before me. Tears of joy and anguish streamed down her cheeks. I was at once distraught and enchanted by her appearance. The barrier stood there between us, the barrier that was intended to prevent us from touching one another, that wanted to resist my attempt to kiss my wife. They had placed a table between us so that I stood in one room, she in the other room; between us the table on which the baby lay, next to it a chief sergeant. I shoved the table to one side as I wanted to hold my wife in my arms. The chief sergeant forbade me to do so and tried to prevent me

---

[65] Saxony was a social-democratic stronghold throughout the early decades of the 20th century.

from starting. I grabbed hold of the table with the words: "One more visible expression of your coarse disposition and I will smash the table into your skull." My wife collapsed into my arms; through her tears flowed the words: "Don't get upset my dearest, ignore this rudeness!" We stood in silence for fifteen minutes, the child began to cry; my wife realized that it had to drink; I implored her to breastfeed the child. But she did not, she could not do it in front of this officer in uniform!

I let myself be led into my cell, collapsed and sank onto my bunk, where I lay down for days like a creature longing for death because that is the only hope of release from all its torments.

These events can only be grasped in their full psychological significance if you look at them from the following perspective: my wife's pregnancy was the result of a deliberate act of procreation, so it was not an accidental and indifferent or even uncomfortable affair, but rather a deliberate design. Her soul heard the inner voice and felt the universal, all-encompassing power to give her blood the germ of a new life and to form a living being, and to form it under the inner urge to do so. This is fundamental and totally changes the sense of expression of the spiritual life of those two people from whose sexual connection the third is about to emerge. In these circumstances, where the woman, as the expectant mother, was wrapped with every fibre of her being around the man, the particular man who stilled the yearning in her blood and nourished her strength of feelings, the man who gave her body the seed, and in so doing fulfilled the conditions that regulate mental equilibrium throughout the imperious will to procreate, she was torn from me. And that was a few days after conception. For me, that was a painful blow that marked me with mental stress; for her it was more: for her it was a single running wound, whose bleeding was accompanied by agonizing sadness and worse. Every psychologist understands this, and yet it is implausible to many a prison governor, because he does not learn to understand it; this is not a part of his nature or his functions. And every psychologist understands that what was going on internally during the said visit between me and my wife was of particular importance.

Typical prisoners, and even more so their women, mostly lack the ability to communicate in writing in a satisfactory manner and thus to ensure a certain level of contact. They lack the vocabulary of the erotic in which to formulate their feelings and moods, quite apart from the fact that, where this possibility does exist, it is usually rendered practically illusory by the schematic process of letter writing. Everything that weighs upon them, everything they feel, everything they do and what they are moved or not moved by, remains unspoken. The intention to empty all the stored memories at the next visit generally breaks down. Supervision and the short visiting time (15 to 30 minutes) frustrate even the best intentions. The two of you then separate, dissatisfied and irritated. That is especially bad for prisoners who are allowed visits only once every three months. With one wet eye and one dry, the law enforcement bodies in the "modern German penal system" already regard a reduction of the interval between visits to two months for category 2 and 3 prisoners as endangering the "penal principle". As most of these visits involve the smuggling in of forbidden items, such as money, tobacco, stimulants and other objects, the focus of the sensory activity of both parties during the visits is: how can I get rid of what I have brought along? Or: how do I get in possession of what has been brought? That is terrible on the nerves. On top of this come the highly agitating, unspoken questions of a sexual nature for both parties.

3. How children are abused in these conditions

Under conditions such as those described in the previous chapter, children – whom women often bring along with them on prison visits – are frequently asked about their mothers' erotic life. Children that have been brought up in a natural environment do not see any "sin", do not see anything bad in it, if their mothers receive a kiss from a man other than their father. It is quite different for the children of prisoners who are in and out of unhealthy relationships. Some already practise spying on their mothers, and they have nothing more important to tell the father in the prison than any incident of a sexual nature. Especially when a prisoner, as father, deliberately assails the child with insistent questions. He not only poses dangerous questions to his child, such as: what does your mother do, does she go out, etc. The child is questioned and interrogated down to the very depths of his soul, in order to draw certain conclusions from the answers as to whether the woman is having intercourse. These are dressed up in the form of questions such as: do men come to visit mother, have strange men have slept at home, has Irma seen a strange man giving mother a kiss? Such are the conversations during prison visits, such are the questions a father asks his child, without even suspecting what he thereby evokes in the child's soul. The child becomes controller of the mother. Imagine the effects this has! Of course, the child gives, in its unhealthy imagination, the answers to these questions that the questioner seeks. Yes, the child tells the father a wealth of "fairy tales" that horrify the mother but give the father a certain "satisfaction". Do not assume that these are individual phenomena. If they were, I would take no notice of them. But these are situations that one hears about almost every day in penal institutions, and that one can witness all too often. Thus, another source of misery breaks forth, one that flows incessantly. After such a conversation with the child the mother gets a beating in the child's presence, and the child now either hates the father or regards the mother as depraved. The prison authorities, protecting their own interests, simply forbid the bringing of children, who have to be spared the bad impression that they could get visiting a prison. No account is taken of the fact that the father longs to see his child.

4. Sexual activities and actual sexual intercourse in the visiting room

It is quite obvious that visits all turn on a single issue: when will the opportunity present itself to give the wife or girlfriend the eagerly desired kiss, unobserved by the supervising warders. Every prisoner hungers for such an opportunity. But they wait and wait; the opportunity never comes. The consequence is nervous tension and an agitated mood.

Nevertheless, intimate caresses, and petting of a non-standard variety take place in the presence of the watching officials. There are some warders who look away during such goings on, but there are also the coarser types who ogle. There are even warders who watch intimate goings-on via the hidden mirror.

Some of the prisoners' wives and girlfriends dress in such a way, partly on their own initiative, partly following instructions, that makes intimate petting easier. The wives or fiancées of prisoners "free" themselves under duress. Women come in dresses that really do not suit them, in so-called "walking skirts", which fulfil a certain purpose, in that they ride up above the knee or even halfway up the thigh. Young girls of 18, 19 and 20 turn up in the prison visiting room in dresses so deeply slashed at the neck and the back that you can almost see their genitals and their *derrière*. Don't get me wrong: I am no prude or moraliser. I love nudity, but only where it is pristine and not simply a bad means to an end. In this case, clothing turns the women into an object of sexual arousal in the prison. And this becomes an ugliness that is repellent rather than attractive, at least as far as bystanders are concerned. I have also observed young girls who came into the jail either with long pigtails or with completely loose and flowing hair, at any rate with a hair style that was purposely arranged for this situation. You can sense this, and you can also hear it when everything sexual is spoken about in a rather trivial manner. You find out, for example, that one girl is wearing no knickers, while another is wearing no blouse.

The facts require more serious consideration. Erotic fantasy demands its right to be satisfied. Under the pressure of their sexual urges, prisoners resort to those forms that they can get away with, given the prevailing circumstances.

One prisoner told me the following about his sexual activities during visits:

"I have often got into very bad situations during visits, so I did not really know what was more expedient here: to accept visits or renounce them entirely. But quite apart from deciding on which course was more suitable for satisfying my own needs, I could not decide on behalf of my wife, to whom I had to leave the decision as to whether she wanted to visit me under these circumstances, or whether she was unable to accept the oppressive predicament under which we had to face each other while being supervised. So, we often stood together in a close embrace. My wife felt my desire and I felt hers; until we fell back, powerless and frustrated, into our chairs. My wife sat on my lap. If she attained the ultimate ecstasy, I was simply exhausted and extremely nervous; conversely, if she was exhausted, I was experiencing the height of desire; I felt in her the highest point of sexual excitement, she with me; I felt the swelling of her breast, she felt the impetuous growth of my penis. All of this happened in the presence of the supervising warden, even if we were doing our best to hide from him what we were up to. But even if he was prevented from seeing anything, he must have noticed what was going on and he certainly heard it, as we were exchanging hot words of passion.

"I gave my wife a *kassiber* in which I implored her, on her next visit, to come without knickers and, if possible, without a blouse, and to alter her dress so with a slit in front and behind. One way or another, I wanted to bring off a "normal" sex act. My wife, who otherwise did virtually everything I whispered to her, turned down this latest request. So, we tortured each other a little longer. But over time, my wife's torment became stronger than mine, so powerful that she lost her balance on one visit: she fell on the stairs into my arms, embraced me and sank to her knees so that she could take hold of my penis with both hands and press it to her breasts. Luckily, we had a sensible sergeant with us on this occasion, who looked away. My wife left, telling me that she could not come back again, as she simply could not endure the frustration anymore."

This prisoner told me that women who are clothed only with the bare necessities, so that they are prepared for any eventualities, very often come into the prison visiting rooms without knickers, without blouses, and have arranged their clothes in a way to facilitate sexual activities.

Another prisoner reported to me that he knew of a case where the wife sat down on the knee of her husband, in such a way that it was in contact with her vagina, and she achieved an orgasm in this way. She managed this several times in the short visiting time of hardly more than a half-hour.

I found out about a case in which a prisoner inserted his penis through the slit at the back of his wife's dress and into her vagina, without the supervising warder noticing or finding out about it later. I heard from another prisoner that for him, visits had only a sexual significance. Through his own skilful manipulation and his wife's help, he managed, at the very least, to feel the naked outline of his wife with every visit. He was often fortunate enough that the supervising warder would leave the visiting room for a few moments. Then he went further and was often surprised by the returning warder, though the latter took no notice of the process.

Do not imagine that such forms of sex in the visiting room of a prison, under the watchful eyes of officers, only occur between prostitutes and pimps. No, respectably married and bridal couples to the same – if it is possible. One can imagine that they experience some terribly embarrassing moments in doing so.

But solutions are found, whatever the cost. I know, for example, of a prisoner who urged his fiancée to bring her friend with her as a means of distracting the warden. With the friend providing cover, the sexual activity could proceed. These were not prostitutes; they were the "daughters of respectable citizens". I would like to reveal to my opponents, who doubtless will raise a hue and cry at the very suggestion, that right-wing lawbreakers do not behave any differently. I am also speaking from experience in this respect. And I would give concrete examples here if I felt no need to spare, as individuals, those active reactionaries in conservative garb with whom I sat behind prison walls. But by no means as stupidly as the press always does when "a case" becomes known. What kind of case? The very sort that could simultaneously demonstrate the sexual torment suffered by all prisoners and prove that "our friends" on the right will become human – all too human – in the "presence" of third parties.

Such visits must at the very least be accompanied by nervous frenzies. And again, it goes without saying that the forms that the effects of such nervous frenzies may take depends entirely on the nature of the supervision. In no cases, however, are such visits spiritually strengthening; they weaken, they destroy nervous energy.

Frequently, several visits take place at the same time in one visiting room. Among them are people who are of a more sensitive nature; because they do not know how to help themselves; they cannot defend themselves against the terrible torments they suffer. What one prisoner once revealed to me about an occurrence in this milieu depressed me so terribly that for days on end I was simply devastated, and on the first evening after hearing this I could find no calming pole of retreat whatsoever. On the afternoon of Christmas day in the year 1924 a member of my group, who had been sentenced with me, told me the following after coming back from a visit:

"Listen, I've just experienced something amazing. My wife came on a visit, and the visit took place together with others. No really, this sexual lust, you should have seen it, you'd have been shocked to the core. The women rode their men and licked each other like cats, snogging, squeezing and crawling over each other as if they were alone with each other in private."

I asked if the supervising warder had allowed this to occur, and my fellow convict said to me: "The warders have no eyes or ears today; it is Christmas. If the supervisor had intervened there would have been a catastrophe. There's no doubt about it. The women were completely sex-crazed. In any case, the officer could not keep an eye on everything, there were too many people in the room."

Here, the women or the men, we do not know which, had entirely lost their self-control, the physical sexual desire was forced from both sides and driven to boiling point by the women. Thus, a kind of officially sanctioned philandering took place on a mass scale in a prison's visiting room, with mutual voyeurism, and driven to the absolute limits, culminating in the sex act itself.

Let us, however, abandon these general considerations, and let us look at a few other deviant acts, which in essence go to show just how bad the sexual plight of two people must be when one of them lives in detention. It is not the actions of such prisoners as are still sufficiently able to exercise self-control, and who are therefore only perpetually *on the edge* of committing acts of desperation that come to the fore here, but rather the actions of those prisoners who habitually commit acts of desperation. I will bring to your attention such an act of desperation that occurred in W. prison and use it to show that it can also lead to the formal sex act itself.

A prisoner, who married young, loses control of himself when his wife visits. The two give each other hugs and kisses in the normal way, but these hugs and kisses become increasingly intense, eventually going so far that the controlling eye of a third party can tolerate them no longer. The supervising official, a Catholic priest, wants to pull them apart. Impossible! They are inseparable in their mutual sexual desire. The priest cries for help, mobilizing the prison warders. The prisoner is verbally abused, arrested, interrogated and eventually declared "insane". I would simply like to know what this emotional discharge has to do with insanity. Admittedly, it provides the simplest and most convenient way to explain away official barbarism. It was not "insanity" that came about here, but rather an explosion of sexual urges that had been repressed for years. This tragedy, which would have to force any halfway normally sensitive and clear-thinking individual to reflect, and then drive out any preconceived notions, offered the warders in W. an inexhaustible source of gossip, the object of cynical, salacious wisecracks.

5. Unsupervised visits in prison

I already mentioned two unsupervised visits that were granted to me, one in May 1924 and the other in March 1927. These two unsupervised visits must be highlighted as characteristic. At Brandenburg prison, the visit went like this: I was summoned by the chief sergeant, who told me that my wife was there while we were on our way. In the conference room, I met my wife in the presence of the police inspector, who informed me that we were to be left without supervision. He then left the room. After about 20 minutes the door reopened; a sergeant looked in and shut the door again. However, we did not take offence at it, even if we weren't indifferent, regarding it as a mistake or a coincidence. After a further 10 minutes a second sergeant entered the room, staying rather longer and coming over to the window. I started to get indignant but held back as I assumed it was still just a coincidence. Another 10 minutes later the first sergeant came back, and I said: Sergeant, we are having an unsupervised visit, to which he replied: Yes, I know. But you are unsupervised! Then he went on. I did not know how to explain what was happening. After a further period, the second sergeant came back again, but this time he was no longer content to step into the room or go to the window, but rather looked in every corner and even took a close look at us. I realized that we were being controlled at irregular intervals and that the policing officers were also intent on surprising us.

Imagine that two people, husband and wife, are forcibly separated for years, are usually allowed to write to each other once every two months and see each other once every three months. Then suddenly they are allowed to be together, unsupervised. Now they think that they can spend hours alone with each other and belong to each other for that time; they live in the belief that this is truly the case – until suddenly the door of the room where they are together is torn open: they are being controlled!

I pointed out to the police inspector that we should have been informed beforehand what exactly "unsupervised" meant so that we could behave accordingly. Either you are granting us an unsupervised visit, or you are not. The procedure adopted here is both outrageous and excruciating at the same time. Given that during the discussions before the visit nobody had denied me the right to use the visit for sexual intercourse, there was a possibility that we might have been found in the highest sexual ecstasy. If that was not the case, it was because for the first ten minutes I was occupied by an endlessly long kiss that my wife gave me with such devotion that I could not really think of anything else; much less could I do anything else. And as our lips parted, our tongues began to speak, while the heart sang and the soul settled into quiet rejoicing. At that moment, I was capable of clearing my intellectual memory for a week, but I was incapable, or not yet capable, of performing physical sexual functions. That would perhaps have been first possible in the twelfth hour of our unsupervised togetherness.

For the unsupervised visit in Luckau prison I got to know the strange disposition of the prison governor. One day my wife announced her visit and asked at the same time if she could bring our boy with her.

This led to a meeting between the Governor and the inspector who would be in charge of controlling the visit, because this official had first started in service the previous Sunday and the second inspector was ill. The inspector agreed to serve on that particular Sunday but remarked that a few weeks ago I assured him that I would have to forego my wife's visits for at least the next five years of my detention if I did not at least have my first opportunity to receive an unattended visit.

At the time there existed once again a state of moodiness and irritability between me and my wife, as can only be the case between two people who have already been separated for five years, in the prime of their life and youthful vigour. This time the condition was such that it could have led to the dissolution of our relationship and thus to catastrophe. Clearly, the harmony between two people must be clouded if one of them is living in prison year after year. In any case, I was not even able to write a letter to my wife, and she could not do that. On top of this, I was unable to speak about the upset between us in the presence of an inspector, even though I did not feel any overpowering inhibitions in this regard and did not greatly feel that the two inspectors, who usually controlled my visits, were foreign interlopers between me and my wife. But given the circumstances, even their presence was unacceptable to me. The stupidest thing I could have done in this situation would have been to agree to the announced visit of my wife and boy. This visit, in the usual form, would not have been helpful. I probably would have sent my wife away after a few minutes, the mood would have gotten even worse. My wife was also aware of this, but she believed she could deal with the danger by bringing our boy along with her. That was certainly true in the sense that in his presence I could not have talked about the oppressive and unbearable state of our relationship, which would have had bad consequences.

The Governor and the inspector reached an agreement that I should be given the opportunity to speak to my wife without being directly supervised. I was therefore first informed about my wife's intention to visit me and bring the boy along, and only then about the concession to allow the visit to take place without supervision. I then pointed out that it would be of little use to us if we could only be together in this way for an hour or two, sitting in the one room, with the official in the next room, and the right to open the door unannounced at any moment and control us. My nature may sometimes be harsh, because of the resentment between me and my wife, which is not sexual in nature, but based on external circumstances, my wife feeling burdened with some guilt. The visit was therefore likely to turn into a kind of courtroom hearing – and I could not greet my wife with the reading of a "charge sheet". The shortness of the time that was available for this visit made a certain nervousness likely from the outset. It is psychologically understandable if my wife, rather than letting me speak, tried to mitigate each harsh word with a kiss or even to choke it entirely in the flow of kisses. Here we would stand on the stage that turns every harshness into indulgence, that obeys the law of emotions: one caress follows another. But I am not in the position of being able to embed myself in my wife's caresses, before my soul is free of the ballast that weighs upon it. This kind of visit could, therefore, have the opposite effect of that intended. Because, of course, my wife would feel hurt and get into an absolutely unbearable state, were I not even to respond to her caresses on this occasion, or perhaps even reject them, whilst we were unable to look at each other in the exultation of our happiness. If the unsupervised visit were to have a truly qualitative purpose, we would have to find ourselves under quite different conditions; conditions that would make it possible for us to grow harmoniously into each other, so to speak, without any kind of pressure, and thus have the most favourable opportunity at our disposal in which we could be inwardly strong enough to be able to speak about the underlying causes of our disharmony. That would certainly be possible and auspicious if we could be completely alone together, without fear of being controlled and thus disturbed in a way that made the thing intolerable: we should be given a truly unsupervised visit of a longer duration, as had been granted to us while I was on remand in Halle; perhaps my wife would be left to me from Saturday evening.

The inspector said: "It will be all right. Speak about it further with the Governor." In fact, the prison governor came to me on the same day and we discussed the matter in all its aspects from six in the evening until eleven at night. In this conversation, I repeated what I had told the inspector and went further, in every respect with absolute frankness, which I was not obliged to do. I summarize the result of this discussion. The Governor said:

"You are talking about forms of caressing, and to be honest I must wonder at the openness with which you talk about the sexual. Obviously, I have given my consent to the unsupervised visit in the chosen form only so that you can talk to your wife without supervision about your points of difference, but not for the purpose of sexual intercourse. Nor do I expect the possibility of this happening, and in my agreement, I have been guided by Herr L.'s view, which emphasized that you will keep your promise. If you cannot and will not now formally promise me, without any preconditions, that this visit will not to be misused for sexual purposes, then I have to retract my agreement. I see absolutely no possibility of allowing you to have sexual intercourse with your wife, and it is quite outrageous for you to talk about such a possibility. The offices are simply not there for such purposes. I have also only given my agreement to this type of meeting on the condition that your wife brings your son with her. If you now insist that she does not bring the boy, then the visit must take place in the usual form.

"Did Herr L. not tell you how the visit was to proceed? You are to go into the small office room of the secretariat with your wife, while Herr. L. is in the next room; he not only has the right, but also the duty, to open the door to your room unannounced and without first knocking. He is to do that at any moment when he cannot hear you speaking, or if he hears untoward noises or notices something of that nature. It is also quite obvious that any hugs and kisses should not go beyond the usual norms, which means they should be restricted to how you might say farewell at a railway station. I will be in the prison on Sunday myself, and I'll give these conditions to your wife in advance and personally attend to the case to ensure the visit takes

place in the way I agreed with Herr. L. You can tell
Herr L. tomorrow morning if you want to agree to
these conditions or not. And the form that the visit
takes depends on your decision."

Despite everything that you see and hear in this, and notice in
general, and whether you like it or not, the conclusion to this
dialogue was outrageous to me. The Governor not only
showed that he lacked any kind of basic psychological understanding or insight into the situation, but also demonstrated a
complete lack of manners by refusing the express wishes of
prisoners in an extremely dire situation. the Governor could
give me an unattended visit and he could refrain from doing
so – he had the opportunity and the right to do either. He did
not have to decide on anything else, he had no duty to decide
anything else, he had no right. If he had granted me an unsupervised visit and in doing so thoroughly tested the question
as to whether there were enough general guarantees that the
visit would not be abused for illegal purposes (escape plans,
etc.), nobody would blame him. However, anything else that
might happen during such an unsupervised visit between two
people who are husband and wife, was something the Governor should not trouble himself about. He should certainly not
impose conditions that were completely impossible to accept.
Only someone who is, as a matter of principle, the enemy of
the prisoner's soul and senses could set out such a thing in the
form of conditions. And he demonstrated that this is exactly
what he was in another way, when at the same time he emphasized that:

"Of course, such conditions are not just a sham as far as
I am concerned. I do not impose such conditions as a
matter of outward form while remaining indifferent as
to whether they are fulfilled or not. A tacit acceptance
of the possibilities offered by such a visit is not part of
my conception of the duties of an official. In any case, I
love correctness, and demand it."

I was unable to accept the conditions given to me because I

did not know if I could abide by them. Moreover, I was unable to accept an unattended visit on the specific condition that our child, a boy of five, was to be placed as a barrier between us; as a prison warden between us, so to speak, who should prevent any intimacy occurring between me and my wife as a consequence of his presence. I did not want to acknowledge these conditions and concern myself with them in practice. I was incapable of accepting such a deceit against myself and against others.

Although I made no promises of wanting to fulfil the conditions set for me, and despite the fact that I forbade my wife to bring our child, she came – and was left to me without supervision. In my absence, the Governor now accepted the promises that I had refused to give from my wife. When I then told my wife about the proceedings and asked her not to embrace me with such passion, as I was supposed to have promised to the Governor that we would "restrict our hugs and kisses to what is normal when parting at the railway station," she replied: "Forget him. He made me aware of these conditions in virtually the same words, so I smiled at him a little before giving my consent. Don't make life so difficult for yourself and certainly no more difficult than necessary. Take people as they are; those who want to be lied to, will be lied to. This does not bother me, because I am not the prisoner of my lies, but merely acting under duress. And white lies are permissible, they do not destroy your core character. Should I first get involved in an hour-long discussion with the Governor that would eat into our time? Only a wretch would do that! Please relieve yourself of all your character-traits that have no place in prison, throw overboard all the ballast that weighs you down in your dealings with those who still regulate your situation."

On seven quarto pages I had written down the "points of difference" that I believed to exist between us and that I now wanted to erase, although it was clear to me that I needed a full week to exhaust every single page of this extraordinary draft. However, when I entered the reception room and flew towards the sobbing girl, the thought that crossed my mind at the sight of my wife was: *Points of difference?* And as we finally kissed each other in private, we asked ourselves, speaking with one voice: *Points of difference?* There are absolutely no points of difference! Or, if there were any, they were washed away under the wave of our emotions.

The "railway station hugs and kisses" did wonders once again: I gave my wife an intimate, powerful foretaste of the joys of spring to send her on her journey. And two days later she sent me the sweetest buds of a high spring, which made me so lively and industrious that once again I thought I could move mountains. And I did move mountains: the delicate, colourful flowers that my wife had brought me blossomed and flourished on the highest peak. The effects of unsupervised visits are always productive, revealing the inner smile in everyone. I find in the published letters of Karl Liebknecht (edited by Franz Pfemfert, Wilmersdorf 1919, in the weekly magazine *Die Aktion*) a letter from Luckau jail dated 18 March 1917, an extract that demonstrates the value of such unsupervised visits. And this despite the fact that Karl Liebknecht was very reticent in expressing his emotions. But even in his reserve Karl Liebknecht shows what he was living and feeling in those days: a unique symphony of joy, known only to those who have experienced it, and which can only be understood by those who for years have been forced to do without woman and womanhood, and therefore without tenderness. I cite the following passage:

> "My dearest beloved! It is so good that I can now write to you again! How delightful your visit was on Tuesday, how we had time entirely to ourselves, however short. It was like one of those visits to Heidelberg, those delicious-happy-agonizing hours; and yet it was different, stronger, more powerful. – How it refreshed you, as though a magic fountain was washing around you. Your eyes sparkled, and yes, mine sparkled too – they

sparkled, because they reflected you, because you lit up my love.

"You will be allowed to visit me alone more often, and I trust that as a result, you will not experience painful *intermezzi* in future." [66]

---

[66] Karl Liebknecht was imprisoned in Luckau from mid-November 1916 until 23 October 1918. Edited by Franz Pfemfert (1879-1954), *Die Aktion* was published between 1911 and 1932 in Berlin-Wilmersdorf, and best known as a vehicle for expressionist art. Its politics favoured the German communist left. Following the Nazi seizure of power, Pfemfert fled to Czechoslovakia, where Stalinists demanded his deportation. From 1929 his wife served as Trotsky's German literary agent and translator, and Pfemfert himself became a close friend of Trotsky, despite their political differences. Pfemfert died in Mexico City.

6. Pregnant women in detention

I now want to look more closely at the conditions faced by a woman who is pregnant while in prison. I am thinking here of the physiological upheavals associated with pregnancy, which determine all the laws of being, encompassing the inner life in the tenderest of sensibilities. The developing fruit of the womb dictates – and the mother has to obey, though she does so willingly, simply surrendering to physiological law, because she is inextricably connected to the unborn child. In other words, the woman who has welcomed pregnancy is fully at the service of reproduction and cannot free herself from this. Concern for the development of the fruit of the womb grows in this soil, partly unconsciously and partly consciously, i.e. mentally and spiritually: "All the powers of the maternal organism are focused on creating a favourable environment for the growing fruit. A planned economy forms itself. External wastage is reduced to the minimum, so that as much as possible remains for nourishing the fruit" (Nemilow). But this implies that "besides this continuing disorganization of the elements of the soul, of the conditioned reflex, the nervous system of a pregnant woman is in a state of fluctuating equilibrium. The slightest impulse suffices for a turn to abnormality. Kräpelin says that 14 percent of all mental disorders in women occur at some point during maternity. Fischer maintains that even the most normal woman exhibits various mental disorders during pregnancy, such as changeability of moods, tastes, moodiness, confusion of consciousness, an inhibited and depressed state of reception and thought processes" (Nemilow).[67]

George Sand describes the energy consumption of a pregnant woman like this: "The needs of the mind, curiosity,

---

[67] A.W. Nemilow, *Die biologische Tragödie der Frau* Oskar Engel Verlag, Berlin. Emil Kräplin (1856–1926) was one of the founders of modern scientific psychiatry, psychopharmacology and psychiatric genetics.

the interest in study and observation, all disappeared as soon as I felt the sweet burden, even before the first impulses announced its existence. Essence, thought, in a word, the whole of intellectual life was gone, erased."

George Sand did not arrive at this wisdom in the laboratory but in her own flesh and blood. And this woman is certainly competent to give judgements that otherwise are only due to authorities. Paul Landau wrote on the 50th anniversary of George Sand's death: "For the first time since the days of Sappho, she has placed the feminine gift alongside the masculine, raising up countless indolent hearts the resounding call of her works, breaking through the barriers of an outmoded order of society. But George Sand did not accomplish her deed by trying to be masculine and imitating men; rather, her greatness is based on being entirely a woman and unfolding from her femininity powers and wonders that had never previously emerged so powerfully in art and life. Her poetry is only immortal and imperative there, where this voice of a woman clearly resounds, accusing and accusatory, besotted and adoring, disappointed and disgusted, yet always swelling out of an unshakable faith in goodness and in nature."[68]

Every educated person should know about the conditions in German jails. And every person with some experience, who is at least halfway in love with the truth, knows that these conditions also apply to an expectant mother in jail. It must be terrible for a woman to have to give birth under the gaze of hardened warders and medical officers in a jail or prison.

I am not theorizing about these things; rather, I am speaking from experience, based on what I know about the conditions in detention and how these conditions affected my wife during her pregnancy at the heart of "Red Saxony", in

---

[68] Paul Landau (1880-1951) was a contemporary journalist and cultural commentator. After the Nazi seizure of power he moved to Palestine.

Dresden jail. My wife does not tend to exaggerate, on the contrary: she is reticent by her very nature; a reticence that has gotten on my nerves on more than one occasion. But my wife could not allow herself to be subjected to the usual treatment. On top of this, she had far too much supervision by outsiders, who took on the role of enforcement authorities. Therefore, first her father took care of her, second, her defence attorney was not completely inactive: both of course paid attention to what my wife told them about her treatment. But how many detainees are there who have no relatives to support them, and at the same time are in no position to defend themselves against bullying treatment! Such female detainees are delivered into despotism without any protection.

My wife was also assisted by bourgeois women's rights activists and welfare workers, who influenced governmental institutions. This was further reinforced by my more or less friendly relations with governing bodies or authorities, so that the people "upstairs" ensured, or took care to ensure, that no "exceptional causes" arose that might lead to "exceptional complaints". At the time there was a purely socialist government in Saxony, that had to take note of communists' criticism of the prison system. Of course, the communist deputies in the Saxon Landtag took special interest in the fate of proletarian political prisoners and were better able to intervene at that time than, for example, the deputies in the Prussian Landtag. Because it does make a difference whether you are taking your complaints or grievances to centrists or to left social-democrats. The former present the well-known insurmountable barrier against which every argument, however robust, collapses as though made of straw. With this statement I am pointing out a relative difference, and no more.

It is also of considerable importance in assessing the treatment of my wife that the Saxon Minister of Justice at the time, Zeigner,[69] visited her and had long discussions with her.

---

[69] Erich Zeigner (1886-1949) was later Prime Minister of the German state of Saxony

This circumstance combined with other events caused the executive organs to exercise caution in ways that one would not normally expect. All this does not change the fact that my wife had to live under the usual and typical conditions of detention.

For example, when she was administered a special diet for the sick instead of the diet for healthy prisoners, this was an easing of the situation, but it could not compensate for the load she was carrying. When she resisted taking a schematically prepared "sick food" and pointed out that she needed a meal tailored to the condition of a pregnant woman, the act of omission was justified by the well-known formula used by the judicial bureaucracy: "That cannot be done, that is out of order!" What falls outside the scope of the "regulations" may not be implemented, even if this denies any elementary requirement and, consequently, people cannot subsist. Every expert knows that for pregnant women, the nutritional question is specific to each one of them. This was even acknowledged during the war, when pregnant women were given special food as a preferential right. A pregnant woman also has a quite unique appetite. The production of substances in bodily organs depends heavily on its satisfaction. Under the conditions of detention, however, this particular appetite of pregnant women cannot or will not be satisfied. Pregnancy is insufficient grounds to declare a person unfit to be incarcerated. In this way they do neither the one thing nor the other, i.e. they neither declare that a pregnant woman is unfit for in-

---

during the attempted communist uprising of 1923. On 10 October 1923 he appointed two members of the Communist Party to his government. Two weeks later the German Chancellor Gustav Stresemann issued an ultimatum demanding a dismissal of the Communist ministers. Zeigner refused to comply and, two days later, was deposed by the President of Germany Friedrich Ebert (SPD) under Article 48 of the Weimar constitution. Zeigner was replaced by a commissioner and did not return to any position of authority. Arrested by the Nazis for anti-fascist activities, he survived the Sachsenhausen and later Buchenwald concentration camps.

carceration, but nor do they take into account her situation in terms of nutrition and appetite. However, this applies only to proletarian women. If a countess has the misfortune of going to prison while pregnant, then a whole regiment of physicians will take care of her and take her to the sanatorium! My wife was locked up together with a below-average woman; allegedly, this was to compensate for her difficult situation, which gave rise to symptoms that are experienced during pregnancy even in normal conditions. Yet it later turned out that this woman, who showed all the signs of moral corruption, had been put there to spy on my wife with the intention of getting information about me; therefore, it was anything but a compensation. And if this pregnant woman was at least allowed to exercise in a confined yard for 45 minutes instead of the usual 15-minutes of exercise time, this does not alter the fact that she was forced to vegetate for the remaining 23 hours in a cell the size of a doll's house, staring at the monotonous grey walls. These conditions could not be eased by the "complex of delicate feelings and experiences" according to which, it is assumed, a pregnant woman is ruled. Quite the opposite: the things that a pregnant woman experiences during her pregnancy are, to a considerable extent, transmitted to the unborn child. A woman needs, during her pregnancy, a serene spiritual life. Before my wife noticed the first stirrings of her "sweet burden", even the doctor denied that she was pregnant, which was already visible to the near-sighted and became more visible every day. But the doctor was not allowed to notice, because as long as her pregnancy was not officially established, the penal system was relieved of certain obligations.

Under these circumstances the question that each pregnant woman faces is understandable: What will be the effect of this abnormal way of life on my child; will he even see the light of day? And if he does, how will his inner predispositions turn out, since during his days in the womb, he could not drink in the power of his mother's soul, which gives him form and shapes his inner being! Every woman held in detention imagines that the foetus will not only be restricted in its development, but the child, once viable, may turn out to be abnormal, crippled, blind; it will show the signs of an abnormal development, as my wife said to me. One must imagine the life of a pregnant woman in jail under these conditions.

Despite all of the defence attorney's efforts to wrest my wife from jail in "Red Saxony", despite all the efforts made by women's rights activists and bourgeois welfare helpers, despite the warm words that the social democratic university lecturer Hennig addressed to key authorities, that the expectant mother, with her complicated nature, should finally be set free, so that the child could develop under the most favourable conditions possible, despite all of this, it did not happen. She stayed locked up. She was also kept in detention after her conviction. Before she was convicted, the former Saxon Minister of Justice Zeigner was compelled to point out that it was impossible for my wife to be released from prison, because this would have meant intervening in a pending process. The law enforcement agency "justified" its position by pointing to the danger of collusion. After her conviction, when the Saxon Minister of Justice's hands were no longer legally bound, he was put under pressure, thus once again there was delay in reaching a clear decision. In this way they declined any interruption to her detention for so long as they could: as a result of her release, the lead that the police supposedly had on me could easily be lost again.

It was shortly before Christmas. My wife went on hunger strike. Her defence attorney approached the Minister three days in a row. Every day he visited again and explained that he would not leave Dresden until my wife was released from prison. Minister Zeigner was inclined to agree to her release but the judicial and ministerial bureaucracy successfully resisted this. They said that my wife's hunger strike showed lack of scruples towards the unborn child, without considering that imprisonment itself must necessarily have a damaging effect on the child's future.

My wife was only released from jail shortly before childbirth. And would not have been were it not for extraordinary pressure. 95 percent of pregnant women in jail lack such means of pressure – the women remain in detention, where they also give birth. I cannot understand how women in freedom, who understand maternal instincts, can tolerate such a situation.[70]

---

[70] Gertrud Gaiewski gave birth early in March 1922. Bureaucratic hurdles prevented a wedding from taking place that summer; eventually Gertrud and Karl were married on 13 October 1922. Source: Volker Ullrich, *Der Ruhelose Rebell*, Karl Plättner 1893-1945 C.H. Beck, Munich 2000, pp 147-8.

VI. Concluding remarks

1. After-effects of sexual abstinence following release from detention

The consequences of sexual abstinence while in detention manifest themselves in various ways after release. I heard from several former prisoners that after they had been let out, they had been "impetuously reckless"; others, however, had become more or less impotent. I have had the occasion to obtain information about the consequences of sexual abstinence on prisoners who were released from prison after the July 1928 Amnesty.[71] With most of these comrades-in-distress, it was hardly possible to talk about anything other than highly erotic issues. Their intention was to conquer several women in one night. In my whole life, I have never observed the effects of sexual hunger as intensively as here, where released prisoners swarmed like bees after years of sexual suppression and rendered entire areas or districts "unsafe". The stories I heard sometimes made me think that these men before me had returned to childhood: mature adults reported sexual encounters in the way that beginners do; they delighted in, and became intoxicated by, basic sexual experiences. They wrote glowing love letters, almost novels on the subject. I also heard – never reported in a smutty way – that they were so awkward and bashful that the girls they met had to teach them sex acts all over again. I noted in others a condition of semi-impotence, which occurs to quite a lot of prisoners after they have been discharged. One of the effects of this condition that comes to the fore is an insatiable need for tenderness, that has

---

[71] The 1928 Koch Amnesty was one of five so-called "Hindenburg Amnesties". They involved the release of approximately 29,000 people at the request of virtually all the political parties represented in the Reichstag, including the Communist Party, which had seen many militants imprisoned as a result of the uprisings between 1919 and 1923. Karl Plättner and Max Hoelz were among those released in 1928.

no limits in time or form. Anyway, when my wife was long since asleep, I sat on her bed, watched her silhouette, trying to touch her softly with my hands, and was happy if I was able to observe all of her body lines in that state. But as soon as I penetrated the frontiers of sexual activity, I was once again overcome by the tendency to "withdraw". For good reasons, I refuse to equate this with a disposition to impotence. It is simply the consequence of a disordered sex life that reveals itself here. And I have no reason to stay silent about the fact that I left prison with a weakened sex drive.

Mühsam, who has a six-year imprisonment behind him, mentioned in his lecture at the Institute for Sexual Science on "Sexual Life and Prison" that most of those released from detention have a weakened potency and a simultaneously strengthened need for love.

As I write down these lines, another political prisoner who spent barely two years in jail, albeit in relatively favourable conditions, told me that he needed to invest an incredible amount of energy to put his sex life back in order; with him, certain manifestations of impotence occurred. In any case, he said, the consequences of sexual abstinence are predominantly individual, but there can hardly be a single prisoner who is released without pathological symptoms in relation to sex.

The question of whether sexual abstinence can lead to complete impotence, I have to leave open; you cannot answer this with a clear yes or a no. Ludwig Levy-Lenz, who deals with Steinach's theory in "Sexual Catastrophes", has this to say on the subject:[72] [73]

---

[72] Ludwig Levy-Lenz (1892-1966) was a German doctor and sex reformer, a colleague of Max Hirschfeld. During the First World War he was ordered to manage a brothel for soldiers, as a result of which he developed an interest and concern for women's sexual health. In 1930 he co-authored the first detailed study on the subject of abortion. He briefly worked with Eugen Steinach on rejuvenation methods.

[73] Eugen Steinach (1861-1944) was an Austrian pioneer of sexual research. He sought to achieve rejuvenation by inhibiting the vas deferens. His most famous

"Steinach found that inhibiting the sperm duct *(vas deferens)* achieved the desired effect to the extent that a degeneration of the seminal gland itself took place. Such an expiration of an organ as a result of the prevention of its functions is known. Thus, a muscle dwindles when it is not needed for a long time, and in this way, unfortunately, at the start of the Great War many injured soldiers lost the mobility of their limbs, which had been in plaster for too long. For the same reason the sperm gland in the testicles die slowly following suppression, because it is functionless; they get smaller and, in their place – this is the crucial point – the interstitial tissue grows all the more powerfully."[74]

Hirschfeld writes in his *Geschlechtskunde*:

"The onset of impotence as a result of sexual abstinence is contested by most physicians and I previously doubted it myself; but I changed my mind after observing a large number of patients who had lived in total abstinence until their marriage."

Since my release from prison in July 1928 I have met eight criminal prisoners, whose acquaintance I made in various penal institutions. Four of them testified to me about the after-effects of sexual abstinence while in detention.

Here are their statements. The first of them reported the following to me:

"I am unable to function sexually as normal. Shortly after my release I was completely under the control of my sexual urges; I was incapable of working and was continuously on the lookout for sexual objects. As a result, I squandered the money that had been paid to me. Finally, I managed to find work. I spent the money I

---

patients for this treatment included Sigmund Freud and William Butler Yeats.

[74] *Sexual-Katastrophen : Bilder aus dem modernen Geschlechts- und Eheleben.* Verlag A. H. Payne, Leipzig.

earned on sex with prostitutes, as sex with a respectable girl in a committed relationship was out of the question. On the one hand I lacked the courage to approach a respectable girl, and on the other hand I knew that no respectable girl would fulfil my particular needs. I hung around in a dissolute way on the street night after night, did not sleep, went into work early and carried on with substitute sex acts during working hours. My condition was not unknown to my work colleagues because I also tried to get them to satisfy my sick needs. Consequently, my employer also found out about my condition. I was sacked. I now operate as a pimp. I am so unhappy, I could fall into despair, because I know that I will go to jail again. And that will be my ruin."

Another made the following statement to me:

"Shortly after my release I was married but stayed with my wife for just two months. The relationship between us was a good one, but it broke down as a result of the sexual idiosyncrasies that I acquired during my seven years in prison. I became impotent and only able to obtain release when masturbating with my wife stand-ing or sitting in front of me. My wife would not join in. She was disgusted by this behaviour. I was ashamed of this, but my wife went further and shamed me herself, made fun of me. Thus, I became incapable of satisfying her and myself. We separated on bad terms. And now my wife not only makes fun of me but tells everyone in my circle of acquaintances about my condition, which pains me all the more because I'm not impotent at all and therefore I am looking for satisfaction in some form."

The third had this to say to me:

"You know from our conversation in Brandenburg that, in matters of a sexual nature, I was not one of those who suffered excessively while in detention; I had enough other distractions. For me, the consequences of sexual abstinence are only just starting now. Unable to connect physically with a girl, I am sinking deeper and deeper into the abyss. I position myself near to a girl but stay out of sight and masturbate. But the urge to expose myself occurs so suddenly and powerfully, for example in the metro, that I can hardly control myself. If this situation gets any worse then I will voluntarily return to prison. I recently came close to raping a girl. And yet I know that I could not have done anything even if I had forced her into my power."

The last statement is as follows:

"For a while after my release I indulged in excessive, though normal, sexual intercourse. Then I entered into homosexual circles, even though I had no homosexual proclivities. For a few months I was completely abstinent, which made my situation even worse. Now my urge for schoolgirls is so strong that I constantly hang about in the vicinity of schools. I already get a great deal of satisfaction just speaking to a schoolgirl. Which I do constantly. I do not know if I will manage to reverse this tendency, which has not yet had any practical consequences. If I do not manage, I will hang myself."

The situations and phenomena that I have described so far are still bearable. But for many released prisoners, things are more dreadful. The prisoner who is released from prison with a warped sexuality will infect his new environment with the deviant inclinations he has developed. As far as those with natural homosexual inclinations are concerned, there is less danger to the general public because such persons will move in homosexual circles. The danger lies elsewhere. A criminal inmate who has been in and out of prison for more than 10 years wrote to me about this:

"Virtually all prisoners strive to compensate for their

privations during imprisonment and in most cases, they become orgiastic rakes, insofar as they were not so already. They fear going back into jail and want to experience as much as they possible can. They are not held back by sexually transmitted diseases; there is nothing left to restrain them, and I have heard about many who take pleasure in infecting healthy women – they regard it as a kind of revenge for their expulsion from human society."

Lumpp confirmed that this is no fantasy with the following comments: "Erotic impulses can also be found in the letters, in which the prisoners lecture their relatives in an idiotic fashion about how to behave in a sexual relationship or give vent to their assumptions about what might be happening in that direction on the outside."

In the most favourable cases, when, after long detention, a man can throw himself into the arms of his wife, who understands and loves him, and who understands his sexual fulminations, the former prisoner will regain normalcy over time. But that is only possible for a few. In most cases, marriage or a free partnership breaks up during detention because of the enforced separation. And where it is not the case that the oneness of two human beings has not been rent asunder by the rapier of the jail house, the consequences reveal themselves after release and have further conse-quences.

Many former prisoners find themselves rootless after their release, disposed to committing new crimes. If one seeks sexual satisfaction, he mainly finds it with prostitutes, who are at his service, but only if he can pay them well.

On the first day of Christmas 1928 a recently discharged prisoner, who had been in prison for eight years, came to me in a state of total annoyance. Before that he had visited Mühsam, Toller and Dr. Magnus Hirschfeld. What he told me about the consequences of his sexual abstinence over the years was harrowing. He asked me to send my wife away, as he wanted to talk to me in private. My wife left, and as soon as she had closed the door, the discharged prisoner began to tremble, and spoke confusedly, because his inner inhibitions meant he did not at first know where to start with the things he thought he needed to tell me. I tried to distract him but did not succeed. Finally, he found the thread, and he gushed:

"I have now been at liberty for three months and my sexual condition is getting worse, my nerves are getting weaker and over-excited. At night I lie sleepless in my bed, sweating in my weak and anxious state, as though I was lying in water. I dread going to sleep and often avoid going to bed entirely. So, I restlessly prowl the streets at night. I am attracted to every woman, putting me in danger of attacking them to satisfy distressing and otherwise sadistic impulses or sadistic desires. At the same time, I am emotionally controlled by a kind of impotence, which makes it impossible for me to achieve sexual release in the normal way. I was under the spell of totally frenzied fantasies, images which followed me everywhere. My wife, who stayed loyal to me through my eight years of detention, can stand it no longer. She is unable to satisfy my needs. Four weeks ago, she chased me away like a mad dog. She said: No, I can no longer live together with you. You have become an animal! So, I wander around the world in search of satisfaction, but cannot find it, as I lack the economic means. When the urge becomes overpowering my conscience evaporates: I no longer see and hear what is going on around me and fall into dangers that will cost me my life. Now, according to well-intentioned advice, I should find a hospital that can help me to restore my nerves to good order. But I dare not do this because then I would fall into the danger of being locked up in an insane asylum."

The man who told me this is an intellectual, well known in journalist circles. Really, one can say here: people are robbed of all their will to control themselves and any last remnants of human dignity are destroyed.

A few days after the lecture that I took part in together with [Felix] Fechenbach, [Ernst] Toller, and [Erich] Zeigner on the sexual dysfunction of prisoners, at a rally held by the German League of Human Rights on 4 December 1928, a woman who had spent about four years behind prison walls came to me. I will give a summary of our conversation. She told me the following:

"When I was 18 years old, I was seduced by an older man, who made me pregnant. Because I was unenlightened at the time, I only realized I was pregnant in the fourth month. My parents threw me out of the house. I was now without means and insecure in the world, because the man who had made me pregnant jilted me. I had learned nothing, and I had to find a job. When my pregnancy became obvious, I lost the job. Because I did not want to starve, I could see no other choice: I started shoplifting. Seeing the impossibility of delivering the child, I had it aborted, which I could not keep secret. For all the crimes I had committed I received a two-year jail sentence. During my detention in a women's prison I witnessed sexually harrowing goings-on. I did not take part in any sexual activity and got through the agonizing situation one way or another, without resorting to masturbation.

"After my release, which took place during the war, I was once again completely rootless. But I then managed to find accommodation in a factory, where I earned my bread as a munitions worker. I made the acquaintance of a combatant, who promised me marriage, got pregnant by him again and only after this did I find out that he was married. After this disappointment I went to pieces, could not work anymore and lost my job. I went off the rails again. I stole, sold my body for a while and committed fraud so that I could finally get another job. After six months they found out who I was: I was fired. I committed more criminal offences and was sentenced to three years' imprisonment. What I experienced in these three years of sexual agony is terrible, but even more terrible was what I observed. I was put in a communal cell and witnessed the most horrible things you can imagine. I demanded to be placed in isolation, which was granted. After several months of abstinence, I turned to self-gratification. But I could only use this means for a short time. I went back into communal custody and took part in sexual orgies. I became addicted to them and will probably remain addicted for the rest of my life.

"After my release I tried to get work, which I managed to do. I worked during the day and at night I took part in sex orgies, sometimes with two or three men at the same time. But it did not stop there. The echo of old habits, combined with my ruined natural instincts, drove me into the arms of women. Four of us joined in at the same time. Men also entered into this circle and made instruments for us. This intercourse, I should explain, took place between people who had all been in prison; they seek each other out because they know that they can best satisfy each other; and this is because only they know what they have been up to behind prison walls.

"Then I summoned up all my willpower and withdrew. That lasted for a while; I worked, earned well, and sought to marry. But in no time at all, after having normal sex with the man, my craving for sex orgies set in once again. The man was disgusted and broke things off. Once again, I went astray. For a full five months I hung around outside prisons in the morning, waiting for newly released prisoners, on some days picking up three, four or five of them to satisfy me; usually one at a time, but sometimes severally. In the end I was physically incapable of doing this any longer; I felt disgust at myself, withdrew once again, and then moved in with a woman. She too had been in jail, but she was a solid woman who has two children at the age of ten and thirteen, a boy and a girl. I seduced both of them. Now it has got to the point that I can only get satisfaction with children. This urge is so powerful that on some days I have sought out two, three, or four boys. I give them everything I own because my nature cries out for satisfaction every hour. So, during the day I work in the factory, and at night I prostitute myself for a few hours, to earn the money I need for the victims who satisfy my craving.

"I have no idea how this will all end. I move this way and that between extremes, I even find animals, dogs and horses attractive."

It is quite clear that among the other after-effects of sexual abstinence and sexual activity practised in custody, a large proportion of sex crimes and sexually motivated murders can be traced back to prison life. Unsatisfied urges – because these persist, despite all substitutes – create the conditions for such crimes. A piece in the *Leipziger Volkszeitung*, which I have cited several times, demonstrates that I am not exaggerating here or making statements that are without proof. It continues:

"When the prisoner returns to freedom one day, his instinctive sex life, which has been stunted, bent and misguided, then breaks forth in a most explosive form. The German public first became aware of these affairs in 1912 through the 'Speckner case'. Directly after serving out a four-year term of imprisonment Speckner committed a really dreadful sexually motivated murder. According to the medical report, enforced sexual abstinence had caused such a nervous over-stimulation that he had completely lost the ability to control his sex drive. Very many do not survive this inner crisis at all. Very many released prisoners disappear for a long time, some of them for the rest of their lives, in the

madhouse."
This is certainly a dark perspective, which fills prisoners with dread, so much so that they feel very conflicted as to whether they should leave prison at all or not simply stay put.

2. Solutions and demands

A critique is only half as valuable as it could be if it casts light on the current state of affairs without saying how this can be overcome. But I would also create disastrous illusions if I did not immediately state that all the damage that has been discovered can only be resolved in a socialist social order. In this respect the only question that must be asked is how can the prisoner's life behind prison walls be made humanely a little more bearable?

A Communist proposal, which was negotiated in the 5th session of the Saxon Parliament (3rd election period), on Thursday, 16 December 1926, and in the 36th session of 16 June 1927, initiated by the Communist Party deputy Robert Siewert, dealt with this question.[75] The petitions request that the government be instructed to make the following arrangements for the coming Christmas holidays:

> 1. That all political prisoners without exception and all criminal inmates, provided their leave of absence does not endanger the lives and health of their fellow human beings, are granted leave;
>
> 2. The families of all prisoners on leave receive an allowance of RM50 for the wife and RM50 for each child. Unmarried prisoners receive an allowance of RM50.

The holiday should last 14 days for short-term imprisonment, three weeks for longer sentences.

As conservative as these requests are, insofar as they should contribute to the solution of the sexual problem in prison, it is also clear that they had mobilized all of the fiscal, administrative and criminal-psychological arguments that are permissible within the capitalist conceptual horizon. The Sax-

---

[75] Robert Siewert (1887-1973) was a "Brandlerist" opponent of Stalinism in the KPD and later fought in the German Resistance against National Socialism. He survived the Buchenwald concentration camp, where he spoke up for many Jewish prisoners.

on Minister of Justice Bünger spoke of a bull market for criminality that would occur in Saxony if these proposals were accepted; he claimed that the prisoners would not come back and that a whole army of police officers would have to be specially recruited for the task of recapturing prisoners on leave and returning them to the "modern German penal system". The Minister finally raised the additional question of who should check the many thousands of files to determine whether the prisoner in question was dangerous to the health and safety of others, i.e. whether the conditions for a leave of absence exist in this general sense. These arguments were, and are, of some validity in the current circumstances, although I also take into account that these circles always have "arguments" at their fingertips against any tendencies towards humane treatment within the prison system. These are typically expressed by the Justice Minister's words: "After all, a prison should not be a pleasure palace." Anyway, these proposals make it all too easy for reactionaries of every stripe to find a majority for their rejection. In fact, the proposals were indeed either rejected or referred to the Legal Committee, where they were later buried, with the same outcome. Had the leave of absence only concerned political prisoners, then the arguments of the main parties would have been meaningless, for the political delinquent, of course, lives under quite different conceptual horizons from those of the criminal. When the political prisoner confronts the question of whether or not he should go back to the torture chamber after being given leave of absence from custody on the basis of such agreements, his outlook is quite different to that of the criminal prisoner, from the very outset. The individual point of view of the average criminal is restricted to the narrowest "I" horizons. The political prisoner, by contrast, must take into account, in such circumstances, the effect his behaviour must have on efforts to modernize the penal system; he must also consider the effect of breaking his word, both with regard to the comrades who are left behind, and with regard to comrades who will be imprisoned later and who will have to pay for the abuse of the system by a single prisoner. He knows that not all political prisoners are on leave at the same time; he also knows that the reactionary bureaucracy generalizes such isolated cases of breaches of trust during leave of absence and will certainly use them as a justification for stifling any attempts to make the prison system more humane. Therefore, he goes on holiday leave with a very different attitude towards his class comrades in general, and a very different sense of responsibility to his comrades in prison in particular, from that of the average criminal prisoner. The exemplary political prisoner therefore returns to prison after such a gen-eral leave of absence, or at least does so as a rule. He stands in relation to his party, to his organization, which for purely objective reasons would now induce him, and if necessary force him, to return to the penal institution, if (hypothetically speaking) this was a case in which the prisoner on leave was deter-mined to continue his vacation. The political combat organization of the proletariat certainly wants to be anything but the police officer for the penal bureaucracy as things stand, and certainly would not feel comfortable about taking on such a function involuntarily. But it would have to take on this role, subject to the condition that there are qualitative opportunities for the humanization of the penal system and that the operation of these opportunities within meaningful limits would be impaired or even completely destroyed by the misplaced behaviour of an individual.

The criminal prisoner usually stands outside of such considerations, which do not fit into his mindset, and certainly not within his narrower field of interest. Whilst the political prisoner of less solid character may now and again be tempted not to return to prison from a leave of absence that has been granted, or at least might waver, even though this might in practice be of very little significance, there will be a not insignificant percentage of average criminal prisoners who will not at first return after such a leave – until they have been caught again, which however is relatively easy in these circles; easier at an rate than with political fugitives, who first of all have a quite different level of protection, and second, move in a quite different social milieu to criminal fugitives, whose flight is for the most part initiated by the anti-social professional criminal fraternity. So, there is little point in endorsing something that the bureaucracy and reaction would take as a welcome opportunity to thwart efforts to make the penal system more humane. It certainly would mean adding grist to the mill for reaction and making all the necessary and improving reforms for the penal system impossible. It would amount to little more than an Echternach dancing procession: one would move three steps forwards and (in practice) two steps backwards; one would achieve practically the opposite of what was purposefully intended. It is important to get something done, also for the criminal prisoners. We may not be enthusiastic about supporting them, but they are in need of our protection, whether they are politically indifferent or even anti-socialist. They are the victims of their circumstances; human beings trying to cope, but with limited faculties. At any rate, they should know that they will find protection within the organized working class. The question thus arises: what sort of control serves them best, in conditions that only allow very few possibilities. For the time being and under the currently prevailing conditions, the experience gained in the penal system in Soviet Russia cannot be transposed schem-atically to the average criminal human material in German prisons. Firstly, because the political conditions in Soviet Russia are quite different from those in Germany, and secondly, because the human material that populates the prisons in Soviet Russia only allows a partial comparison with the pro-fessional criminal in Germany. What Dr. Hirschfeld, who visited Soviet Russia in his capacity as a sexual researcher, explained to social-democratic workers about the nature of the penal system there, is very interesting. According to a report in the *Leipziger Volkszeitung* of 1 December 1926, he noted the following, among other things, in the tenth point of his lecture on the new law governing sexual offences in Soviet Russia: [76]

> "The penal system in the new Russia is more humane than anywhere else in the world; prison psychoses no longer occur hardly at all. Less serious offenders get a holiday on Sundays, when they can visit their wives, and receive 75% of the wages paid to normal workers. More serious offenders may, at certain intervals, receive visits from their wives."

How very different it is in Germany: here, every prisoner is driven to the utmost limit of nervous weakness and nervous irritation; every tenth prisoner is ruled by the flight of his psyche into psychosis, and every twentieth prisoner is constantly on the very edge of committing terrible, desperate acts.

Obviously, all of the activity of the average criminal prisoner is anchored in such conditions, if they have been given a one or two-week leave of absence from hell: a large percentage of these prisoners will in fact not return to prison; not just a large percentage, but a strikingly large percentage. And the bureaucracy would have what it needs: seemingly sound evidence of a failed experiment. We will not give the bureaucracy such evidence, indeed we must not give it, on penalty of the consequences that will inevitably follow: allowing the bureaucracy to win over a public, which is unqualified to judge for itself, to its side. However, the crucial passage in the petitions of the Communist parliamentary group in the Saxon State Parliament itself already states that all criminal prisoners are to be granted leave "unless their leave of absence endangers the life and health of their fellow human beings". This

---

[76] Hirschfeld had a significant influence on sexual policies in the early years of the Soviet Union. His work was cited for example in the discussions that led to the decriminalization of homosexuality in 1922. Soviet Health Commissar Nikolai Semashko and Institute of Neuropsychiatric Prophylaxis director Lev Rozenshtein visited the Institute for Sexual Science; Hirschfeld reciprocated with a visit to Moscow in 1926.

passage is very elastic in its conception and conceptualization and must open up impossible perspectives in the hands of a judicial bureaucracy in its current guise. However, there would be a further limit placed on this restriction: lifelong prisoners or prisoners serving long-term sentences, for example 10 to 15 or perhaps even five years, would certainly not experience this general leave of absence. Remand prisoners would also not enjoy these leaves of absence, since remand is justified in law specifically because there is a risk of the prisoners absconding or entering into collusion with others; therefore, even the most favourable political regime would apply the most unfavourable conditions, whereby it is significant that remand prisoners not infrequently have to sit out detention for one and often even two years.

Let's take a look at the social conditions of criminal prisoners, especially professional criminals. Their leave of absence leads them into the circles with which they are involved and intimately connected in their wrongdoing. Thus, the opportunity serves as a prerequisite for committing further criminal acts. And this opportunity must be combined with the fact that they are rooted in decadence and accustomed to living a dissolute life. But this, in turn, is intertwined with the downright inhumane abstinences and deprivations that lie behind them, for which they, now that the opportunity has arisen, want to compensate themselves and will compensate themselves: this is the pillar that supports a new reality. And the penal superstructure is then applied to this substructure. Our penal code only recognizes two maximum penalties: life imprisonment or a fixed term of up to 15 years. This basic principle of the penal system would be broken if, for example, a person sentenced to 15 years' imprisonment commits new offences during a 14-day furlough. Although a life sentence for a prison sentence cannot be reduced, a fixed prison sentence of five years can easily be extended to 10, 20, 30 and more. This presents unlimited possibilities to the diligent jurist who goes by the book.

But quite apart from the fact that lifelong prisoners and those sentenced to long prison terms do not receive a vacation, the example also has significance for those serving short sentences. And in this respect psycho-sexual factors must not be underestimated. Short-term leaves of absence must be considered in light of the prisoners' sexual excesses and in this connection the prisoner's awareness that he must go back again: he wants to compensate himself for the sexual deprivations that lie behind him; this is entirely understand-able from a psychological point of view. But more than this, he wants to compensate for the deprivations that lie ahead, with the difference that he now knows exactly the nature of those deprivations that lie ahead. He therefore not only goes on a sexual rampage because he is "catching up" but also because he is "stocking up". But how is he going to do that? That is not even possible with his wife; very often the prisoner has no wife; often the marriage has broken down, as previously mentioned. And where that is not the case, only in the rarest cases will the wife be able to satisfy his needs, even if she herself has an inordinate sex drive: he therefore has to sow his oats in brothels, where, so long as he is able to pay, he can satisfy all of his needs, even if they are of an eccentric nature. But how is he going to get hold of the money? He simply has to get it. He will be led astray, one way or another. This can take a thousand forms, whether he commits robberies or serious burglaries, or works as a big-time pimp during his vacation, or it could be that he flogs his home furnishings for the price of three nights of pleasure, thereby completely destroying what is left of his marital relationship and funding the bloody tragedy that ensues. And where this is not within the realms of possibility, under the prevailing circumstances it is understandable that sexual lust is transformed into sexual voraciousness, which is the basis for further sex crimes, and perhaps the first stage on the way to a sexually motivated murder. In any case, we can foresee serious consequences and dangerous situations that demand a completely different approach and cannot be solved by means of a general leave of absence.

I consider that the proposals referred to, insofar as they are intended to remedy the sexual problem in prison, are also inappropriate because such leave would take place only once a year, at best twice, for two or three weeks. Does this present a solution to the sexual problem in the penal system?

This problem will only be solved if regular intercourse is assured according to individual needs. This is only possible if it is taken for granted that sexual functions must be integrated within the framework of the penal system. This should apply to all prisoners who are sexually mature, not just those who are married, as demanded in the requests of the Communist parliamentary fraction in the Prussian parliament. Marriage in the bourgeois sense is not a biological matter, but rather a temporal concept that changes as the structure of society evolves; bourgeois marriage is an outward form of, but not a prerequisite for, sexual activity. In order to meet the prisoner's necessities of life in the psycho-sexual field, the subsequent demands must be raised and fought for by all parliamentary and extra-parliamentary means.

1. The ban on speaking and interacting with one another must be entirely abolished for all detainees.

2. No prisoner may be locked up in solitary confinement against his will, especially not as a means of punishment; likewise no prisoner may be held in communal detention against his will. The individual needs of the prisoners must be taken into account, and in particular, all prisoners are granted the general right to commune with all prisoners within the prison walls, without a waiting period. Doors remain unlocked.

3. Day rooms are to be furnished comfortably. The character of the cells is to be done away with. In particular, the following are to be removed or altered:

a) The folding beds, folding chairs and folding tables; the inventory in the living rooms must meet normal needs;

b) The blinds in front of the windows and the opaque windowpanes. Window casements are to be constructed normally. In particular, windows should not be locked; the windows are to have tasteful curtains;

c) Walls are to be painted colourfully with oil-paint;

d) The prisoner is allowed to decorate the walls of the living rooms according to his taste and needs. Should the prison administration feel obliged to intervene because of gross bad taste, this must be done using suitably qualified educational methods;

e) The unhygienic slopping out system is to be done away with and replaced with lavatories;

f) Only work that is suitable in living quarters should be performed there. All other work is to be performed in work rooms;

g) In winter there is adequate heating, and above all, the principle that prisoners can be further punished with incarceration in a cold cell is to be done away with;

h) For reasons of social education, meals in general are administered in communal rooms, not by a rigid system of allocation, but following principles of qualified need; The prisoners eliminate any possible bad situations among themselves by means of "communal corrective measures";

i) Prison lighting is to be installed such that the prisoners can turn on the light themselves at any time; and

k) The spyholes in the doors are to be removed.

4. All prisoners have the right to freely acquire and read political newspapers, periodicals, books and bro-

chures of all persuasions.

5. All religious tracts are to be removed from prison libraries. They are to be replaced with books that have literary and scientific value, also those with a political or party-political direction.

6. Borrowing takes place flexibly; any system that takes books out of service is to be avoided.

7. All prisoners are to be employed according to their wishes and abilities with the exclusion of all unproductive and soul-destroying activity. All employment is to be designed with a view to later productive activity. To increase productivity and give employment meaningful purpose, the aim is to industrialize prisons. Leased properties and estates are taken over and operated by the State and worked by prisoners.

8. Nourishment is not to be based on calorie intake alone, but also based on mental and cultural requirements. Individual tastes and appetites are to be taken into account as far as possible. The principle that has applied up until now, according to which the food allowance should also be used as a means to punish prisoners, is to be set aside. The nutritional regime in all prisoner groups will in future depend on the self-management and co-determination of the prisoners.

9. Punishment in arrest cells, as with all forms of physical punishment (such as denial of hot food) shall be abolished; the same applies to isolation, insofar as this is only a disguised form of arrest punishment.

10. Pregnant women and breastfeeding mothers may not be taken into custody or held on remand. The exclusion from detention also comes into effect for mothers for at least three years after delivery, provided that the birth is normal and the child is alive. Mothers who are taken into custody beyond this time have the right to take their children into custody with them, insofar as they are in need of maternal care. Care should be taken

to ensure suitable accommodation for both mothers and children. Likewise, care must be taken to ensure that these children can leave the grounds of the penal institution daily under the supervision of a carer.

11. Scientific, literary, entertaining and musical lectures and performances are held regularly every week.

12. Prisoners may keep their own musical instruments in their cells.

13. In consequence of sexual-scientific learning, which teaches that the arbitrary separation of the sexes unnaturally increases the natural sexual tension between the two, the separation of the sexes is rejected as harmful and abolished.

14. Completely free, unimpeded and uncontrolled correspondence of all prisoners with their relatives.

15. Prisoners have the right to receive enough visits. In principle, the visits are not to be supervised and must take place in a psychologically satisfying environment.

16. Each prisoner may receive the visits of his sexual partner at regular intervals of at least four weeks, such that normal and satisfying sexual intercourse can take place. This type of visit is to extend to at least 48 hours.

17. A holiday is to be granted every six months.

18. Prisoners may have their children with them at regular intervals for the exercise of parental purposes. The duration of these visits by prisoners' children must be in accordance with the purpose and must not be less than three days.

It is not, and cannot be, my task to write the regulations to be implemented in this context; it must be enough that we have broadly hinted at the direction of elementary demands.

This is exactly what Ibrahim Nierndl suggested in the *Berliner Volkszeitung* of 6 December 1928. His courageous confession states: "The Punishment of Sexual Distress":

"Prisons are worse than cages for predatory beasts. Because they are based on the violent suppression of the most elemental life instincts. By dividing them into men's and women's departments, by strictly keeping away all persons of the opposite sex, we corral and constrict the most powerful instinct, the instinct that dominates the human being and which, according to the psychoanalytic school, defines the very essence of man. .... It is good that in our time we are now starting to feel deep sympathy with this form of distress that was formerly kept secret, and it is worthy of note that the Ministry of Justice is also working to protect prisoners from this most inhumane punishment, which is not intended in law ...

"No, a game of hide and seek is unhelpful in this matter. Just as you do not let the prisoners starve, because you must satisfy the instinctual drive for nourishment, so you must ensure that their sexual instinct is satisfied. If you assume the right to imprison them, you also have the duty to provide for their most elementary urges. You can place limitations on them, as is done with food, but you must not let them grow to terrible torments. Give the married prisoners the opportunity to come together with their wives now and again. And the others? My God, you were not ashamed, in fact you felt it necessary to build brothels openly and freely during the war for the sexually hungry soldiers. Do the same thing for prisoners! A way will be found! Above all, just as you have a pastoral worker in every prison, create sex workers. For those of us in freedom, who are not so much in need of welfare, you have long since done this."

Magnus Hirschfeld, a great among greats, Magnus Hirschfeld, the counsel and aide for many in the deepest sexual distress, finishes the first volume of his Geschlechtskunde with Goethe's aphorism: *Die Erde wird durch die Liebe frei* – love makes the world free.

I will close my work with a quote from Hirschfeld:

"Love is the shared desire, the reciprocal will of two people in giving and receiving. This means there are not only rights to sex and love, but even: obligations."

Only he whose pulse beats in this sense has the will and possesses the ability to help prisoners, a constituent part of humanity, and to lead them out of the depths of sexual distress with the watchword: All for one and one for all!

We owe this mission to the human race; this mission must be fulfilled by all those who have lived just once with this sexual misery; fulfilling this mission is also within the power of relatives of those in custody.

Come on, you people, struggle alongside the prisoner and win for him what belongs to all humans: the free sexual activity that is the root of life itself!

Be not content simply to destroy the prisons that are today like cages for wild animals but help to build a social life that no longer needs prisons at all!

Bibliography

Other Works by Karl Plättner

Before his imprisonment, Plättner was a prolific political theorist and polemicist. His publications (apart from the one presented here) include *Der Weg zur Räte-Diktatur* (The Path to the Council Dictatorship, 1919); *Das Fundament und die Organisierung der sozialen Revolution* (The Foundation and the Organization of the Social Revolution, 1919); *Das Todesurteil : Moskau über Spartakus : Kronzeuge Radek als Verteidiger der Kommunistischen Arbeiter-Partei Deutschlands* (The Death Sentence; Moscow on Spartacus: Crown Witness Radek as Defender of the Communist Workers' Party of Germany, 1920); *Rühle im Dienste der Konterrevolution; Das ostsächs[ische]. Sportkommunisten-Kartell oder Die revolutionäre Klassenkampf-Partei* ([Otto] Rühle in the Service of the Counter-Revolution; the East Saxon Sport-Communists-Cartel or the Revolutionary Party of Class Struggle, 1920); and *Der organisierte rote Schrecken! Die kommunistischen Paradearmeen oder organisierter Bandenkampf im Bürgerkrieg* (The Organized Red Scare! Communist Paradeground Armies or Organized Guerrilla Warfare in the Civil War, 1921).

After his release, Plättner published *Der mitteldeutsche Bandenführer. Mein Leben hinter Kerkermauern*, (The Central German Gang Leader. My Life behind Prison Walls, Berlin 1930). Many of these works can be found online in the Anton Pannekoek archives at www.aaap.de

Biography

Volker Ullrich: *Der Ruhelose Rebell, Karl Plättner 1893-1945;* C.H. Beck Verlag; Munich 2000.

Bergbauer, Knut: Karl Plättner: Anmerkungen zur Biographie eines politischen Partisanen. In Graf, Andreas G. (Hg.): *Anarchisten gegen Hitler. Anarchisten, Anarcho-Syndikalisten, Rätekommunisten in Widerstand und Exil*; Lukas Verlag; 2001.

Manfred Asendorf und Rolf von Bockel (Hg.): *Demokratische*

Wege. Deutsche Lebensläufe aus fünf Jahrhunderten, S. 481 ff.

Material in English
There is very little written on Plättner in English.
Kuhn, Gabriel (Ed.): *All Power to the Councils! A Documentary History of the German Revolution of 1918-19*; PM Press; 2012; contains an extract from *Das Fundament und die Organisierung der sozialen Revolution*.
A short biography can be found on the LibCom website: https://libcom.org

Also from RedLines Press

The German Robin Hood
The Extraordinary Life of Max Hoelz

He was dubbed "the German Robin Hood" in England; to his enemies in Germany he was better known as "the Dictator of the Vogtland". Max Hoelz was a worker, engineer, soldier – and an irresistible womanizer – who became one of the most fascinating and charismatic figures during the working-class insurrections in Germany that followed the First World War. *From the 'White Cross' to the Red Flag* was the title of his autobiography, which appeared in 1929.It follows Hoelz's progress from simple farmhand through Germany to London, his efforts to educate himself, and the breathtaking action and horrors he experienced as a cavalry messenger and front-line soldier. He returns from the fighting to lead his local unemployed workers' committee, before taking up the armed struggle and a life on the run from the authorities. As leader of the Red Army in Central Germany during the Kapp Putsch of 1920 and again during the March Action a year later, Hoelz robs from the rich to give to the poor – but runs afoul of the Communist Party bureaucracy in the process. Framed for a murder he did not commit, Hoelz is sentenced to life imprisonment and begins a new struggle against the cruel regimes of Münster, Gross-Strehlitz and Sonnenburg prisons.

This book also includes Hoelz's *Indictment against Bourgeois Society*, his speech to the Moabit Special Court in Berlin on 22 June 1922, and an introduction by the translator, Ed Walker.

Also from Redlines Press

We Are Prisoners
Oskar Maria Graf

The autobiography of Oskar Maria Graf, his first major work,
was published in 1927. It covers his early youth growing up in
the village of Berg by Lake Starnberg, his cruel abuse by his
older brother, his escape to Munich, where he worked as a
baker, and then to anarchist communes in Switzerland. Graf is
drafted into the army, where he reluctantly serves as a horse-
groom on the supply trains. He is discharged as mentally unfit, spends a year in an asylum, then returns to Munich, working in a biscuit factory, starting his literary career and making
money on the black market. *We Are Prisoners* paints a fascinating picture of bohemian life in Schwabing and the radical politics of the time, and climaxes with the short-lived Bavarian
Soviet Republic of 1919. Many of the characters in the novel
became well known artists and writers in Weimar Germany.
The book is an honest and blithe personal account of momen-
tous events. Graf's quirky literary style combines a self-
deprecating and anarchic sense of humour, sympathy for the
downtrodden and the Heimat genre of German culture.

"He behaves disgracefully and provokes laughter and disbe-
lief, but in so doing, he wins our hearts."
THOMAS MANN

The book is translated, introduced and annotated by
Ed Walker.